Financial Accounting and Information Systems

Financial Accounting and Information Systems

Edited by
Rory Nolan

MURPHY & MOORE
www.murphy-moorepublishing.com

Published by Murphy & Moore Publishing,
1 Rockefeller Plaza,
New York City, NY 10020, USA

ISBN: 978-1-63987-225-1

Cataloging-in-Publication Data

Financial accounting and information systems / edited by Rory Nolan.
p. cm.
Includes bibliographical references and index.
ISBN 978-1-63987-225-1
1. Information storage and retrieval systems--Accounting.
2. Accounting--Data processing. 3. Accounting. 4. Financial statements. I. Nolan, Rory.
HF5679 .F56 2021
657.028 5--dc23

For information on all Murphy & Moore Publications
visit our website at www.murphy-moorepublishing.com

MURPHY & MOORE

Contents

Preface

The field of accounting that deals with the analysis, reporting and summarization of financial transactions is known as financial accounting. Such financial reports are made available to banks, stockholders, government agencies and business owners to aid decision making. Statement of cash flows, statement of financial position and statement of financial performance are elementary to financial accounting. Accounting information systems enable the storage, collection, and processing of accounting and financial data. It can be used to support accounting functions and activities, such as management accounting and tax, financial accounting and reporting, and auditing. This book is a compilation of chapters that discuss the most vital concepts and emerging trends in the field of financial accounting. The ever growing need of advanced technology in financial accounting is the reason that has fueled the research in the field of accounting information systems in recent times. With state-of-the-art inputs by acclaimed experts of this field, this book targets students and professionals.

Various studies have approached the subject by analyzing it with a single perspective, but the present book provides diverse methodologies and techniques to address this field. This book contains theories and applications needed for understanding the subject from different perspectives. The aim is to keep the readers informed about the progresses in the field; therefore, the contributions were carefully examined to compile novel researches by specialists from across the globe.

Indeed, the job of the editor is the most crucial and challenging in compiling all chapters into a single book. In the end, I would extend my sincere thanks to the chapter authors for their profound work. I am also thankful for the support provided by my family and colleagues during the compilation of this book.

Editor

1

Implementation of international financial reporting standards in Ukraine

Ruslana Kuzina [a,1]

[a] *Odessa National University of Economics, Ukraine*

Abstract: Since Ukraine gained independence in 1991, the Ukrainian economy has been undergoing constant transformation. Legislative, institutional and structural reforms have been driven by the rapidly changing business environment and much progress towards a market economy has been made. The Ukrainian economy now comprises a spectrum of economic subjects, ranging from large financial-industrial groups (FIGs) and banking institutions to small, privately financed enterprises. One necessary precondition for access to such cheaper investment finance is reliable, high quality financial information; thus, the pace and extent of Ukraine's economic reform is being held back by the widespread lack of such information. In this article author describes the evolution of the implementation of International Financial Reporting Standards in Ukraine, makes an attempt to identify some problems of methodological, organizational and practical nature. In this article author describes the evolution of the implementation of International Financial Reporting Standards in Ukraine, makes an attempt to identify some problems of methodological, organizational and practical nature.

Keywords: IFRS studies, Turkey, accounting developments

1. Introduction

In Ukraine, the process of harmonization of financial reporting is carried out by the introduction of IFRS to socially significant enterprises – joint-stock companies, insurance companies, banks, pawn shops and so on. However, the process of transition of the Ukrainian enterprises to IFRS reporting has its specific features related first of all to the occurrence in nineties of joint-stock companies. Usually, they were formed by reorganizing the state enterprises and are now in poor

[1] *Corresponding author:* Ruslana Kuzina, associate professor of accounting and auditing of the Odessa National University of Economics, rws_1@ukr.net

condition – suffer losses, have multimillion salary debts, etc. But Joint Stock Companies Law assumes a transition of all the JSCs to international standards, regardless of whether the enterprise is listed or is not. Thus, the accountants faced an urgent issue: how to make the transition to IFRS reporting, how much does it cost and what are the consequences for business?

The need for high quality "global GAAP" (Ampofo & Sellani, 2005: 228) was officially recognized in 1966, when professional accounting bodies first began working towards a set of international accounting standards (IASC/IASB Chronology, 2006). Since then world capital markets have become increasingly tied to one another (Turner, 2001: 1), and so "integrated and interdependent" that "the stability of one market affects others" (UNCTAD, 2005: 5). As the barriers between nations have become more "porous" (Harris, 2002: 417-418), domestic economies have become increasingly vulnerable to the "external shocks" caused by an "expanding world economy", necessitating the adoption of globalized practices if they are to function effectively (Lehman, 2005). The development of IFRS is one manifestation of that institutional logic, with the globalization of IFRS described as "part of a general wave of standardization that has taken place in broader, non-accounting contexts over the last 150 years" (Rodrigues and Craig, 2007: 740).

In this study, we tried to examine the main stages of development of legal provision introduction of international financial reporting standards, assess the level of convergence of IFRS and national standards.

2. Financial reporting in Ukraine: convergence process to IFRS

Since it gained independence in 1991, Ukraine has adopted a civil law system based on codes and acts. The Law on Companies (1992), and the Civil and Commercial Codes (2004) define various legal structures which can be used by businesses operating in Ukraine. The most commonly used types of legal entities include joint-stock companies, (which can be open joint-stock companies or closed joint-stock companies), limited liability companies, additional liability companies, general and limited partnerships10. The most common are limited liability companies and joint-stock companies. Enterprises with foreign capital are generally established in the form of joint-stock companies or limited liability companies, or operated through representative offices.

Responsibility for financial reporting at limited liability companies and joint-stock companies is set out in the Law on Companies. In both, the Management Board and/or the General Directorate are responsible for the day-to-day activities of the company, including accounting and financial reporting. In addition there is a Supervisory Board, which is roughly equivalent to a Board of Directors in Anglo-Saxon jurisdictions. For joint-stock companies, there is a legal requirement for a

Revision Commission, a body with certain oversight responsibilities. However, the Revision Commission does not fulfill many of the necessary functions of an „Audit Committee", such as the approval of the appointment of independent auditors and the review of the audit report. Company legislation should be amended to either replace the Revision Committee, or significantly amend its structure, composition, role and responsibilities, to require that companies have an audit committee in accordance with international best practice. Banking legislation already requires this for banks; the requirement should be extended to all joint-stock companies.

Securities Market in Ukraine began its formation in 1991 after the Law of Ukraine "On Securities and the Stock Market." Then Ukraine in law got the tools and the professional securities market participants who actively participated in the creation of the domestic financial sector.

In recent years the trend of increasing in trading volume on the stock market continues. Thus, this figure in 2012 was 2 530 870 000 000 UAH, which is more than the volume of executed contracts in 2011 on 359 770 000 000 UAH. At the same time, the growth of the stock market was accelerated compared to GDP - volume of trading on the stock market exceeded GDP almost doubled. It shows the development of the state economy in general and the development of the stock market in particular, as well as the rapid pace of development.

The ratio of the share capitalization of listed companies to GDP is an important indicator of the stock market and the financial system in general. If we trace the dynamics of this figure in Ukraine since 2008, when it was 9.0%, it should be noted that the figure rose to 13.7%. At the end of 2012 it was 19.66%. In 2012, the capitalization was moderately increasing, which is primarily due to the increasing of number of issuers who have been listed. Such index as the volume of investments in the economy of Ukraine through the stock market instruments on the results of 2012 totaled 67 230 000 000 UAH. It may be noted the stability of this index in recent years. As for the certain indexes of performance of the stock market, as the results of trading on the stock exchanges, the volume of exchange contracts on securities in 2012 was 263 670 000 000 UAH. an increase of 11.99% compared to 2011 year.

Over the past three years, the total number of issues of shares that are traded on stock exchanges was also increasing. By the end of 2012, 1731 shares were included to exchange lists of trade organizers, up almost 40% in comparison with the end of 2011. If we talk about the bond market, in 2012 there were registered 332 bonds in the amount of 51 390 000 000 UAH. Comparing with 2011, the volume of registered bonds rose to 15 480 000 000 UAH or by 43.11%.

The process of reorganization of open and closed joint stock companies into public and private companies in accordance with the Law of Ukraine "On Joint Stock

Companies" continued for last 3 years (2011-2013). According to the National Commission on Securities and Stock Market as of December 31, 2011 registered as legal entities are 26 631 joint-stock companies, of which open – 5 761 (public – 2 161), closed – 15 798 (private – 2 911). The vast majority of corporations is concentrated in Kiev and Kiev region – 9 197 (or 34, 53% of the total), Kharkov – 2 371 (or 8.90%), Dnepropetrovsk – 2 059 (or 7.73%), Donetsk – 1 887 (7.08%) and Zaporozhye – 971 (or 3.65%) regions.

Given a number of joint stock companies (5 761) which are required to file IFRS financial statements, it is worthy of note that only 773 companies are listed, i.e. only 12.68% of joint stock companies demonstrate direct interest in attracting investments. As we can see the vast majority of shares listed on the domestic market, so in our study we turn our attention to the similarity of Ukrainian and international accounting standards.

The formation of new economic relations between business entities, processes of integration into the world economy, the need to remove economic and trade barriers, to energize foreign investments, to access the world capital markets, the formation of a competitive market environment stipulated the reform of accounting and reporting in Ukraine.

The process was initiated in May of 1992 by Ukrainian President Leonid Kravchuk signing the Decree on Ukraine's transition to the common practice in international accounting and statistics (Decree on Ukraine's transition to the common practice in international accounting and statistics, 1992). Basing on this Decree the Cabinet of Ministers by its Regulation no. 326 of May 4, 1993 approved the Concept of building a Ukrainian national statistics system and the State program of transition to international system of accounting and statistics. This program included the creation of normative-methodological basis of accounting in next three years.

By the Decree of the Cabinet of Ministers of Ukraine issued February 27, 1993 the function of regulating through the development, implementation of common methodological bases of accounting and reporting for enterprises, organizations and institutions (excluding banks) was reserved for the Ministry of Finance of Ukraine, in which a Board of accounting methodology was established. The Board has developed various Guidelines and instructions regarding the operations, relatively new for Ukrainian enterprises. Enterprises received the right to establish an internal system of accounting and control, to introduce the necessary sub-accounts, to create reserves for future expenses and payments. Small businesses were allowed to keep simplified accounting.

However, some authors considered (Pushkar, 1999) that the accounting remained socialistic in Ukraine, which was focused on monitoring the accomplishment of plans and not providing the necessary information to managers. Soon, by the Decree of Parliament, the Audit Law was adopted in Ukraine.

The important factors of accounting reforming in Ukraine in 1996-99 were the requirements of the World Bank regarding loans to Ukraine, tax reform and professional accounting organizations (UFPAA) activity.

Hallmark of Ukrainian accounting in those years was the focus on the needs of tax accounting. Because of the rule of law of the relative tax accounting over the statutory accounting any changes in tax laws caused the relative changes in accounting methodology. Thus, accounting in Ukraine did not provide information about the financial position of the companies needed to attract investment, that's why one of the conditions of the obtaining of the World Bank loans was the transition of the National Bank of Ukraine and commercial banks in 1998 to the International Accounting Standards, as well as the implementation of IAS by the stock market traders.

Given the experience of accounting reforming in banks and in order to make the national accounting system to meet the requirements of the market economy and the IAS a program of reforming the accounting system using international standards was approved by the Regulation № 1706 of the Cabinet of Ministers of Ukraine on October 28, 1998. Hence, Ukraine has made the strategic choice in the orientation of accounting to IFRS. Reform program contained an action plan, according to which in 1998-2001 the development of the Regulations (standards) of accounting, chart of accounts, revision of the universities curricula, development and publication of a new training-methodical literature was provided.

The first step in the implementation of this program was the adoption of the Law on Accounting and Financial Reporting in Ukraine, dated July 16, 1999. This Law:

- legislated rights of all user groups to obtain reliable information on business activities by implementation of accounting and reporting, according to national regulations (standards) of accounting, which are not inconsistent with international standards;
- determined the subjects of accounting rulemaking;
- established the basic requirements for accounting and reporting.

Table 1. The evolution of the development of national standards in Ukraine

Period	Adoption	Results
1999-2003	24 accounting and reporting standards were approved	Government activities in the field of accounting and reporting were aimed at further rapprochement of Ukrainian laws to the European Union's legislation and International Financial Reporting Standards, as well as stepping up the accountants' proficiency requirements

Period	Adoption	Results
2004-2007	6 accounting and reporting standards were approved	Period is characterized by the inconsistent steps in reforming the accounting and reporting, approved by the IFRS Methodology council in May 2004, declared N(S)BU (Ukrainian accounting standards) improvement considering the current Ukrainian legislation and the Provisions of IFRS, which led to the diversity of the accounting reform directions. The issue of harmonization of accounting was actualized also in connection with the uncovering of prospects of partnership, economic integration and cooperation due to the expansion of the European Union in 2004. This caused the signing on the February 12 2005 of the "Ukraine - EU" Action Plan, which envisaged the need to adapt and to ensure effective implementation of the basic principles of relevant international rules and standards, as well as the rules and standards of the EU.
2007-2011	4 accounting and reporting standards were approved	Period is characterized by significant efforts and achievements in reforming the Ukrainian accounting system. During this period the transition of state-financed organizations to IFRS was started. Although, of course, the process of full transition to international accounting standards is still far from complete.
2012-2014	2 accounting and reporting standards were approved	National N(S)BU and international standards will co-exist in Ukraine.

However, in the 2001-2003 period the criticism continued from scientists who considered the main cause of the shortcomings of accounting reform the lack of scientific justification and adequate funding. For example, according to Kuzhelny and Parkhomenko (2001) the funds should have been allocated and international aid targeted funds should have been directed since 1992 to the important accounting reform. This work, on self-financing conditions, should have been done by academic scientists.

It can be concluded that the system of national accounting in Ukraine has been radically reformed since 2000. Ukrainian Provisions (standards) of accounting – N(S)BU – are generally agreed upon, and are largely based on the general provisions of IFRS – International Financial Reporting Standards.

The process of implementation of IFRS in Ukraine passed synchronously with the reform of the accounting and auditing system and with the formation of state regulators, that are part of the institutional economic environment of the country: Ministry of Finance, the National Bank of Ukraine, State Commission on

Securities and Stock Market of Ukraine, the Audit Chamber of Ukraine, National Commission on Financial Services, public organizations (ACS, UFPAA).

In 10 years (2000-2010) several attempts of IFRS implementation were undertaken in Ukraine, but the actual date of transfer was continually delayed and postponed. 2010 can be considered the starting point of joint-stock enterprises transition to IFRS, when the Procedure of filling forms of disclosure and amendments thereto by listed issuers of stocks and bonds came into effect (Decision of the State Commission on Securities and Stock Market no. 981 of July 22, 2010) in which the following requirement appeared: public joint-stock companies disclose further information about their activities on the basis of international accounting standards.

In accordance with the action plan to implement the strategy of application of International financial reporting standards in Ukraine (Decree of the Cabinet of Ministers of Ukraine on the adoption of the Strategy implementation of international financial reporting standards in Ukraine, 2007), changes were made to the Law on accounting and financial reporting in Ukraine, with effect from January 1, 2012. Recent changes assert that to prepare financial statements the international standards should be used if they are officially published on the Ministry of Finance website. While public joint-stock companies, banks, insurance companies, and enterprises engaged in various activities in accordance with the list of the Cabinet, prepare financial statements and consolidated financial statements according to international standards. Yet other companies independently determine the appropriateness of the application of international standards for financial reporting.

Thus, since 2012, national N(S)BU and international standards will co-exist in Ukraine. Let's mention one important fact – following the adoption of the Tax Code, which entered into force on January 1, 2011, quite serious changes in the N(S)BU were made (Tax Code of Ukraine, 2010). Obviously, such a situation cannot have a positive impact on the organization of accounting of economic entities. Attempts to adapt the accounting under the requirements of the taxation management will not succeed, because the existing differences are objectively conditioned by the various purposes, principles laid in their base, by the mismatch of accounting objects, methods of tax base calculation, etc.

The opinions of scientists on the evaluation of accounting reform in Ukraine are often opposing. Some scientists interpreted reform processes negatively: Borodkin (1997) believed that radical reform in accounting is premature and inappropriate since neither companies, nor authorities are not ready for it, and personnel training and retraining require significant investments. According to Butinetz (2003), during a lasting accounting pseudo-reform Ukraine has almost lost the former accounting, human resources, who understood the importance and role of theory and practice of accounting, its essence and function. There is generally no need in accounting reform, because the accounting system already provides all market participants with relevant accounting information, says Ohiychuk (1997). This conclusion was based on the assertion of full Convergence of Ukrainian accounting regulations with the international accounting standards.

Opposite point of view is shared by Kuz'minskii (2006), Sopko (2006), Gutsaylyuk (2006) and others. In particular, Lastovetskiy (2002) believes that national standards are not IFRS copies but consider specific and positive heritage of the Soviet period, to be the main positive trait. Mossakovskii (2003) wrote that regarding the accounting system that develops in Ukraine in recent years, it should be noted that it used to a certain extent the foundations that have been used in the USSR, in conjunction with those that are inherent to the international practices. And thereby create conditions for successful development in Ukraine of accounting system that would match the highest international standards.

Debatable is also a question – which accounting model accounting in Ukraine belongs to. According to some scholars (Pushkar, 1999) basing on the characteristics of the main accounting schools, accounting in Ukraine belongs to the continental model. Other opinions are more radical (Golov, 2007) such as that Ukrainian system did not share any of the approaches and did not have any construction concept before year 2000. Moreover, after July 1, 1997 Ukrainian accounting system has become a tax-accounting surrogate because, unlike income and expenses, fixed assets accounting was bound tightly to the tax laws. Meanwhile, the system of accounts and the financial reporting format in Ukraine is more close to the Anglo-Saxon model.

3. Status and prospects of IFRS implementation in Ukraine

The legislative basis for the implementation of IFRS in Ukraine is the Law on Accounting and Financial Reporting in Ukraine, which provides for the IFRS application:

- Public stock companies, banks, insurance companies prepare financial statements and consolidated financial statements according to international standards since 2012;
- Businesses providing financial services, except insurance and pension funding since 2013;
- Companies performing support activities in the financial services and insurance since 2014;
- All other companies determine the appropriateness of the use of international standards for financial reporting independently.

3.1 The use of international standards

The international standards are used for financial reporting if they do not contradict the Law and are officially published on the website of the central executive body of the state financial policy. The main condition of IFRS use for the financial reporting in Ukraine is "non-contradiction" to the Ukrainian Law on Accounting and Financial Reporting in Ukraine, namely:

- Objectives of accounting and financial reporting, according to the law are to provide users with full, truthful and impartial information about the financial position, operations results and cash flows of the enterprise for decision-making;
- Essential principles accounting and financial reporting are based on.

Practically Ukrainian enterprises frequently undermined those accounting rules. The most serious IFRS system deviations are usually included in the regulations that are not called "standard". It gives the Ministry of Finance a formal excuse to use the regulation not named "standard" and not warranted by the Law on Accounting and Financial Reporting in Ukraine, or state regulators, defending their requirements, began to refer to the IFRS conceptual framework which allegedly allows expressing their professional opinion (Ministry of Finance letter of May 11, 2011). Mentioned in the introduction to IFRS Conceptual Framework, the opportunity to nominate "other or additional" reporting requirements for governments does not mean a possibility to violate the norm of the Accounting Law, which states that national standards cannot contradict IFRS.

Many Ukrainian accountants confuse "does not contradict IFRS" with the term "comply with IFRS." A promising disclaimer appears in reports: "Financial report is prepared in accordance with IFRS, enterprise accounting realized according to the current Ukrainian legislation" (Financial Statements SATP 0904). Thus, regardless of the package of standards, business entities required to comply with provisions of the Law on Accounting and Financial Reporting in Ukraine, the Procedure for filing financial statements, as well as normative-legal acts concerning accounting records, inventory, etc.

Accountants experience certain difficulties filling accounting reporting forms and handing it to the regulator. The problem is that informing about the selected standards package is made by checking the relevant box in financial report and no additional information is required by the state statistical agencies. Enterprises preparing consolidated financial reports under IFRS send information to the statistics authorities by mail. But reports prepared in accordance with IFRS do not comply with the approved Ukrainian reporting format.

Ukrainian Ministry of Finance is working with the IASB on a regular basis. Agreements were concluded on getting:

- IFRS texts for translation into Ukrainian and publishing;
- IFRS for SMEs texts for translation into Ukrainian and publishing;
- IFRS projects and its discussion.

But the Ministry of Finance did not pay for the translation of standards texts – Ukrainian translation was made by a public organization – the Ukrainian Federation of Professional Accountants and Auditors (UFPAA), and then posted on the Ministry of Finance website. Significant part of the information – samples, decision-making basis, etc. – is an IASB intellectual property and may be published for extra charge only.

In order to coordinate IFRS implementation activities and understanding the complexity of using, as well as referring to the need for joint efforts of all participants in this process the Ministry of Finance and the National Bank of Ukraine initiated the association of the professional community to solve the task, which is formalized by relevant Memorandums. Parties to the Memorandum were: Ministry of Finance, the National Bank, the National Commission on Securities and Stock Market, the National Commission for state regulation of the financial services markets, the State Tax Service of Ukraine, the State Statistics Service, the Financial Sector Development Project (FINREP), non-governmental organizations. Parties to the Memorandum agreed to coordinate activities in the field of IFRS use in Ukraine to form common approaches to IFRS application, translation, information support, dealing with issues and building effective relationships in this area. The coordinator is Ukrainian Ministry of Finance.

The first step in the IFRS implementation was to create a special website by the Ministry of Finance together with the FINREP. Website msfz.minfin.gov.ua was presented in February 2012. The aim of the site is gratuitous and free access of business entities, accounting practitioners and students to the best IFRS application practices.

Many businesses that conducted revaluation of fixed assets at the time the letter appeared faced with a choice – when to submit the final package and, in order to save funds for the transformation, filed financial position report for 2 years, and the statement of comprehensive income in one year. The final package under IFRS will be report for 2013. Then the fixed assets revaluation was held not by the date of transition.

Situation with IFRS basics training for JSC accountants was also sad. Accountants certification was not conditioned by and the state regulator believe that to be a definite plus, but not during the transition to IFRS. Due to national peculiarities, accountants were generally nowhere near the statutory accounting and most companies had to use the third-party organizations services for consultation on transition to IFRS. The cost of the auditor's report on IFRS compatibility was significantly increased with no effect for the enterprise – accountants have not received enough experience of IFRS accountancy, moreover significant expenses incurred for the transition and reporting confirmation.

Consider a few more reasons of Ukrainian enterprises formal attitude to the transition to IFRS.

- Accounting in Ukraine is focused primarily on tax accounting, statutory accounting is secondary. Accountants are trying to harmonize the tax and statutory accounting, giving preference to the correct taxation. Another reason for this situation was low over time demand for financial reporting in Ukraine. High corruption level and the shadow turnover do not allow investors to base their decisions on the official set of financial statements. Public authorities represented by the State Statistics Committee established dirt-cheap penalties for failing reports. A whole generation of bookkeepers grew, who consider themselves accountants without even knowing the depreciation methods. According to Kirsch (2007): "Except for accounting services in couple of dozens of large JSC, the vast majority of Ukrainian accountants express extremely formal attitude to the accounting standards. Everybody ceased their serious engagement in accounting, and, in fact, have switched to a tax accounting – undated and penalty-threatening".
- Accounting reporting in Ukraine was traditionally based on the legal form, not on the economic content. Moreover, in fact managers can manually adjust the "book profit" figure. Auditors warn investors about such approach because it can lead to abuse: "Problem of juridically detailed, based on the law standards, determining the exact legal bound, is that they encourage to operate in close proximity of this bound, or even test it for strength. They encourage the search for holes in the legislation and devalue professional judgment" (Levitsky, 2002).
- Ukrainian analysts estimate the national standards to be 65% compliant with international standards. This suggests that businesses that keep accounts properly will face minimal adjusting entry under IFRS. However reality is far from it. Accountants of Ukrainian companies often ignore the requirements of national standards due to the fact that non-Convergence is not punished either at the corporate level or at the level of state regulators.

Outstanding issues are:

- *Submission of quarterly reports:* interim reporting is provided by IFRS. The law requires filing quarterly financial statements – accordingly business entities that use IFRS are required to file quarterly financial reports. The law establishes a minimum amount of quarterly reports which may be required by government users of financial statements.
- *Financial reporting forms* – based on the state statistics bodies needs and the conditions of the transition period by order of the Ministry of Finance the standard financial reporting forms are approved. Before compiling the first annual financial statements that fully comply with IFRS, issues of reporting form filing will be resolved based on alternative approaches. Here are some of them:
    - improvement of standard financial reporting forms in respect of the IFRS mandatory requirements;

- approval of the financial statements items nomenclature with possibility for economic entities to choose the form of financial statements;
- implementation of electronically filed financial reports.

While using improved standard forms of financial reporting, information about filing in a different form is disclosed at the request of the investor in the Annotations to the financial statements. Based on the foregoing, it can be concluded that the transition to IFRS, declared by the Government of Ukraine took place in the year 2012-2013. But is it possible for investors to fully base their decision on public financial statements prepared by the Ukrainian enterprises and what are the consequences of IFRS implementation?

It should be noted that the informal, unofficial or shadow economy in Ukraine exceeds the official and is the largest among the CIS countries and other countries of the near abroad. This condition is confirmed by the data of the Sociology Institute of the Academy of Sciences of Ukraine project "Monitoring of social change", presented August 18, 2011 (Yurchenko, 2011). In addition, the experts noted that “the Austrian economist Schneider, who over 30 years has been studying the informal economy in the world, defines the 56% of Ukrainian economy as informal. Certainly "informal sector exists in any economy, and is usually 12% to 15%”. So Ukraine has exceeded the normal level of shady business by more than four times. Under such conditions is simply senseless to speak about the completeness and truthfulness of the financial statements. Thereby one of the main qualitative characteristics of IFRS reporting – truthful representation – is violated. The author believes, the introduction of IFRS for all companies was premature, only some companies that listing or plan to attract loans from foreign banks have actually benefited from the introduction of IFRS, other companies have approached this issue formally, as evidenced by the following facts.

We studied 30 Ukrainian companies at the date of transition to IFRS which were divided within samples into profitable, average and unprofitable. Performance evaluation was based on circumstantial evidence: increase in the fixed assets value (analyzed the facts of revaluation), items of additional capital - should be minimized to retained earnings, items of deferred taxes, the doubtful debt reserve and provision for holidays.

Sample shows that only 3 of large companies (Azovsteel, Arselormital, Steel Works of Mariupol) have indirect signs of IFRS 1 "First-time IFRS Application", namely: passed fixed assets revaluation , deferred taxes were calculated, items of additional capital were folded. Situation with medium-sized enterprises is much worse – only two enterprises Dobropolskaya CPP plant and Donetsk electrical plant meet the requirements of IFRS, when it comes to the small businesses it’s obvious that no Convergence with IFRS can be traced - no deferred taxes or vacation reserves were calculated, fixed asset revaluation wasn’t conducted.

3.2 Level of convergence Ukrainian standards with the international standards

Ukrainian provisions (standards) of accounting (*here in after **P(S)BU***) cover the majority of IAS but do not copy it. Some national standards (e. g. P(S)BU 12 "Financial investments", P(S)BU 16 "Expenses", etc.) combine principles of several IAS, on the other hand, there are national standards not corresponding to the international standards.

In contrast to the IAS, Ukrainian standards do not provide for alternative approaches in determining accounting policies, in particular with respect to:

- correction of fundamental errors and changes in accounting policies (IAS 8);
- goodwill and fair value adjustments after the acquisition of a foreign operation (IAS 21);
- borrowing costs (IAS 23);
- investments in subsidiaries (IAS 27);
- investments in associates (IAS 28);
- display in the consolidated statements of equity in a jointly controlled entity (IAS 31).

There are significant differences between the IFRS and Ukrainian accounting standards. P(S)BUs are developed and approved by the Ministry of Finance, the accounting law require that they do not contradict the IFRS. Comparative analysis suggests that there are some differences between the two standards systems (see Table 1), and it should be noted that a number of IFRS doesn't exist in the national system. In particular P(S)BU does not cover:

- IAS 20 "Accounting for Government Grants and Disclosure of Government Assistance";
- IAS 26 "Accounting and Reporting by Retirement Benefit Plans";
- IAS 34 "Interim Financial Reporting";
- IFRS 1 "First-Time Application of International Financial Reporting Standards";
- IFRS 2 "Share-Based Payments";
- IFRS 3 "Business Combinations";
- IFRS 4 "Insurance Contracts".

Table 2. Comparative analysis of the P(S)BU and IFRS

IFRS	P(S)BU
IFRS 1 "First-time Adoption of International Financial Reporting Standards" (2008)	none
IFRS 2 "Share-based Payment" (2005)	P(S)BU 34 "Share-based payment"
IFRS 3 "Business Combinations" (2008)	P(S)BU 19 "Business Combinations" (2012)
IFRS 4 "Insurance Contracts" (2005)	none

IFRS	P(S)BU
IFRS 5 "Non-current Assets Held for Sale and Discontinued Operations" (2005)	P(S)BU 27 "Non-current Assets Held for Sale and Discontinued Operations" (2012)
IFRS 6 "Exploration for and Evaluation of Mineral Resources" (2006)	P(S)BU 33 "Mineral Resources exploration costs"
IFRS 7 "Financial Instruments: Disclosures" (2007)	P(S)BU 12 "Financial investments" (2012)
IFRS 8 "Operating Segments" (2009)	P(S)BU 29 "Financial Reporting by Segments" (2012)
IFRS 9 "Financial Instruments"	P(S)BU 12 "Financial investments" (2012)
IFRS 10 "Consolidated Financial Statements" (2013)	NP(S)BU 2 "Consolidated Financial Statements" (2013) P(S)BU 20 "Consolidated Financial Statements" (2012)
IFRS 11 "Joint Arrangements" (2013)	none
IFRS 12 "Disclosure of Interests in Other Entities" (2013)	none
IFRS 13 "Fair Value Measurement" (2013)	none
IAS 1 "Presentation of Financial Statements" (2009)	NP(S)BU 1 "General Requirements for Financial Statements" (2013)
IAS 2 "Inventories" (2005)	P(S)BU 9 "Inventories" (2012)
IAS 7 "Cash Flow Statements" (1994)	NP(S)BU 1 "General Requirements for Financial Statements" (2013)
IAS 8 "Net Profit of Loss for the Period, Fundamental Errors and Changes in Accounting Policies" (2005)	P(S)BU 6 "Correction of errors and changes in the financial statements" (2012)
IAS 10 "Events After the Balance Sheet Date" (2005)	P(S)BU 6 "Correction of errors and changes in the financial statements" (2012)
IAS 11 "Construction Contract" (1995)	P(S)BU 18 "Construction Contracts" (2012)
IAS 12 "Income Taxes" (1998)	P(S)BU 17 "Income Tax" (2012)
IAS 16 "Property, Plant and Equipment" (2005)	P(S)BU 7 "Fixed Assets" (2012)
IAS 17 "Leases" (2005)	P(S)BU 14 "Leases" (2012)
IAS 18 "Revenue" (1995)	P(S)BU 15 "Revenue" (2012)
IAS 19 "Employee Benefits" (1999)	P(S)BU 26 "Employees Compensation" (2012)
IAS 20 "Accounting for Government Grants and Disclosure of Government Assistance" (1984)	none
IAS 21 "The Effects of Changes in Foreign Exchange Rates" (2005)	P(S)BU 21 "Effects of Changes in Foreign Exchange Rates" (2012)
IAS 23 "Borrowing Costs" (2009)	P(S)BU 31 "Financial expenses" (2012)
IAS 24 "Related Party Disclosures" (2011)	P(S)BU 23 "Related Parties Disclosures" (2012)
IAS 26 "Accounting and Reporting by Retirement Benefit Plants" (1998)	None

IFRS	P(S)BU
IAS 27 "Consolidated and Separate Financial Statements" (2008)	NP(S)BU 2 "Consolidated Financial Statements" (2013) P(S)BU 20"Consolidated Financial Statements" (2012)
IAS 28 "Investments in Associates and Joint Ventures" (2011)	P(S)BU 12 "Financial investments" (2012)
IAS 29 "Financial reporting in Hyperinflationary Economies" (1990)	P(S)BU 22 "Effect of inflation" (2012)
IAS 31 "Financial Reporting of Interests in Joint Ventures" (2005)	P(S)BU 12 "Financial investments" (2012)
IAS 32 "Financial Instruments: Disclosures and Presentation" (2005)	P(S)BU 13 "Financial Instruments" (2012)
IAS 33 "Earning Per Share" (2005)	P(S)BU 24 "Earnings per Share" (2012)
IAS 34 "Interim Financial Reporting" (1999)	P(S)BU 1 "General Requirements for Financial Statements" (2013)
IAS 36 "Impairment of Assets" (2004)	P(S)BU 28 "Impairment of Assets" (2012)
IAS 37 "Provisions, Contingent Liabilities and Contingent Assets" (1999)	none
IAS 38 "Intangible Assets" (2004)	P(S)BU 8 "Intangible Assets" (2012)
IAS 39 "Financial Instruments: Recognition and Measurement" (2005)	P(S)BU 10 "Receivables" P(S)BU 11 "Liabilities" (2012) P(S)BU 12 "Financial investments" (2012) P(S)BU 13 "Financial Instruments" (2012)
IAS 40 "Investment Property" (2005)	P(S)BU 32 "Investment Property" (2012)
IAS 41 "Agriculture" (2003)	P(S)BU 30 "Biological Assets" (2012)
IFRS FOR SME	P(S)BU 25 " Small Enterprise Financial Report"
none	P(S)BU 10 "Receivables"
none	P(S)BU 11 "Liabilities"
none	P(S)BU 16 "Expenses"

The following are selected key differences between statutory accounting and IFRS, which may have a significant impact on the comparability of companies P(S)BU financial statements to those made in accordance with IFRS:

- some aspects of IFRS , in particular the requirement to disclose the ultimate owners and some of the requirements of IAS 24 "Related Party Disclosures", as well as methods of accounting for derivative financial instruments are not covered by the P(S)BU;
- according to the national standards the enterprise has to submit the consolidated financial statements, however, there is no regulatory support for adjusting the scope of consolidation, hence significant investments in subsidiaries, associated companies and mutual funds may remain beyond consolidation.
- P(S)BU do not cover accrual of unused leave allowance and other reserves accumulation, in accordance with IAS 37.

P(S)BU, although developed on the IFRS basis, however do not fully reflect recent changes in IFRS. For example, P(S)BU do not cover several latest standards (IFRS 7 "Financial Instruments: Disclosures", IFRS 4 "Insurance Contracts"), as well as other standards approved some time ago (IAS 37 "Provisions, Contingent Liabilities and Contingent Assets ", IAS 34 "Interim Financial statements").

Disclosure requirements in the P(S)BU are not so strict; e. g. IFRS requires disclosure of payments to key employees of the enterprise, and P(S)BU do not. The impact of these differences on the usefulness of financial statements may in some cases be significant. Discrepancies may result in the impossibility to compare the financial statements prepared under P(S)BU to those prepared under IFRS, and limits the usefulness of the P(S)BU financial statements for users unfamiliar with the Ukrainian national accounting standards.

Another source of "gap in standards" are the cases of setting the accounting rules by the regulating authority such as the National Bank of Ukraine, which are different or inconsistent with the requirements of accounting standards. Usually, regulators require information, including financial information, from entities regulated by them on a larger scale than one contained in the of general purpose mandatory reporting. Regulatory reporting framework may be different from the existing accounting standards and regulated companies have to coordinate one with the other. Such "gap in standards" is evident in the Ukrainian banking sector; banks generate statutory financial statements according to P(S)BU and separate financial statements in accordance with National Bank of Ukraine accounting rules (based on IFRS) contained in the regulations of the NBU.

The result of such inconsistency is obvious complexity for companies to meet both – the requirements of IFRS and the accounting regulations of the NBU, so their financial statements may not comply with IFRS. So any request of IFRS implementation to the entities such as banks, other financial institutions and listed companies, as was recently suggested in Ukraine, should be accompanied by a revision of relevant legal documents for IFRS compatibility that apply to such entities.

3.3 Convergence with P(S)BU

Companies must submit annual financial information to the State Statistics Committee and the tax authorities with tax returns. Notable examples of non-Convergence with standards are:

- lack of related party transactions disclosure;
- lack of existing accounting policies disclosure;
- lack of charging provisions against liabilities, whose evaluation is not supported by third-party primary documentation; accrual of such provisions are not usually allowed by tax accounting rules, in particular, accrual of leave allowance and the reserve for losses on doubtful receivables;

- lack of accrual of deferred taxes;
- lack of disclosure of earnings per share;
- recording assets at cost if there is evidence of impairment, as well as
- non-inclusion of cash flow report to the statements.

The biggest problem in achieving Convergence with P(S)BU remain the differences in the assessment base between the key articles of general purpose financial statements prepared in accordance with P(S)BU, and the calculation of tax liabilities of the enterprise. In cases of differences between the tax accounting standards and P(S)BU, many preparers use tax rules. This leads to inconsistency in terms of accounting estimates (because the tax calculations, as a rule, do not allow the use of accounting estimates), the valuation of assets and liabilities (tax accounting often requires the use of formulas, but liabilities are recognized only if they are supported by primary paper documents) and misuse of accrual basis.

3.4 Convergence with IFRS

As noted above, the financial statements in accordance with IFRS are not required by law; such reports are prepared to meet the needs of investors and other stakeholders. It is usually prepared with the help of the international accounting firm and often audited by the same firm (which may lead to potential conflicts of interest); company financial statements in accordance with P(S)BU are usually prepared unassisted and audited by another, often domestic, firm. Examples of apparent non-Convergence with IFRS are:

- lack of disclosure of related party transactions and the real side carrying out control;
- that some consolidated financial statements do not include all controlled subsidiaries and special purpose entities;
- low level of Convergence to reporting requirements by business segments;
- that disclosure of revalued fixed assets was mainly weak even when there is evidence of significant revaluation;
- weakness of intangible assets disclosure, particularly in view of impairment;
- that disclosure of significant assumptions and estimates were obviously better in banks and worse in industrial plants;
- that in some cases, the fair value of financial instruments, assessed at amortized cost were not provided, and the explanation of considerable coincidence in the assessment of the fair value and the amortized cost were weak and
- the information about purchases and sales of subsidiaries is not always disclosed.

Preparers of the insurance companies reporting noted particular difficulties associated with lack of proper methodological support and support in matters directly related to insurance. Calculation of required reserves ("reservation") is one of the biggest challenges for the insurance companies of Ukraine. Orientation of insurance operations (primarily in property damage insurance) and fixed rules applicable to certain passive operations, lead to the fact that the requirements of insurance claims are now more short-term than that is required by international standards; it simplifies the process of reservation. However, with the development of the insurance industry insurance procedures and policies will become more complex, the life insurance market will expand, prolonging the requirements term and complicating the process of reservation. Adherence to standards of accounting estimates is likely to become an even greater challenge. In addition, the project is being implemented by the IASB which concerns IFRS for insurance operations; authorities should monitor developments in this project.

With the publication of new and significant changes to existing international standards, discrepancies between national and international standards will deepen. Such a prospect is quite realistic, given the program of the Council on International Accounting Standards. This raises the problem of making the appropriate changes in the national provisions (standards) of accounting, according to the issue of new or replacement of existing international standards.

Golov (2007) shows that: "Implementation of the principles and methods of IAS by P(S)BU proves that IAS is not only the methods and approaches for accounting and reporting, but also, to a certain extent, an imprint of the ideology and democracy of the society, the ability of its institutions to adapt the norms of civilized relations. Consequently, the full implementation of IAS is impossible without appropriate political, economic and social changes in the environment in which they will be applied. It is clear that such changes cannot be instantaneous".

Building an effective regulatory and institutional framework at the national level is a challenging task. Under the terms of a practical guide for the development of the accounting system, during the evaluation of the process of development of the regulatory and institutional standards for high-quality corporate reporting the following aspects and related indicators should be considered (TD/B/C.II/ISAR/63):

- Auditing quality and cost – foreign and domestic auditing companies are presented at the audit services market in Ukraine. Most large manufacturing companies, as well as listed companies use the services of international companies and it's justified by their goals. All other companies, stock companies by configuration, use the services of local auditing firms. Fees for IFRS reporting confirmation have increased by 30-40%;
- Licensing of auditors in Ukraine is carried out since the adoption of the Law of Ukraine "On Auditing" in 1993. Moreover, each auditor must have a certificate and passes the annual advanced training.

- Corporate governance quality – evaluation of the quality of corporate governance is stipulated by the Law of Ukraine "On Joint Stock Companies".
- Inspections, disciplinary measures and appeals – no body is inspecting the IFRS Convergence. Report with "IFRS Compliant" field is submitted to the State Statistics Service, audited report is submitted to the National Securities Commission, the experts of the National Commission does not have the right to inspect and make any decisions regarding the quality of submitted reports.
- Ethics – submitted IFRS reports are often inconsistent not only with the format, but also with the meaning of IFRS. All of them are certified by the auditing company. Often the level of audited reports is very low. This fact is explained by the ignorance of auditors who do not have even the most common international certification diplomas CAP, ACCA DipFR, and the acquisition of the auditor certificate in Ukraine is also highly criminalized.
- Clear institutional responsibilities – a major concern in Ukraine is the large number of state regulators, which are not connected with each other and do not coordinate their work with any higher authority. The situation is chaotic and confusing for all participants of the transition to IFRS reporting process.
- Efficiency of financing mechanisms – as we've mentioned earlier no financing mechanism of transition to IFRS is provided. According to the author this is nonsense, and points out a formal approach to the problem by the state.
- Professional accountancy bodies – today in Ukraine a large number of professional organizations is presented, one of which is a full member of IFAC - Federation of Professional Accountants and Auditors of Ukraine, as well as - the Union of Auditors of Ukraine; - Ukrainian Association of Accountants and Auditors and others. Professional organizations should increase certification of accountants and monitor quality of service. In fact, this is not happening.

The role of “Big 4” in the implementation of IFRS in Ukraine is difficult to estimate. Most of the major Ukrainian companies are audited just at them. The site http://msfz.minfin.gov.ua/ presents instructional materials to facilitate understanding of IFRS, as well as business cases on the application of IFRS for the first implementation. In the period of 2005-2014, with the participation of specialists “Big 4” were held a series of round tables, conferences on IFRS implementation in Ukraine. So during a public discussion "Future of audit", which was organized by ACCA were discussed questions such as: The role of audit in society, lack of transparency, corruption, appeals for stricter adherence to existing laws and for more close cooperation with regulators, audit economy in crisis, proportional and fair limitation of liability of auditors.

In his speech, Gerry Parfitt (Parfitt, 2010), Audit Partner of KPMG in Ukraine, said that the profession had not done enough to reduce the level of corruption and ensure transparency. "What would I like to see in Ukraine is transparency, where society and businesses appoint auditors to ensure the transparency of the business. In the UK every single company has to provide their accounting annually to the State Registration Department of companies. This is a public document, which is easy to find on the Internet." Essentially, no discussion or implementation of IFRS for SME occurs at the state level. There were organized a series of activities and discussions by private entities and educational centers. For example, in 2012 the International Business Conference took place a presentation of the IFRS for SME, which was introduced by Michael Wells - Director of IFRS Education Initiative.

4. Conclusions

Based on the conducted study it can be concluded that the accounting system of Ukraine during its independence has undergone fundamental change. First of all a system of accounting regulation was created, Plan of National Accounts and accounting standards were developed, strategic choice in favor of the use of IFRS was made.

Attempts to apply the IFRS led on one hand to decrease in the number of rules, strict regulation of accounting due to the replacement of multipage instructions by the concise standards, on the other hand there are still the rules of reflecting the account transactions, regulated by chart of accounts, instructions for chart of accounts use, rules of drafting financial reporting, standardized financial reporting forms. Thus, a problem remains with accounting in Ukraine, which is based on rules rather than on principles.

Modern Ukrainian accounting system combines the features of several Western models. From the perspective of accounting regulation in Ukraine dominates continental model, which is characterized by government regulation, standardized reporting forms and centralized chart of accounts. On the other hand, an integrated system of accounts and functional approach based on the definition of a financial result is used, which is specific to the Anglo-Saxon system. Such mixed system of accounting is typical for most countries with economies in transition.

Financial reporting international standards are used if they do not contradict the local law and are officially published on the website of the central executive body providing the state financial policy. Ukrainian analysts estimate the national standards to be 65% compliant with international standards, so it may be concluded that Ukraine took the way of convergence of national and international standards.

The first step in the IFRS implementation was to create a special website by the Ministry of Finance together with the FINREP. The purpose of the site is easy and free access of business entities, accounting practitioners and students to the best IFRS application practices. Ministry of Finance declared that the transition to IFRS is implemented with minimal transaction costs. This applies to both business entities, which is not imposed neither mandatory training nor certification of professionals, who are provided with free training materials, and the state, which did not spend extra budgetary resources on the transition process.

The transition to IFRS, declared by the Government of Ukraine took place in 2012-2013. But, as a matter of fact, it is not possible for investors to fully base their judgments on Ukrainian enterprises public financial statements because of the distortion of primary information in the financial reporting. Ukraine has exceeded the common level of shadowization by more than four times. Under such conditions there's no completeness and truthfulness in financial reporting because of the violation of one of the main qualitative characteristics of IFRS reporting – truthful representation.

According to the author, the introduction of IFRS for all joint stock companies was precipitate, only few companies (12.68% of the total number of existing public companies) which were listed or planned to attract loans from foreign banks actually benefited from the introduction of IFRS, all other companies have approached this issue formally.

Indirect signs of transition to IFRS evidence the formal attitude: no change in the book value of fixed assets, items of added capital, deferred taxes are not taken into account; the doubtful debt reserve and provision for holidays are not assessed.

Thus enterprises by marking "comply with IFRS," practically did not accomplish the transformation from national reporting standards to the IFRS financial statements. State regulators have failed to provide effective legal and institutional frameworks at the national level for the process of full implementation of IFRS.

Ukraine's experience in the implementation of IFRS shows that initially was elected approach adapting national accounting standards to the international standards. Further, this process has been refocused on the progressive convergence to IFRS. Convergence does not imply a direct transition to IFRS, limiting by practical aspects of IFRS convergence with national standards, providing for involvement in the development and improvement of IFRS professionals from around the world and thus the achievement of common approaches to deal with accounting and reporting at the national level.

References

Ampofo, A. A. & Sellani, R. J. (2005) "Examining the differences between United States Generally Accepted Accounting Principles (U.S. GAAP) and InternationalAccounting Standards (IAS): implications for the harmonization of accounting standards", *Accounting Forum*, vol. 29: 219-231

Borodkin, A. S. (1997) "Shock therapy for accounting", *Svit buh.obliku*, vol. 1: 4-45

Butinetz, F.F. (2003) "Accounting in Ukraine", *Mythology*, vol. 2 - Zhitomir: ZHDTU, p. 524

Golov, S. F. (2007) *Accounting in Ukraine: Status and prospects of development*, Kiev: Centre

Golov S. F. (2007) Implementation of the principles and methods of IAS available on-line at http://www.mim.kiev.ua/ common/ua/activities/publications/ mim_kostuchenko.pdf

Gutsaylyuk, Z. V. (2006) "Strategic accounting", *Kiev Accounting Review*, no. 2

Harris, P. R. (2002) "European challenge: developing global organizations", *European Business Review*, vol. 14(6): 416-425

IASC/IASB Chronology (2006) available on-line at http://www.iasplus.com/ restruct/chrono.htm. Accessed on 19th April 2006.

Kirsch, A (2007) "Formal attitude of Ukrainian accountants", *Business*, vol. 5: 12

Kuzhelny, M.V. & Parkhomenko N. M. (2001) "PSBU: current status, completion and implementation processes", *Bulletin of the KNU*, vol. 52: 12-18

Kuz'minskii A. M. (2006) "What is the system of accounting?", *Kiev Accounting Review*, no. 6

Levitsky, O.L. (2002) "Enron - what's next", *Accounting Report*, Feb. 2002, p. 18-23

Lehman, G. (2005) "A critical perspective on the harmonization of accounting in a globalizing world", *Critical Perspectives on Accounting*, vol. 16: 975-992

Lastovetskiy, V. O. (2002) "About accounting science", *Ukrainian Accounting Review*, vol.1: 35-38

Mossakovskii, V.B. (2003) "Harmonization of financial reporting", *Accounting and Auditing in Ukraine?*, vol. 4: 24-32

Ohiychuk, M. F. (1997) "A uniform methodological basis Soviet of accounting", vol. 5: 3-9

Pushkar, M. S. (1999) *Trends and patterns of accounting development in Ukraine (theoretical-methodological aspects): monograph*, Ternopil: Economicheskaya misl, 422 p.

Parfitt, G. (2010) working paper available on-line at http://www.bakertilly.ua/ ru/news/id113

Rodrigues, L. L. & Craig, R. (2007) "Assessing international accounting harmonization using Hegelian dialectic, isomorphism and Foucault", *Critical Perspectives on Accounting*, vol. 18, no. 6: 739 – 757

Sopko, V. V. (2006) “Accounting for management”, *Kiev Accounting Review*, no. 6

Turner, L. E. (2001) “Disclosure and Accounting in a Global Market: looking to the future”, Securities Regulation in the Global Internet Economy Conference, November 14-15. available on-line at http://www.iasplus.com/usa/0111turner.pdf. Accessed on 19th April 2006.

UNCTAD (2005) Review of Practical Implementation Issues of International Financial Reporting Standards, available on-line at http://www.iasplus.com/resource/0511unctad.pdf, Accessed on 19th April 2006.

Financial Statements SATP 0904 available on-line at http://smida.gov.ua/db/participant/00435560.

Yurchenko, N. (2011) “Ukrainian shadow economy exceeds the official one”, sociologist/ UKRINFORM official website. available on-line at http://www.ukrinform.ua/ukr/order/?Id=1036033)

*** Decision of the State Commission on Securities and Stock Market no. 981 of July 22, 2010

*** Decree of the Cabinet of Ministers of Ukraine on the adoption of the Strategy implementation of international financial reporting standards in Ukraine" dated October 24, no. 911, 2007

*** Decree on Ukraine's transition to the common practice in international accounting and statistics, available on-line at http://zakon4.rada.gov.ua/laws/show/303/92)

*** Ministry of Finance letter of May 11, 2011 no. 31-08410-07-10/12036.

*** Normative and institutional framework for high-quality corporate reporting: main trends and challenges TD/B/C.II/ISAR/63

*** Tax Code of Ukraine of 02.12.2010 no. 2755-VI

2

Some issues related to cash flow statement in accounting education: The case of Turkey

Can Öztürk [a,1]

[a] *Çankaya University, Ankara, Turkey*

Abstract: This paper focuses on some issues related to the cash flow statement in the context of accounting education in Turkey. I identify eight aspects related to the cash flow statement based on my experience in teaching IAS 7 *Statement of Cash Flows*, and discuss their evolution over time. The paper also incorporates the educational perspective of Turkish accounting academics who teach an undergraduate level accounting course that covers this statement. For the purpose of this study, a survey of Turkish academics was conducted. The findings provide insights on how the students' competencies related to the cash flow statement should be improved in the context of undergraduate level accounting education in Turkey and, by extension, in Central and Eastern European countries. While the paper is focused on the Turkish context, the findings might be of interest for other countries in the region, embarked in the modernization of financial reporting and International Financial Reporting Standards-based accounting education.

Keywords: cash flow statement, accounting higher education, Turkey

1. Introduction

In Turkey, the cash flow statement (CFS) was prepared in 1989 as an optional financial statement by entities that are subject to the regulation of the Capital Markets Board (CMB) (Çiftçi & Sarıoğlu, 2007). In 1992, the CFS became a compulsory financial statement for all Turkish entities, but in 1994, the reporting of

[1] *Corresponding author*: Department of Management, Çankaya University; Eskişehir Yolu 29. Km, Yukarıyurtçu Mahallesi Mimar Sinan Caddesi No:4 06790, Etimesgut/ANKARA Turkey;
Email address: cozturk@cankaya.edu.tr

a CFS by all entities became optional unless their total assets or net sales revenue exceeded a certain amount. It should be noted that the role of this financial statement was not a very important one in the Turkish accounting system, because of the tax driven structure of this system (rather than financial reporting) until recently. Starting in 2005 however, the role of the CFS began to increase. The Turkish Accounting Standards Board (TASB) and subsequently the Turkish Public Oversight, Accounting and Auditing Standards Authority (TPOAASA) started to regulate the financial reporting in Turkey. Currently, CFS is a compulsory financial statement for the entities that are subject to independent audit, and an optional one for the entities that are not subject to independent audit if their total assets or net sales revenue do not exceed certain amount.

From the educational perspective, CFS has never lost its importance and its existing importance moved ahead within the Turkish accounting education after the adoption of International Financial Reporting Standards (IFRS) in 2005. In this context, the objective of this paper is to investigate some issues related to the CFS in accounting education in Turkey, and to contribute to the global accounting education in the context of the CFS from the perspective of Turkish accounting academics.

In this regard, this research is important because it investigates and discusses the trends on the eight aspects of the CFS in undergraduate level accounting education in Turkey. These aspects that are based on the author's experience in teaching IAS 7 *Statement of Cash Flows* are as follows: (1) courses that cover the CFS, (2) methods taught to calculate the cash inflows and cash outflows in a CFS, (3) accounting regulations taught to prepare a CFS, (4) accounting policies taught to prepare a CFS, (5) accounting policies taught to classify and/or exemplify some items of a CFS, (6) methods used to exemplify the financial analysis of a CFS, (7) methods used to assess and evaluate the preparation of CFS, and (8) tools of educational technology used to prepare a CFS.

The observations and discussions of my research will be of interest to both Turkish and non-Turkish accounting academics who teach undergraduate level accounting courses that cover the CFS. This research will draw a picture on some issues related to the CFS in accounting education and offer suggestions, of interest for Turkish accounting academics. On the other hand, it is expected that non-Turkish academics will also benefit from this research because it provides a starting point (i.e. the eight aspects of the CFS) to analyze the teaching of CFS at the undergraduate level within their country, and to implement some improvements.

The paper has the following structure: section 2 presents the review of the debate on CFS in accounting education; section 3 explains the data and the research methodology; section 4 discusses the eight aspects related to CFS. Finally, section 5 presents concluding remarks along with main findings.

2. Review of the debate on CFS in accounting education

As I stated before, this paper focuses on eight aspects of the CFS from the perspective of accounting academics teaching undergraduate level accounting courses in Turkey. That is why the literature review section of this paper was developed according to those aspects. However, before the literature review, I should say that there are four papers that specifically refer to the literature review on accounting education, which are Apostolou *et al.* (2001; 2010; 2013), and Watson *et al.* (2007). These papers cover the literature review of accounting education from 1997 to 2012. As far as these papers and my additional analysis of literature are concerned, I did not find any prior research that specifically refers to the matters in my paper.

2.1 Courses that cover the CFS

In order to determine the undergraduate level accounting courses that cover the CFS in Turkey, I examined the content of undergraduate level accounting courses in the global context and determined that the CFS is generally covered within the content of Financial Statement Analysis, IFRS, and Managerial Accounting.

In the context of the course of Managerial Accounting, I gave particular attention to the United States of America (USA) higher education system because preparation and analysis of a CFS has been one of the chapters covered in the courses and textbooks of managerial accounting for many years within business related majors when I was a student in the US. For instance, the well-known US managerial accounting textbooks co-authored by Garrison and Noreen (2003) as well as Weygandt *et al.* (2012) cover the CFS.

Within the framework of this global analysis, I questioned and discussed which courses related to CFS are mostly taught in Turkey.

2.2 Methods taught to calculate the cash inflows and cash outflows in a CFS

In order to prepare a CFS, traditional methods taught to calculate the cash inflows and cash outflows are T-Account approach and Worksheet approach (Weygandt *et al.*, 2013). However, other than these methods, it is known that O'Bryan *et al.* (2000) designed the user-oriented pedagogical approach to be used in the first financial accounting course by providing a direct linkage from accounting equation analysis to the statement of cash flows within the framework of direct method. In addition, Brickner and Mccombs (2004) presented an instructional approach to be used in the introductory financial accounting course to teach the indirect approach with a specific focus on journal entries and T-Accounts. Fletcher and Ulrich (2010) created an alternative and algebraic approach for student instruction in the creation of the CFS under direct and indirect methods based on financial equation relationships to be used in a graduate level course. Overall all the methods try to emphasize the interrelationships between the CFS, balance sheet and income statement from different perspectives.

Within the framework of traditional methods and prior research, I questioned and discussed which calculation methods are taught by Turkish accounting academics.

2.3 Accounting regulations taught to prepare a CFS

In Turkey, financial reporting is currently regulated by the TPOAASA. In this context, this Authority organizes financial reporting from two perspectives: financial reporting for entities that are subject to independent audit and financial reporting for entities that are not subject to independent audit.

In this context, entities that are subject to independent audit as well as have public accountability must prepare their financial statements in accordance with IFRS. In addition, entities that are subject to independent audit but do not have public accountability can prepare their financial statements in accordance with the first communiqué on accounting system(published in 1992) or IFRS. On the other hand, financial reporting of entities that are not subject to independent audit is regulated by the first communiqué on accounting system.

This indicates that entities that are subject to independent audit are required to prepare a CFS regardless of the regulation adopted. However, entities that are not subject to independent audit are required to prepare a CFS if their total assets or net sales revenue exceed certain amounts determined by every year. This restriction has been in force since 3rd communiqué on accounting system was published in 1994.
Within the framework of this analysis, I questioned and discussed according to which accounting regulation(s) a CFS is currently taught by Turkish accounting academics.

2.4 Accounting policies taught to prepare a CFS

Accounting policies to prepare a CFS refers to the direct and indirect method in terms of IAS 7. From the financial reporting perspective, Nobes (2013) indicates that direct method is preferred by Australian listed entities versus Canadian and European listed entities (entities from Britain, France, Germany, Italy, Netherlands, Spain, Sweden) are inclined to prefer indirect method. In the same context, Pekdemir and Yönet (2010) using 2007, 2008, and 2009 IFRS financial statements, Öztürk (2011) using 2008 IFRS financial statements, Bahadır and

Tolga (2013) using 2011 IFRS financial statements, and Özdemir (2014) using 2012 IFRS financial statements, show that Turkish listed companies are inclined to prepare their CFSs under indirect method.

From an educational perspective, through the participation of thirty eight accounting students, Kojima (2012) determined that the presentation format of operating cash flow either direct or indirect influences lending decisions by using financial information about a hypothetical retail company. This research states that participants did not make any additional calculations under direct approach. This means that they directly and easily observed cash inflows and outflows compared to indirect approach. Farshadfar and Monem (2013) indicates that direct method is useful in predicting the cash flows. Hales and Orpurt (2013) supports the idea that the direct method cash flow information is decision useful within the framework of their review of academic research.

Within the framework of the financial reporting, educational, and academic perspective, I questioned and discussed which accounting policies are taught by Turkish accounting academics to prepare a CFS.

2.5 Accounting policies taught to classify and/or exemplify some items of a CFS

In terms of IAS 7, it is possible to see the reporting of interest received, interest paid, dividend received and dividend paid under different activities of the CFS in practice.

In terms of interest received, interest paid, dividend received and dividend paid, IAS 7 requires these cash flows to be disclosed separately and classified in a consistent manner from one period to another as operating, investing, and financing activities (Alfredson *et al.*, 2013: 710). In this context, Nobes (2013) indicates that Australian, Canadian and European listed entities (entities from France, Netherlands, Italy, and Sweden) are inclined to classify all interest payments under cash flows from operating activities.

However, TPOAASA does not accept such a sole classification. Depending on the consistent classification under operating, investing, and financing activities, it regulates its exemplary IFRS financial statements stating that interest paid should be allocated to operating, investing, and financing activities as well as interest received should be allocated to operating, and investing activities. That is why I did not question and discuss interest received and interest paid from an academic perspective.

In this section, I focused on dividend paid, dividend received, taxes paid, and cash flows from discontinued operations.

Dividend paid: According to IAS 7, dividend paid may be classified either in the cash flows from operating activities or in the cash flows from financing activities in terms of non-financial companies (Alfredson *et al.,* 2013: 710). In this context, Öztürk (2011) states that Australian, Turkish, and European (entities from Britain, France, Germany, and Italy) listed entities are inclined to classify dividend payments in the cash flows from financing activities. By taking accounting policy applied in practice into account, I questioned and discussed whether Turkish accounting academics exemplify dividend paid in the cash flows from operating or financing activities.

Dividend received: IAS 7 does not prescribe how dividend received should be classified for non-financial companies (Alfredson *et al*., 2013: 710). However, it is possible to classify dividend received either in the cash flows from operating activities or in the cash flows from investing activities in terms of non-financial companies depending on the accountant's perspective. In this context, Kvaal and Nobes (2010) indicates that listed entities from Australia, France and Germany are inclined to classify their dividend received under operating activities versus British entities prefer investing activities. By taking accounting policy applied in practice into account, I questioned and discussed whether Turkish accounting academics exemplify dividend received in the cash flows from operating or investing activities.

Taxes paid: IAS 7 makes taxes paid possible to classify in the cash flows from operating activities unless it can be specifically identified with investing and financing activities. However, the tax expense may be readily identifiable with investing and financing activities although this is not often the case (Alfredson *et al*., 2013: 710). In this context, Öztürk (2011) shows that Turkish, Australian and European listed entities are inclined to classify their tax payments in the cash flows from operating activities. By taking the accounting policy applied in practice into account, I questioned and discussed whether Turkish accounting academics directly exemplify taxes paid in operating activities or they exemplify it by allocating to related activities.

Cash flow from discontinued operations: According to the relationship between IAS 7 and IFRS 5 Non-Current Assets Held for Sale and Discontinued Operations, if there are discontinued operations in a business organization, cash flows from discontinued operations must be reported in the CFS or in the notes. In this context, I questioned and discussed whether there are any Turkish accounting academics teaching the cash flows from discontinued operations in undergraduate level accounting education and, if any, where they report those cash flows.

2.6 Methods used to exemplify the financial analysis of a CFS

mIn terms of the use of a CFS in the context of financial analysis, Gup *et al.* In terms of the use of a CFS in the context of financial analysis, Gup *et al.* (1993) from an American perspective and Aktaş *et al.* (2012) from a Turkish perspective examined the cash flow patterns by using the CFS to analyze a firm's economic condition. Ibarra (2009) used the CFS to evaluate company's liquidity, efficiency, profitability and ability to protect long-term investors and creditors via cash flow ratios. In addition, Karğın and Aktaş (2011) analyzed the CFSs of a Turkish listed construction company through comparative, trend, ratio, and cash flow patterns' analysis. Kirkham (2012) uses the CFS in order to support the traditional ratios with cash flow ratios for a better liquidity analysis.

Within the framework of the prior research, I questioned and discussed which methods of financial analysis could be used by Turkish accounting academics to analyze the CFS in an undergraduate level accounting course.

2.7 Methods used to assess and evaluate the preparation of CFS

Gelbal (2013) states that there are three fundamental characteristics of the methods of assessment and evaluation: reliability, validity, and practicability. Reliability consists of how the methods of assessment and evaluation sensitively measure the variable or how the results of assessment and evaluation are free from error. In this context, reliability covers consistency, persistency, and sensitivity. Validity is possible as long as the method of assessment and evaluation meets its objectives. Practicability refers to the methods whose preparation and application period is short, and easy as well as that are economically reasonable, and grading-friendly.

Within the framework of these characteristics and my teaching experience, I questioned and discussed which methods of assessment and evaluation could be used by Turkish accounting academics to assess and evaluate their students' preparation of a CFS in an undergraduate level accounting course.

2.8 Tools of educational technology used to prepare a CFS

According to the recent research made by Yalçın (2012), Turkish employers expect that potential and existing accounting professionals should be familiar with the tools of information systems in terms of bookkeeping, preparing comparative financial information, and utilizing managerial and cost accounting information in the context of financial and managerial decision making within the business.

Related to these expectations, Cengiz and Uyar (2012), by examining 900 job advertisements related to accounting on February 6, 2012, found out that 96% of Turkish employers look for a potential accounting employee who has the ability to use office programs and 24% them look for a potential accounting employee who is capable of using the accounting software "Logo" when they advertise an accounting related position.

Despite the expectations of Turkish employers, Hatunoğlu (2006) and Erol Fidan and Subaşı (2014) shows that the use of accounting software in Turkish accounting higher education is generally rare in terms of some courses such as Financial Statement Analysis, Managerial/Cost/Corporate Accounting, and Auditing versus the use of accounting software in a General Accounting course is around 20% of academics contributing to both researches. Overall, the findings of both researches indicate that accounting courses in Turkish accounting higher education are mostly taught theoretically and the use of accounting software is primarily devoted to the specific course "Computerized Accounting".

In this context, Sultanoğlu *et al.* (2007) state that Computerized Accounting is generally offered as an elective course for students majoring in management by examining a sample set of 30 Turkish universities and found out that 9 of these universities (33%) have this course in their list of electives. According to Hatunoğlu (2006), the number of academics teaching this course refers to 29 academics in a sample set of 102 academics versus the number of academics teaching this course consists of 45 academics in a sample set of 136 academics according to Erol Fidan and Subaşı (2014). Both in 2006 and 2014, around 30% of academics teach this course. Overall, prior research indicate that this course is taught in more than 9 universities; however, it is expected that it will remain as an elective course due to the adoption of EU's Bologna Process.

Other than the use of the accounting software, the use of office programs is expected from potential accounting employees as I stated before. As a reflection of this, what needs to be done is to question which one of the office programs is particularly used to teach accounting applications.

In this context, Hatunoğlu (2006) states that 77% of academics, generally, prefer using Excel in journalizing accounting transactions in a sample set of 92 academics but does not establish a relationship between the course title and Excel usage. In the same perspective, Erol Fidan and Subaşı (2014) states that the use of office programs in accounting courses consists of 80% of 136 academics, but this research does not specifically answer which one of the office programs is particularly used to teach accounting applications.

In terms of the CFS, it should be noted that Eesley (2013) developed a simpler method to introduce the CFS to entrepreneurship and other non-accounting majors so that they can construct a simple CFS under indirect method using basic spreadsheet skills. In addition, Sultanoğlu *et al.* (2014) indicates that spreadsheet based accounting applications including the CFS were integrated into an undergraduate level principles of accounting course at Bilkent University in Turkey.

Within the framework of the prior research, I questioned and discussed whether there are any Turkish accounting academics who use any software in teaching the CFS and which accounting software and/or office programs are used by these academics to teach the preparation of CFS.

3. Data and research methodology

3.1. Sample set

This research is based on the survey whose answers were collected from the Turkish accounting academics regardless of their academic levels. In this sense, this survey was sent to approximately 300 academics via e-mail. However, 105 academics contributed to this survey and 43 of them, positively, responded to the question whether they teach a course that covers the CFS. That is why the sample set is analyzed below in terms of 43 academics in the numerical, regional and academic context.

If the sample set is analyzed in the numerical context, the survey based research of Hatunoğlu (2006) and Erol Fidan and Subaşı (2014) helped me to defend my sample. According to Hatunoğlu (2006), the number of Turkish accounting academics teaching the course "General Accounting"(including Principles of Accounting, and Financial Accounting) consists of 81 academics versus the number of academics teaching a course related to CFS, primarily, "Financial Statement Analysis" refers to 45 academics in a sample set of 102 academics. In the same context, Erol Fidan and Subaşı (2014) indicate that the number of Turkish accounting academics teaching the course "General Accounting" refers to 119 academics versus the number of academics teaching the course "Financial Statement Analysis" consists of 66 academics in a sample set of 136 academics. Both researches show that the majority of academics, primarily, teach "General Accounting" in Turkey as the common course of business related majors versus teaching the course "Financial Statement Analysis" is limited compared to "General Accounting". That is one of the factors that negatively influenced my sample set.

However, this is not the only case. There are other factors that negatively influenced my sample size. In this context, some of the academics let me know that CFS is not within their specialization area or a course related to CFS is not within their major's curriculum. Some of them told me that it is within their specialization area but related courses were transferred from the list of compulsory courses to the list of elective courses due to the adoption of European Union's Bologna Process. That is why they are not able to teach those courses at this point in time. This situation was also verified by Terzi *et al.* (2013) stating that the number of elective courses was increased due to Bologna Process. In addition, one of the academics informed me that the business major has been recently introduced and the course related to CFS has not yet been taught by him. Also, it should be considered that some of the academics did not want to contribute to my survey as well as I did find any accounting academics at some universities and I did reach some of the accounting academics due to their missing e-mail addresses.

Within the framework of all these factors/constraints, I believe that my sample size is reasonable compared to the sample size of Hatunoğlu (2006) and Erol Fidan and Subaşı (2014) and relatively reflects the Turkish case.

If the sample set is analyzed in the regional context[1], the following results are pointed out in Table 1. The regional results show that the majority of academics (86%) who, positively, answered this question are from the universities located in Central Anatolia, Marmara and Aegean regions of Turkey. In addition, it reflects mainly the perspective of accounting academics from relatively major universities located in the following cities: Ankara, Istanbul, and Izmir.

Kaya and Daştan (2004) state that undergraduate level of accounting education in Turkey has taken place within the Faculty of Business Administration or within Faculty of Economics and Administrative Sciences for students majoring in management, economics, finance, and international relations. Even if the prior research indicates this fact, new business related majors such as Health Care Management, Accounting and Financial Management, Banking and Finance, Accounting Information Systems, and International Finance and Trade have been introduced within the Faculty of Health Sciences, Faculty of Economics and Administrative Sciences, within the Faculty of Commercial Sciences or within the School of Applied Sciences since 2004.

By taking this situation into account, if the sample set is analyzed in the academic context, we pointed out that 84% of academics are employed in the major of management and the remaining 16% are the academic members of other majors stated above. This shows that the finding of Kaya and Daştan (2004) is still valid.

With respect to academic levels, professors (assistant, associate and full) refer to 88% of all academics who teach a course that covers the CFS. The remaining 12% consist of instructors (with or without PhD).

Table 1. Summary of the regional distribution of the Turkish accounting academics who teach a course covering the CFS

Regions	Cities	Number of Academics Teaching CFS per City	Number of Academics Teaching CFS in the Regional Context	% of Academics Teaching CFS in the Regional Context
Central Anatolia	Ankara	17	18	42%
	Konya	1		
Marmara	Bursa	3	15	35%
	Çanakkale	2		
	Edirne	2		
	İstanbul	6		
	Yalova	2		
Aegean	İzmir	4	5	12%
	Muğla	1		
Mediterranean	Antalya	1	1	2%
Black Sea	Tokat	1	1	2%
Southeastern Anatolia	Gaziantep	1	2	5%
	Şanlıurfa	1		
Unclassified	Unclassified	1	1	2%
Eastern Anatolia	-	-	-	-
Total	**-**	**43**	**43**	**100%**

Universities of Turkish accounting academics from:
Ankara: Atılım University, Başkent University, Bilkent University, Çankaya University, Gazi University, Middle-East Technical University and TOBB University of Economics and Technology
Konya: Selçuk University
Bursa: Uludağ University
Çanakkale: Onsekiz Mart University
Istanbul: Doğuş University, Galatasaray University, Istanbul University, Marmara University, Yeditepe University
Yalova: Yalova University
Izmir: Dokuz Eylül University, Izmir University of Economics, Yaşar University
Muğla: Sıtkı Koçman University
Antalya: Akdeniz University
Tokat: Gaziosmanpaşa University
Gaziantep: Zirve University
Şanlıurfa: Harran University

Unclassified: The academic's university name is unknown.

Within the framework of the regional analysis, this sample set does not lead us to make comparative regional analysis due to its specific focus to Ankara, Istanbul, and Izmir. In addition, academic levels do not make difference in determining the trends on issues related to CFS in accounting education. That is why the sample set is taken into account regardless of regional distribution and academic levels of academics to analyze the survey questions.

3.2 Research methodology

This research uses the frequency distribution method as the research tool. In this context, this survey was prepared in summer of 2014, uploaded to Google Survey in November 2014 and sent to Turkish accounting academics via e-mail to almost all universities within Turkey as long as the university employs accounting academics. Collected answers through survey system were transferred to Excel and evaluated using the frequency distribution method. In addition, all the findings were supported through the author's observations and experiences of other accounting academics.

4. Empirical results and discussion

4.1 Courses that cover the CFS

Compared to my course research in the global context, my survey findings indicate that the courses that the CFS is taught in undergraduate level accounting education in Turkey, covers Specifically Designed Financial Accounting courses and some other courses in addition to Financial Statement Analysis, IFRS, and Managerial Accounting. In this context, while Table 2 presents how these courses are frequently taught by Turkish accounting academics, these findings are discussed below.

Table 2. Courses related to the CFS

N^2=76	Frequency Distribution of Courses	%
Financial Statement Analysis	33	44
IFRS	19	25
Managerial Accounting	7	9
Specifically Designed Financial Accounting	14	18
Other Courses	3	4
Total	**76**	**100**

Financial Statement Analysis: This course, primarily, deals with the analysis of a firm's working capital management, debt to equity structure and profitability management. In order to learn how to analyze all these financial aspects of a firm, it is required to know what the financial statements are, which items are reported in the financial statements, how they are valued in terms of accounting policies and how they will be analyzed within the framework of the tools of financial analysis.

In this context, the historical development of financial statements in Turkey is based on the existence of State Economic Enterprises (SEE) (Özerhan & Yanık, 2008). While SEEs were preparing their balance sheets and income statements in different formats in 1930s, they adopted a quite uniform balance sheet and an income statement formats in 1939. However, these formats were not able to provide the opportunity to financially analyze these enterprises. Around 1950s, balance sheet formats were reorganized in such a way that assets were classified according to non-current/current distinction. This reclassification provided these enterprises the possibility to make financial analysis in the context of trend and ratio analysis. In 1972, a uniform chart of accounts for all firms except for banks and insurance companies was adopted and accounts were classified according to the balance sheet and income statement formats. Since then, asset items were classified according to current/non-current distinction, net working capital began to be easily calculated, regulatory accounts were reflected to balance sheet as a deduction item and the income statement was started to be prepared by function.

If the relatively recent developments were taken into account in terms of financial statements in Turkey, the first communiqué on accounting system was published in 1992 in order to regulate accurate, reliable and comparable financial statements (Koç Yalkın & Demir, 2012: 193).

One of the issues that the first communiqué on accounting system regulates is the preparation and presentation of financial statements. In this context, financial statements prepared in the context of Turkish accounting practice have to include a balance sheet, an income statement, a statement of cost of goods sold, a funds flow statement, a CFS, a profit distribution statement, a statement of owners' equity and notes to these statements (Şımga-Muğan, 1995: 357). The balance sheet, income statement and notes consist of the fundamental statements and the others are supplementary statements.

At the time that this communiqué entered into force, all business entities had to report all financial statements. In 1994, however; the third communiqué on accounting system was published in order to regulate the reporting of supplementary financial statements. According to this regulation, supplementary statements became compulsory for business entities whose total assets or net sales revenue exceed a certain monetary amount that is determined every year. Due to this constraint, the number of entities that have to report all financial statements have been limited since 1994 and this situation emphasized that accounting in Turkey is for tax purposes rather than financial accounting.

Even if this is the case, a CFS has been kept in Turkish accounting education and specifically in the content of the course and textbooks of Financial Statement Analysis. It was taught according to the Turkish format presented in the first communiqué on accounting system until the adoption of IFRS. For instance, the preparation of CFS was retained in one of the textbooks on financial analysis co-authored by Akdoğan and Tenker (2005) after the adoption of third communiqué. In this context, one of my interviewees described the situation as follows:

> "After accounting authorities restricted the reporting of supplementary financial statements, accounting academics believed that they have to cover these financial statements, no matter what, in order to have well-educated potential accountants. That is why I should emphasize that CFS has never lost its position, its character, and its significance in Turkish accounting education despite the third communiqué."

In 2005, IAS 7 that was published by the former TASB made the reporting of a CFS compulsory for listed entities, banks and insurance companies. Since then, Turkish accounting academics have reorganized their courses or textbooks. For instance, it was observed that the textbook of Akdoğan and Tenker (2007) was reorganized according to IAS 7 while preserving the Turkish CFS.

In addition, new financial analysis books that cover solely the CFS in accordance with IAS 7 were introduced such as the textbook co-authored by Karapınar and Zaif (2009). On the other hand, some others, still, focus on the Turkish format presented in the first communiqué on accounting system such as Savcı (2013), and Bektöre *et al.* (2013).

This situation shows that the preparation and analysis of a CFS has been a part of a course or a chapter of a textbook in Turkish accounting education regardless of adopted regulations in Turkey. That is why the findings of this research indicate that Financial Statement Analysis is the most frequently taught course that covers the CFS in Turkish undergraduate level accounting education.

IFRS: After the full adoption of IFRS in 2005, IFRSs started to be offered as a required or elective undergraduate course in majors related to business and accounting and CFS of IAS 7 became a part of the course content as well. In this context, IFRS consists of the second frequently taught course that covers the CFS in Turkish undergraduate level accounting education. In addition, Turkish accounting academics started to publish IFRS related textbooks (Gücenme Gençoğlu, 2007; Gökçen *et al.*, 2011; Özerhan & Yanık, 2012; Kızıl *et al.*, 2013; Örten *et al.*, 2013) and IFRS related subject specific books (Demir & Bahadır, 2009; Demir, 2009; Akdoğan *et al.*, 2011; Kaya, 2011).

Specifically Designed Financial Accounting Courses: In most of business related majors in Turkish higher education, General Accounting courses are generally designed for two terms to teach the accounting cycle, to introduce the items of balance sheet and income statement as well as the preparation of these financial statements. Sultanoğlu *et al.* (2007) state that these courses are also called Principles of Accounting or Financial Accounting. Generally speaking, the preparation and analysis of a CFS is not included in these courses. Even the Turkish textbooks on principles of accounting does not generally cover the CFS. In this context, the great majority of the textbooks on general accounting (Civan, 2005; Çaldağ & Ayanoğlu, 2012; Arıkboğa, 2013; Atabey *et al.*, 2013; Koç Yalkın, 2013; Şengel, 2013; Ataman, 2014; Erdamar & Basık, 2014; Karasioğlu, 2014; Sevilengül, 2014; Yükçü, 2014a) do not cover the CFS.

However, it is possible to see some specifically designed courses on accounting principles in some business related majors. These courses such as Principles of Accounting, Principles of Financial Accounting or Financial Accounting as stated in the survey answers, are designed as either one semester or two semester courses and cover specifically the preparation and analysis of a CFS in addition to the traditional content of such courses. In this context, one of my interviewees explained the situation in her university as follows:

> "In my university, I taught principles of accounting as a two semester course until the major of management's curriculum was revised. After the revision, this course was transformed to a one-semester course and the CFS was included into the traditional course content. The reason of doing this change in course content was generated from the direct linkage between the CFS and other specific courses such as Business Finance, and Financial Statement Analysis. In this context, my students think that learning the CFS in this introductory course is complicated but familiarity to the CFS makes them happy when they take upper level accounting and finance courses because those courses teach them how to use the CFS in financial and managerial decision making."

The results of this research indicate that specifically designed financial accounting courses are the third frequently taught courses that cover the CFS in Turkish accounting education.

Managerial Accounting: By taking the US perspective of the course on managerial accounting into account, this research questioned whether there is any Turkish accounting academic who teaches a managerial accounting course by covering the CFS. My findings are not surprising and show that Managerial Accounting is the fourth frequently taught course that covers the CFS in Turkish accounting education in the sense that Turkish accounting academics are inclined to teach managerial accounting without CFS compared to their American peers.

These findings were also proved by the Turkish managerial accounting textbooks (Gürsoy, 2009; Civelek & Özkan, 2011; Haftacı, 2013; Büyükmirza, 2014; Gökçen *et al.*, 2014; Saban & Erdoğan, 2014; Yükçü, 2014b). None of them includes the CFS in their content.

In this regard, Turkish accounting education assumes that CFS is part of the financial accounting and other related courses rather than managerial accounting. That is why Turkish accounting academics, rarely, build a bridge between CFS and managerial accounting as seen in this survey.

Other Courses: There are two other courses that were received from survey answers. One of them is a two term Business Finance course whose first term is devoted to financial statements analysis which also covers the CFS. The other course is called Financial Reporting which covers financial reporting theory, alternative approaches in financial reporting, the role of financial reporting in market economy, the problem of measurement in financial reporting, alternative measurement approaches, recognition and qualitative characteristics of financial statements, and international accounting (international financial reporting) including the CFS. Other courses are the least frequently taught courses.

4.2 Methods taught to calculate the cash inflows and cash outflows in a CFS

In accounting literature, there are mainly two methods to calculate the cash inflows and cash outflows: Worksheet approach and T-Account approach. However, prior research also shows that other calculation methods were developed to facilitate the preparation of a CFS as I stated before. In this context, Table 3 presents my findings and those findings are discussed below.

Table 3. Calculation methods for cash inflows and cash outflows

N=43	Frequency Distribution of Calculation Methods	%
Worksheet Approach	23	53
T-Account Approach	5	12
Both Approaches	11	26
Other Calculation Methods	4	9
Total	**43**	**100**

In terms of the Worksheet approach and T-Account approach, it seems to me that T-Account approach is more convenient than Worksheet approach in undergraduate level accounting education from the students' perspective. In order to defend my opinion, I would like to share my experience based on two different courses.[3] On one hand, I taught a course on IFRS for the students majoring in accounting information systems in Fall 2012, 2013, and 2014. For them, I designed my example of CFS according to T-Account approach. On the other hand, I taught a course on principles of financial accounting for the students majoring in management in Summer of 2012, 2013, and 2014. For them, it was required to design the course material according to Worksheet approach. During the final exam, I asked both group of students to prepare a full CFS. As a result of the final exams given every year, I observed that the students who prepared the cash statement using T-Account approach is more successful than the students who applied the Worksheet approach. This is not a coincidence for all years because what I experienced is the fact that as long as students concretely follow cash inflows, and cash outflows by applying T-Account approach, they feel confident and they are able to prepare a CFS almost correctly. However, those applying the Worksheet approach, mostly, memorize the application process and finally get confused. Overall, I am in favor of teaching the T-Account approach in undergraduate level accounting education if I am free to choose one or the other within the framework of the key word "***concreteness***".

In addition to my experiences, there are other Turkish accounting academics who solely teach the T-Account approach by experiencing that T-Account approach is easier, more concrete, and understandable than Worksheet approach in terms of students.

On the other hand, some Turkish accounting academics who solely teach the Worksheet approach find this approach less time consuming because they think that this approach provides students the opportunity to directly benefit from the balance sheet and income statement and students do not have examine accounting books. At some point, it is true but I believe that time should not be an accounting academic's perspective in order to select the Worksheet approach.

In this context, academics should primarily teach the method that clearly reflects the cash inflows and outflows regardless of time because their audience are students who learn what is going on in a CFS. Therefore, accounting books should not be ignored in teaching the CFS in order to decidedly establish the infrastructure of cash inflows and cash outflows for students in determining the amount cash received and cash paid. That is why I use T-Accounts whenever I need while teaching because they help students to observe changes made on accounts.

A final word of this discussion comes from the academics preferring to teach both approaches. They believe that both approaches complement each other. This is theoretically true from an academic perspective. However, I am not sure about whether students are capable of complementing both approaches with each other in their minds. Also, some academics prefer both approaches by believing that T-Account approach is more explicative than Worksheet approach but Worksheet approach is also exists in practice. I agree with them but I believe that the optimality would be possible through the full knowledge of T-Account approach and the familiarity to the Worksheet approach.

4.3. Accounting regulations taught to prepare a CFS

In Turkey, financial reporting regulations are currently based on the first communiqué on accounting system and IFRS under different circumstances as I stated before. Within the framework of this fact, I discuss below the findings of my research while presenting them in Table 4.

Table 4. Accounting regulations related to CFS

N=43	Frequency Distribution of Calculation Methods	%
IFRS - IAS 7	30	70
First Communiqué on Accounting System	5	12
Both Regulations	8	18
Total	**43**	**100**

The findings mentioned above shows that the majority of Turkish accounting academics switched from the first communiqué on accounting system to IAS 7 in teaching the CFS as if the first communiqué on accounting system is not in force anymore. However, this should not be the case because Turkish entities do not have a single financial reporting regulation at this point in time and financial reporting regulations that will be adopted, primarily, depends on whether entities are subject to independent audit or not. That is why I don't agree with accounting academics who solely teach the CFS in accordance with the first communiqué on accounting system or IAS 7. The knowledge of a CFS in accordance with the first communiqué on accounting system[4] and IAS 7 is still necessary in undergraduate level accounting education.

4.4 Accounting policies taught to prepare a CFS

In teaching the preparation of a CFS, cash flows from operating activities can be taught under direct method, indirect method or both. In this context, I discuss below the findings of my research while presenting them in Table 5.

Table 5. Accounting policy choice related to CFS

N[5]=38	Frequency Distribution of Accounting Policy Choice	%
Direct Method	11	29
Indirect Method	6	16
Both	21	55
Total	**38**	**100**

In order to determine the rationale behind the academics' accounting policy choice, I designed specific questions to concretely understand the academics' perspective.

In order to prefer the direct method when teaching the cash flow from operating activities section of the CFS, essentially, there would be four reasons in the Turkish and academic context as seen in Table 6.

Table 6. The rationale to prefer the direct method

	N^6=20	Frequency Distribution to Prefer the Direct Method	%
a.	The former TASB expressed a preference for the direct method by allowing the use of both methods (TASB, 2010: 391). That's why, I am stick to this preference.	6	30
b.	Cash inflows and outflows are directly observed under direct method with specific reference to Kojima (2012).	7	35
c.	Students easily understand cash inflows and outflows under this method with specific reference to Kojima (2012).	6	30
d.	The cancellation of indirect method has been planning by the International Accounting Standards Board since 2011 (IASB, 2010: 43).	1	5
Total		**20**	**100**

In this context, I believe that the direct method combined with the T-Account approach is the most effective and efficient methodology to be able reach the minds of the students when teaching the CFS because direct method is straightforward and does not challenge the minds of students as far as my experience is concerned. Therefore, I am primarily in favor of choice b and choice c in preferring the direct method.

In order to prefer the indirect method when teaching the cash flows from operating activities section of the CFS, essentially, there would be two reasons in the Turkish and academic context as seen in Table 7.

Table 7. The rationale to prefer the indirect method

	N^7=8	Frequency Distribution to Prefer Indirect Method	%
a.	A great majority of entities listed on Turkish Stock Exchange "Borsa Istanbul" use indirect method (Pekdemir & Yönet, 2010; Öztürk, 2011; Bahadır & Tolga, 2013; Özdemir, 2014).	5	62
b.	Students easily understand the transition from accrual basis to cash basis of accounting when adjusting net income for the period.	3	38
	Total	**8**	**100**

In this context, one of my interviewees explained the situation in her university as follows:

> "My accounting course on principles of accounting was designed to meet what is expected from the accounting market. In terms of the CFS, what is expected from the potential accountants in Turkey is to be able prepare a CFS under indirect method. It is known that potential accountants who would particularly work for Big 4's need to know indirect method. Academic research generated from audited financial statements, also, proves this fact. In addition, indirect method is relatively easy and less costly for independent audit firms."

I agree with my interviewee in meeting the demand generated from the accounting market. However; from the students' perspective, I believe that teaching the CFS under indirect method combined with T-Account approach would be more concrete than teaching the CFS under indirect method combined with Worksheet approach as indicated by Weygandt *et al.* (2013: 659-660) because transition from accrual basis to cash basis of accounting when adjusting net income for the period would be concretely perceived by the students by posting and adjusting numbers on T-Accounts.

In order to prefer both methods when teaching the cash flow from operating activities section of the CFS, essentially, there would be four reasons in the Turkish and academic context as seen in Table 8.

Table 8. The rationale to prefer both methods

	N[8]=32	Frequency Distribution to Prefer Both Methods	%
a.	Students should able to prepare a CFS under both methods.	15	47
b.	Both direct and indirect method exist in accordance with IAS 7.	8	25
c.	TPOAASA did not express preference to any of these methods (TPOAASA, 2013).	4	13
d.	Other reasons expected from academics (e.g. to compare both methods with each other)	5	16
	Total	**32**	**100**

In this context, I believe that potential accountants should know both methods. Teaching should reflect a current and future perspective. Even if indirect method is trendy in Turkey at this point in time, it is expected that IASB cancels this method in the future or even TPOAASA may switch from indirect method to direct method depending on a regulation. That is why potential accountants should be fully educated in undergraduate level accounting education.

4.5 Accounting policies taught to classify and/or exemplify some items of the CFS

This section covers the classification of dividend paid, dividend received and exemplification of taxes paid and cash flows from discontinued operations from the perspective of Turkish accounting academics.

Dividend paid: To classify dividend paid in the CFS of non-financial companies, three possible choices were provided to Turkish accounting academics as seen in Table 9.

Table 9. The classification and the rationale for dividend paid

N=38	Frequency Distribution for Dividend Paid	%
a. They classify dividend paid in the cash flows from operating activities (Reason: Dividend paid is taken into account in the calculation of net income for the period).	3	8
b. They classify dividend paid in the cash flows from financing activities (Reason: Companies want to show their dividend payment capability which constitute a return on equity (ROE) to their shareholders).	29	76
c. They classify dividend paid in the cash flows from financing activities (Reason: The former TASB (2010: 394) expressed preference to classification in cash flows from financial activities in order to uniformly present dividend payments).	1	3
Both b & c	5	13
Total	**38**	**100**

In terms of dividend payment from the perspective of non-financial business entities what I believe is to uniformly classify dividend paid. For instance, when company A distributes dividends to Company B, this dividend from the perspective of Company A should be classified under financing section of the CFS as a cash outflow.

Dividend received: To classify dividend received in the CFS of non-financial companies, two possible choices were provided to academics as seen in Table 10.

In terms of dividend received from the perspective of non-financial business entities what I believe is to uniformly classify dividend received. For instance, when company A distributes dividends to Company B, this dividend from the perspective of Company B should be classified under investing section of the CFS as a cash inflow.

Table 10. The classification and rationale to classify dividend received

N=38	Frequency Distribution for Dividend Received	%
a. They classify dividend received in the cash flows from operating activities (Reason: Dividend received is used in the calculation of net income for the period).	15	39
b. They classify dividend received in the cash flows from investing activities (Reason: Dividend received constitute a return on investment (ROI) through common stock purchased by the company).	23	61
Total	**38**	**100**

Uniformity in terms of dividend paid and dividend received is necessary to make the CFSs comparable. In this regard, it looks like that more than 50% Turkish accounting academics teaching the CFS established such a uniformity with each other in undergraduate level accounting education.

Taxes paid: To report taxes paid, two choices were provided to accounting academics as seen in Table 11 whether they solely exemplify taxes paid in the cash flows from operating activities or they allocate taxes paid under operating, investing or financing activities.

Table 11. Exemplification of taxes paid

N=38	Frequency Distribution for Taxes Paid	%
a. Taxes paid is classified in the cash flows from operating activities.	29	76
b. Taxes paid is allocated to operating, investing, and financing activities.	9	24
Total	**38**	**100**

In this context, I believe that exemplifying all taxes paid in the cash flows from operating activities is more convenient than allocation of all taxes to different sections of this statement in undergraduate level accounting education. The reason why I defend this opinion is the fact that this financial statement is relatively difficult and allocation is expected to make this financial statement even more complicated than it is.

In addition, the usual practice of the financial statement preparers is not to allocate taxes paid according to Öztürk (2011) even if they are capable of determining the amounts that should be recorded to investing and financing sections. I believe that their preference is based on the fact that reporting taxes paid directly in the operating cash flows is easier and less time consuming than allocating them into specific sections of this statement.

Within the framework of this analysis, I observe that the policy choice of accounting academics and the preparers of financial statements are in compliance with each other. So, there is no reason to create pressure on students. There is a uniformity between teaching and practice.

Cash flows from discontinued operations: According to the relationship between IAS 7 and IFRS 5 Non-Current Assets Held for Sale and Discontinued Operations, cash flows from discontinued operations may be exemplified when the CFS is taught. In this regard, my findings show that this is rare in teaching the CFS in undergraduate level accounting education by referring to 8 academics, only.

In this context, one of my interviewees explained the situation in her university as follows:

> "I currently teach Financial Statement Analysis and IFRS. In the Financial Statement Analysis course, I introduce how discontinued operations will influence the financial statements and specifically focus on the income statement and statement of cash flows. In IFRS course, I teach how to recognize discontinued operations".

Depending on my interviewee and my experiences, I should state that teaching the cash flows from discontinued operations is based on the course level that accounting academics teach. Cash flows from discontinued operations should be taught in upper or advanced level accounting courses after having some degree of accounting background in accounting education.

For the academics teaching the cash flows from discontinued operations, two choices were provided in accordance with IAS 7 and IFRS 5 on how they exemplify the reporting of them as seen in Table 12.

Table 12. Classification of cash flows from discontinued operations

N=8		Frequency Distribution for Cash Flows from Discontinued Operations	%
a.	Cash flows from discontinued operations are reported in the notes.	6	75
b.	Cash flows from discontinued operations are reported as a separate item of the statement of cash flows.	2	25
	Total	**8**	**100**

In this context, I believe that reporting in the notes is expected to help the students to clearly understand how much the cash flows from discontinued operations are through detailed explanations.

4.6 Methods used to exemplify the financial analysis of a CFS

In terms of the financial analysis of the CFS, it is possible to determine different methods as I stated before. In this context, four possible choices as seen in Table 13 were provided to academics as they should be as the methods to exemplify the CFS in terms of financial analysis.

Table 13. Methods to exemplify the CFS in terms of financial analysis

N⁹=50		Frequency Distribution for Financial Analysis of the Cash Flows Statement	%
a.	Financial analysis of a firm's CFS for a specific year	11	22
b.	Comparative financial analysis of a firm's CFS from one year to another	20	40
c.	Comparative financial analysis of firms' CFSs whose operating activities are the same	15	30
d.	Other possibilities that are expected from academics (e.g. analysis of balance sheet, income statement and CFS together)	4	8
	Total	**50**	**100**

In my opinion, comparative financial analysis of the CFS from one year to another and/or comparative financial analysis of firms' CFSs whose operating activities are the same should be essential in undergraduate level accounting education. In addition, it is possible to strengthen this analysis with vertical analysis if the CFS is prepared under direct method. That is why direct method is also important.

Overall, through comparative and vertical analysis, students can have more meaningful, concrete and sound results than the financial analysis of a firm's CFS for a specific year, only.

4.7 Methods used to assess and evaluate the preparation of CFS

In terms of the assessment and evaluation methods for the preparation of a CFS, I provided five possible choices to the academics as seen in Table 14.

In this context, one of my interviewees explained the situation in her university as follows:

> "I am in favor of asking a full CFS. However, it is not the case from time to time. As an accounting professor for students majoring in accounting, I always consider the capability of my students in undergraduate level accounting education. So, I am prudent. That's why, I sometimes prepare my question to ask one or two sections of the CFS rather than asking a full CFS".

Table 14. Methods used to assess and evaluate the preparation of CFS

	N[10]=66	Frequency Distribution of Assessment Methods	%
a.	Preparation of a full CFS in the midterm or final exam	20	30
b.	Preparation of one or more than one section of the CFS in the midterm or final exam	28	42
c.	Preparation of a CFS through a quiz	11	17
d.	Preparation of a CFS through a case study	6	9
e.	Other possibilities that are expected from academics (e.g. in-class assignment)	1	2
	Total	**66**	**100**

In my opinion, I am in favor of asking a full CFS when I teach for the students majoring in accounting information systems because they are potential accountants. However, I am a little flexible when I teach for the students majoring in management. In asking a full CFS, the audience is really important. For instance, if I teach for an audience covered by the students majoring in engineering (70%) as well as management (30%) in summer, I feel confident because I know engineering students have stronger quantitative skills than management students. That is why my preference is to ask a full CFS in such a case.

4.8 Tools of educational technology used to prepare a CFS

The use of educational technology is important but its use in Turkey is rare in the context of the preparation of CFS. My research findings show that the number of academics who use the educational technologies in teaching the CFS is quite rare by referring to 4 academics.

In this context, my survey results pointed out that two academics make their students practice a CFS using Excel specifically at Bilkent University and the other two academics benefit from the accounting software called "Link Paket" specifically at Uludağ University.

My results show that the use of accounting software and spreadsheet application in the context of the preparation of CFS in an undergraduate level accounting course is extremely rare in Turkey in parallel to the results of prior research papers that I stated before.

In this context, one of my interviewees explained the situation in her university as follows:

> "I teach principles of accounting for the students majoring in management. This course was designed to combine accounting with spreadsheet applications so that students can continue to use their computer skills based on what they learnt in Introduction to Business. Within a semester, I have four or five lab sessions. I provide my students spreadsheet templates and questions. They prepare journal

> entries, T-Accounts, Trial Balances, depreciation schedules, and all financial statements including the CFS on the spreadsheets. They like these practices so far".

In addition, Sultanoğlu *et al.* (2014) prepared a paper to compare the success of their students in terms of before and after the adoption of spreadsheet applications in an undergraduate level course on financial accounting at Bilkent University. Their research shows that students who took this course after integrating the spreadsheet applications into the course content are more successful than the former students.

In addition, Mazhin (1989), Çakıcı (2006), and Eesley (2013) show that Excel can be easily applied in order to prepare a CFS in any format.

Within the framework of this analysis, I believe that spreadsheets or accounting software should be used to teach accounting and specifically to teach the CFS. As it is in the CFS, I am in favor of supporting difficult accounting issues with computerized applications, if possible, so that students can learn complicated issues through the help of computers as one of the tools that they enjoy.

5. Conclusions

Based on the author's experience in teaching IAS 7, eight issues related to teaching the CFS were identified and further analyzed in the context of undergraduate level accounting education in Turkey. As concluding remarks, I discuss each issue within the framework of my suggestions to improve the students' competencies in a CFS, as follows:

1. **Courses that cover the CFS:** Since the number of entities that have report a CFS increased, teaching the CFS should be required for business students. In this case, CFS should be integrated into General Accounting or Financial Statement Analysis should be a compulsory course in the business curriculum.
2. **Methods taught to calculate the cash inflows and cash outflows in a CFS:** In teaching a CFS, my keyword was "***concreteness***" from the perspective of students. For this reason, teaching should be primarily done through T-Account approach to establish a strong infrastructure to observe the cash inflows and outflows.
3. **Accounting regulations taught to prepare a CFS:** Turkish accounting academics should not ignore the first communiqué on accounting system in addition to IFRS because it is still in force. For this reason, business students should be familiar with the CFS prepared under both regulations.
4. **Accounting policies taught to prepare a CFS:** In teaching a CFS, direct method to meet learning objectives and indirect method to meet the demand from accounting market should be taught. But, my preference is to

combine both methods with T-Account approach to establish "***concreteness***".

5. **Accounting policies taught to classify and/or exemplify some items of the CFS**: To facilitate the students' learning and to establish uniformity, I believe that dividend paid should be reported under financing activities and dividend received should be reported under investing activities for non-financial entities. In addition, taxes paid should not be allocated and cash flows from discontinued operations would remain into an advanced IFRS course.
6. **Methods used to exemplify the financial analysis of a CFS:** I believe that "comparative financial analysis of a company's CFS from one year to another" and "comparative financial analysis of companies' CFSs whose operating activity is the same" should be essential. I would prefer direct method to also make a vertical analysis in all sections of the CFS.
7. **Methods used to assess and evaluate the preparation of a CFS**: Since this statement is important within the framework of the developments in financial reporting regulations, my expectation from undergraduate business students is to be able to prepare a full CFS in the exams. However, an accounting academic should be "***prudent***" by taking their students' capability into account.
8. **Tools of educational technology used to prepare a CFS:** Computer is a tool of educational technology that students, usually, enjoy. For this reason, a Financial Statement Analysis course would be designed to integrate spreadsheet applications to make horizontal, vertical, and ratio analysis through posting financial statements into spreadsheets. A CFS can, also, be prepared. This is what I do on my own use and I enjoy using spreadsheets in this course.

Within the framework of my suggestions, I believe that students would improve their competencies on CFS.

Further research would be the analysis of these issues in undergraduate or graduate level accounting education in the global context, and particularly in the context of Central and Eastern European countries, in order to investigate how teaching CFS was developed in these countries, and how it should be improved for the purpose of students' competencies by benefiting from the results of Turkish accounting academics, the author's experiences and the views of other academics.

Acknowledgements

I would like to thank Prof. Dr. Cătălin Albu and the reviewer of my paper for providing me constructive support while developing this paper.

References

Akdoğan, N., Aktaş. R., Deran, A., Erhan, D. U. & Acar, A. (2011) *Türkiye muhasebe standartları ile uyumlu sektörel muhasebe* [Sectoral accounting in compliance with Turkish accounting standards], Turkey: Gazi Publications, 1st Edition

Akdoğan, N. & Tenker, N. (2005) *Finansal tablolar ve mali analiz teknikleri* [Financial statements and methods of financial analysis], Turkey: Gazi Publications, 10th Edition

Akdoğan, N. & Tenker, N. (2007) *Finansal tablolar ve mali analiz teknikleri* [Financial statements and methods of financial analysis], Turkey: Gazi Publications, 11th Edition

Aktaş, R., Karğın, S., & Karğın, M. (2012) "Nakit Akışlarının Sağlandığı Faaliyetler Yöntemi İle İşletmelerin Nakit Akış Profillerinin İncelenmesi" [Analyzing the Cash Flow Profiles of Firms Using the Cash Flow Patterns Method], *Muhasebe ve Finansman Dergisi/Journal of Accounting & Finance*, no. 56: 101-118

Alfredson, K., Leo, K., Picker, R., Loftus, J., Clark, K. & Wise, V. (2013) *Applying International Financial Reporting Standards*, John Wiley & Sons, 3rd Edition

Apostolou, B., Watson, S.F., Hassell, J.M. & Webber, S.A. (2001) "Accounting Education Literature Review (1997–1999)", *Journal of Accounting Education*, vol. 19, no. 1: 1-61

Apostolou, B., Hassell, J. M., Rebele, J.E. & Watson, S. F. (2010) "Accounting Education Literature Review (2006–2009)", *Journal of Accounting Education*, vol. 28, no. 3: 145-197

Apostolou, B., Hassell, J. M., Rebele, J. E. & Watson, S. F. (2013) "Accounting Education Literature Review (2010–2012)", *Journal of Accounting Education*, no. 31:107-161

Arıkboğa, D. (2013) *Finansal muhasebe* [Financial accounting], Turkey: Der Publications, 2nd dition

Atabey, A., Parlakkaya, R. & Alagöz, A. (2013) *Genel muhasebe - dönem sonu işlemleri* [General accounting - end of accounting period transactions], Turkey: Nobel Publications, 3rd Edition

Ataman, Ü. (2014) *Genel muhasebe - Muhasebede dönem sonu işlemleri* [General accounting - end of accounting period transactions], Turkey: Seçkin Publications, 16th Edition

Bahadır, O. & Tolga, B. (2013) "Accounting Policy Options Under IFRS: Evidence from Turkey", *Accounting and Management Information Systems,* vol. 12, no. 3: 388–404

Bektöre, S., Çömlekçi, F. & Sözbilir, H. (2013) *Tekdüzen hesap planı ile uyumlu mali tablolar analizi*, [Financial Statement Analysis in compliance with the Uniform Chart of Accounts], Turkey: Nisan Bookstore, 1st Edition

Brickner, D. R., & Mccombs, G. B. (2004) "Teaching the Indirect Method of the Statement of Cash Flows in Introductory Financial Accounting: A Comprehensive, Problem-Based Approach", *Journal of Education for Business*, vol. 80, no. 1: 41-46

Büyükmirza, K. (2014) *Maliyet ve yönetim muhasebesi* [Cost and managerial accounting], Gazi Publications, 19th Edition, Turkey

Cengiz, E. & Uyar, S. (2012) "Bilgi Teknolojileri ve Muhasebe Eğitimi" [Information Systems and Accounting Education], *XXXI. Sympozium of Turkish Accounting Education - Interdisciplinary Approach to Accounting Education*, 25-29 April 2012

Civan. M. (2005) *Finansal muhasebe* [Financial accounting], Turkey: Gazi Publications, 2nd Edition

Civelek, M. & Özkan, A. (2011) *Maliyet ve yönetim muhasebesi* [Cost and managerial accounting], Turkey: Detay Publications, 6th Edition

Çaldağ Y., & Ayanoğlu, Y. (2012) *Genel muhasebe* [General accounting], Turkey: Gazi Publications, 9th Edition

Çakıcı, C. (2006) *Excel ile muhasebe* [Accounting by using Excel], Turkey: Beta Publications, 2nd Edition

Çiftçi, Y., & Sarıoğlu, L. (2007) "Nakit Akış Tablosu İle İlgili Türkiye'deki Düzenlemeler ve Uluslararası Uygulamalarla Karşılaştırılması" [Regulations related to the Cash Flows Statement in Turkey and their Comparisons with International Applications], *Selçuk Üniversitesi Sosyal Bilimler MYO Dergisi/ Selçuk University Journal of Vocational School of Social Sciences*, vol. 10, no.1-2: 181-200

Demir, V. (2009) *UFRS/TFRS kapsamında finansal araçlar* [Financial instruments in the context of IFRS/TFRS], Turkey: Nobel Publications, 1st Edition

Demir, V. & Bahadır, O. (2009) *UFRS/TFRS kapsamında işletme birleşmeleri ve konsolidasyon: açıklamalar ve uygulamalar* [Business combinations and consolidation in the context of IFRS/TFRS: explanations and applications], Turkey: Nobel Publications, 2nd Edition

Eesley, D. T. (2013) "A Simplified Method for Teaching Cash Flow Statement Construction to Entreupreneurship and Non-Accounting Majors", *Mountain Plains Journal of Business and Economics*, Pedagogy, vol. 14: 16-33

Erdamar, C. & Orhon Basık, F. (2014) *Finansal muhasebe ve tekdüzen hesap* sistemi [Financial accounting and uniform accounting system], Turkey: Türkmen Bookstore, 4th Edition

Erol Fidan M. & Subaşı, Ş. (2014)"Türkiye'deki Muhasebe Öğretim Elemanlarının Sayısal Çağda Teknoloji Kullanımına İlişkin Durum Tespiti" [Assessment of Technology Use by Academic Staff of Accounting in Turkey in Digital Age], *Proceedings Book of XXXIII. Symposium of Turkish Accounting Education - New Approaches in Accounting Education in Digital Age*, 23-27 April 2014

Farshadfar, S. & Monem, R. (2013) "The Usefulness of Operating Cash Flow and Accrual Components in Improving the Predictive Ability of Earnings: a Re-examination and Extension", *Accounting & Finance*, vol. 53, no. 4: 1061-1082

Fletcher, H. & Ulrich, T. (2010) "The Statement of Cash Flows Using Financial Statement Equations", *Business Education & Administration*, vol. 2, no. 1: 15-26

Garrion, R.H. & Noreen, E. W. (2003) *Managerial accounting*, USA: Mc-Grawhill Companies, 10th Edition

Gelbal, S. (2013) *Ölçme ve değerlendirme*[Assessment and evaluation], Turkey: Anadolu University Publications

Gökçen, G., Ataman, B. & Çakıcı, C. (2011) *Türkiye Muhasebe Standartları uygulamalar*ı [Applications of Turkish Accounting Standards], Turkey: Türkmen Bookstore, 2nd Edition

Gökçen, G., Çelenk, H. & Horasan, E. (2014) *Yönetim muhasebesi ve uygulamaları* [Managerial accounting and applications]. Turkey: Beta Publications, 1st Edition

Gup, B. E., Samson, W. D., Dugan, M. T., Kim, M. J. & Jittrapanun, T. (1993) "An Analysis of Patterns from the Statement of Cash Flows", *Financial Practice and Education*, vol. 3, no. 2: 73-79

Gücenme Gençoğlu, Ü. (2007) *Türkiye Muhasebe Standartları ve uygulamalar* [Turkish Accounting Standards and applications], Turkey: Türkmen Bookstore, 1st Edition

Gürsoy, C.T. (2009) *Yönetim ve maliyet muhasebesi* [Managerial and cost accounting], Turkey: Beta Publications, 3rd Edition

Haftacı, V. (2013) *Yönetim muhasebesi* [Managerial accounting], Turkey: Umuttepe Publications, 5th Edition

Hales, J. & Orpurt, S. F. (2013) "A Review of Academic Research on the Reporting of Cash Flows from Operations", *Accounting Horizons*, vol. 27, no. 3: 539-578

Hatunoğlu, Z. (2006) "Muhasebe Öğretim Elemanlarının Bilgi Teknolojisinden Yararlanma Oranlarının Tespitine İlişkin Bir Araştırma" [A Research related to the Determination of Accounting Academics' Usage Level of Information Technology]. *Çukurova Üniversitesi Sosyal Bilimler Enstitüsü Dergisi/Çukurova University Journal of the Institute of Social Sciences*, 15(1)

International Accounting Standards Board (IASB) (2010) "Staff Draft of Exposure Draft IFRS X Financial Statement Presentation", UK: IFRS Foundation Publications Department. http://www.ifrs.org/Current-Projects/IASB-Projects/Financial-Statement-Presentation/PhaseB/Documents/FSPStandard.pdf (accessed on June 6, 2014)

Ibarra, V. C. (2009) "Cash Flow Ratios: Tools For Financial Analysis", *Journal of International Business Research*, vol. 8, SI. 1: 91-107

Karapınar, A. & Zaif, F. (2013) *Uluslarararası Finansal Raporlama Standartları ile uyumlu finansal analiz* [Financial analysis in compliance with International Financial Reporting Standards], Turkey: Gazi Publications, 3rd Edition

Karasioğlu, F. (2014) *Finansal muhasebe - dönemsonu işlemleri* [Financial accounting - end of accounting period transactions], Turkey: Nobel Publications, 1st Edition

Karğın, M. & Aktaş, R. (2011) "Türkiye Muhasebe Standartlarına Göre Raporlanmış Nakit Akış Tablosu ve Analizi" [Cash Flow Statement Reported in accordance with Turkish Accounting Standards and its Analysis], *Muhasebe ve Finansman Dergisi/Journal of Accounting & Finance*, no. 52: 1-24

Kaya, İ. (2011) *Türkiye Muhasebe ve Finansal Raporlama Standartlarında konsolide finansal tablolar* [Consolidated financial statements according to Turkish Accounting and Financial Reporting Standards]. İstanbul: Türkmen Bookstore, 2nd Edition

Kaya, U. & Daştan, A. (2004) "Türkiye'de Lisans Düzeyinde Verilen Muhasebe Eğitiminin Öğrenci-Öğretici ve Uygulayıcılar Açısından Değerlendirilmesi" [Assessment of Undergraduate Level Accounting Education in terms of Students, Academic Staff and Practitioners in Turkey], *Proceedings Book of XXIII. Symposium of Turkish Accounting Education*

Kızıl, A., Fidan, M.M., Kızıl, C. & Keskin, İ. (2013) *Türkiye Muhasebe ve Finansal Raporlama Standartları: uygulamalar, yorumlar, muhasebeleştirme* [Turkish Accounting and Financial Reporting Standards: applications, interpretations, recognition], Turkey: Der Bookstore, 1st Edition

Kirkham, R. (2012) "Liquidity Analysis Using Cash Flow Ratios and Traditional Ratios: the Telecommunications Sector in Australia", *Journal of New Business Ideas & Trends*, vol. 10, no. 1: 1-13

Koç Yalkın, Y. & Demir V. (2012) "Turkey", *A Global History of Accounting, Financial Reporting and Public Policy: Eurasia, the Middle East and Africa*. Studies in the Development of Accounting Thought. vol.14D: 183-207

Koç Yalkın, Y. (2013) *Genel muhasebe ilkeler ve uygulamalar* [Principles and applications of general accounting], Turkey: Nobel Publications, 19th Edition

Kojima, K. (2012) "Decision Usefulness of Cash Flow Information Format: An Experimental Study", *International Review of Business*, no. 12: 23-44

Kvaal, E. & Nobes, C. (2010) "International differences in IFRS policy choice: a research note", *Accounting and Business Research*, vol. 40, no. 2: 173-187

Mazhin, R. (1989) "A Spreadsheet Template for the Statement of Cash Flows", *Journal of Accountancy*, vol. 167, no. 3: 110-113

Nobes, C. (2013) "The Continued Survival of International Differences under IFRS", *Accounting and Business Research*, vol. 43, no. 2: 83-111

O'Bryan, D., Berry, K. T., Troutman, C. & Quirin, J. J. (2000) "Using Accounting Equation Analysis to Teach the Statement of Cash Flows in the First Financial Accounting Course", *Journal of Accounting Education*, vol. 18, no. 2: 147-155

Örten, R., Kaval. H. & Karapınar, A. (2013) *Türkiye Muhasebe - Finansal Raporlama Standartları uygulama ve yorumları* [Applications and interpretations of Turkish Accounting and Financial Reporting Standards]. Turkey: Gazi Publications, 7th Edition

Özdemir, S. (2014) "Nakit Akış Tablosunun Hazırlanmasında Yöntem Tartışmaları ve TMS 7 Standardı Şartlarına Uygun Brüt (Dolaysız) Yönteme Göre Örnek Bir Uygulama" [Discussion on Methods of Preparing a Cash Flow Statement and a Sample Case According to the Gross(Direct) Method in compliance with TMS 7 Requirements], *Mali Çözüm Dergisi/Journal of Financial Analysis*, no. 24(125)

Özerhan, Y. & Yanık, S. (2008) *Türkiye'de finansal tabloların tarihsel gelişim süreci (1923 - 2008)* [Historical development process of financial statements in Turkey (1923 - 2008)], Gazi Publications. Turkey

Özerhan, Y. & Yanık, S. (2012) *Açıklamalı ve örnek uygulamalı Türkiye Muhasebe Standartları–Türkiye Finansal Raporlama Standartları* [Turkish Accounting Standards - Turkish Financial Reporting Standards with explanations and examples], TÜRMOB Publication, No: 427, 2nd Edition Turkey

Öztürk, C. (2011) *Finansal tabloların dipnotlarında sunulan muhasebe politikalarının Uluslararası Finansal Raporlama Standartları açısından incelenmesi* [Examination of the accounting policies presented in the notes of financial statements in terms of International Financial Reporting Standards], Unpublished Doctorate Dissertation, Ankara, Turkey

Pekdemir, R. & Yönet, N. K. (2010) "Exploratory Evidence for the Adoption of the IAS 7 in Turkey", *Accounting and Management Information Systems*, vol. 9, no. 4:524-538

Saban, M. & Erdoğan, N. (2014) *Maliyet ve yönetim muhasebesi* [Cost and managerial Accounting], Turkey: Beta Publications, 5th Edition

Savcı, M. (2013) *Mali tablolar analizi* [Analysis of financial statements]. Turkey: Ekin Publications, 6th Edition

Sevilengül, O. (2014) *Genel muhasebe* [General accounting], Turkey: Gazi Publications, 17th edition

Sultanoğlu, B., Akman, H. N. & Şımga-Muğan, C. (2007) "Lisans ve Yüksek Lisans İşletme Programları'nda Muhasebe Dersleri-Yeniden Ele Alış" [Accounting Courses in Undergraduate and Graduate Programs - Revised], *Proceedings Book of XXVI. Sympozium of Turkish Accounting Education - Influence of Globalisation on Accounting Education and Applications*. 23-27 May 2007

Sultanoğlu, B., Aydoğmuş, C. & Akman, H.N. (2014) "Muhasebe Eğitiminde Tablolama (EXCEL) Uygulamasının Öğrenci Başarısı Üzerindeki Etkisi" [Influence of the Spreadsheet (Excel) Application over the Student's Success in Accounting Education], *Muhasebe Bilim Dünyası/World of Accounting Science*, vol. 16(3)

Şengel, S. (2013) *Genel muhasebe* [General accounting], Turkey: Detay Publications, 1st Edition

Şımga-Muğan, C. (1995) "Accounting in Turkey", *European Accounting Review*, vol. 4, no. 2: 351-371

Turkish Accounting Standards Board (TASB) (2010) *Uluslararası Finansal Raporlama Standartları ile Uyumlu Türkiye Muhasebe Standartları* [Turkish Accounting Standards in compliance with International Financial Reporting Standards], Turkey

Terzi, S., Şen, İ. K. & Solak, B. (2013) "Bologna Sürecinin Muhasebe Eğitimine Etkisi: Üniversitelerin İşletme Bölümlerinin Ders Programları Üzerine Bir İnceleme" [Influence of Bologna Process on Accounting Education: Observations on the Curriculum of Management Departments]. *Muhasebe ve Finansman Dergisi/Journal of Accounting & Finance*, (59)

Turkish Public Oversight Accounting and Auditing Standards Authority (TPOAASA) (2013) Örnek UFRS Finansal Tabloları [Examples of IFRS based Financial Statements] http://www.kgk.gov.tr/contents/files/Pdf/Finansal_Tablo_Ornekleri_20.5.2013.pdf (accessed on June 6, 2014)

Turkish Public Oversight Accounting and Auditing Standards Authority (TPOAASA) (2015) Türk Ticaret Kanununa göre Finansal Raporlama [Financial Reporting in accordance with Turkish Commercial Code]. http://www.kgk.gov.tr/contents/files/Pdf/Basın%20Duyurusu_2015.pdf (accessed on April 1, 2015)

Turkish Ministry of Finance. 1 no'lu Muhasebe Sistemi Uygulama Genel Tebliği [The First Communiqué on Accounting System]. http://www.resmigazete.gov.tr/main.aspx?home=http://www.resmigazete.gov.tr/arsiv/21447_1.pdf&main=http://www.resmigazete.gov.tr/arsiv/21447_1.pdf (accessed on June 6, 2014)

Turkish Ministry of Finance. 3 no'lu Muhasebe Sistemi Uygulama Genel Tebliği [The Third Communiqué on Accounting System]. http://www.resmigazete.gov.tr/main.aspx?home=http://www.resmigazete.gov.tr/arsiv/22055.pdf&main=http://www.resmigazete.gov.tr/arsiv/22055.pdf (accessed on June 6, 2014)

Yalçın, S. (2012) "Büyük İşletmelerin Muhasebe Meslek Mensuplarından Bilgisayar Becerileri Hakkında Beklentileri - Disiplinlerarası Yüksek Lisans Önerisi" [Expectations of Large Entities from Accounting Professionals with respect to Computer Literacy - Proposal of Interdisciplinary Graduate Program], *Proceedings Book of XXXI. Sympozium of Turkish Accounting Education - Interdisciplinary Approach to Accounting Education*. 25-29 April 2012

Yükçü, S. (2014a) *Yeni Türk Ticaret Kanunu ile uyumlu TMS ve UFRS örnekli genel muhasebe* [General accounting in compliance with the new Turkish Commercial Code with examples related to TAS and IFRS], Turkey: Altın Nokta Publications, 7th Edition

Yükçü, S. (2014b) *Herkes için yönetim muhasebesi* [Managerial accounting for everbody], Turkey: Altın Nokta Publications. 2nd Edition

Watson, S. F., Apostolou, B., Hassell, J. M. & Webber, S. A. (2007) "Accounting education literature review (2003–2005)", *Journal of Accounting Education*, vol. 25, no. 1: 1-58

Weygandt, J., Kimmel, P. & Kieso, D.E. (2012) *Managerial accounting*, Singapore: John Wiley & Sons, 6th Edition

Weygandt, J. J., Kimmel, P. D. & Kieso, D. E. (2013) *Financial accounting: IFRS edition*, John Wiley & Sons, 2nd Edition

---

1 In Turkey, there are seven geographical regions that were determined according to the climate character.

2 N is equal to the total number frequencies and is based on the course selection of 43 academics who stated that they teach courses that cover the cash flow statement. Some of the academics teach more than course related to the cash flow statement.

3 Regarding my case, teaching an advanced course on one side, teaching an introductory course on the other side may be questionable. In this context, I don't expect that the course level is a determinant of success. If the same introductory accounting course that I taught is reorganized according to T-Account approach, I believe that students would improve their success.

4 Cash flow statement in the first communiqué on accounting system (Turkish cash flow statement) and in IAS 7 is not the same. According to the Turkish cash flow statement, all cash inflows and all cash outflows are reported under direct method without classifying them under operating, investing and financing activities (Akdoğan & Tenker, 2005: 287).

5 N is equal to the number of academics who stated that they teach courses that cover the cash flow statement in accordance with IAS 7.

6 N is equal to the number of frequencies and is based on the selection of direct method made by 11 academics. Some of the academics stated more than reason.

7 N is equal to the number of frequencies and is based on the selection of indirect method made by 6 academics. Some of the academics stated more than reason.

8 N is equal to the number of frequencies and is based on the selection of both direct and indirect methods made by 21 academics. Some of the academics stated more than reason.

9 N is equal to the number of frequencies and is based on the selection of methods of financial analysis made by 43 academics who stated that they teach courses that cover the cash flow statement. Some of the academics stated more than method.

10 N is equal to the number of frequencies and is based on the selection of methods of assessment and evaluation made by 43 academics who stated that they teach courses that cover the cash flow statement. Some of the academics stated more than method.

3

The value relevance of financial distress risk in the case of RASDAQ companies

Ioan-Bogdan Robu[a], Mihaela-Alina Robu[a], Marilena Mironiuc[a] and Florentina Olivia Bălu[b,1]

[a] *Alexandru Ioan Cuza University of Iasi, Romania,*
[b] *University of Geneva, Switzerland*

Abstract: The financial distress risk concept has been referred as follow: negative net assets, insolvency, bond default, overdraft, unpaid dividends for the preferred stocks, bankruptcy etc. From all the stakeholders, investors are interested in the financial position and performance of a company and its ability to continue as a going concern, without knowing the appearance of financial distress status. The purpose of this study aims to test the value relevance of the appearance of distress risk on investors' decisions on the purchase or sale of stock, with impact on stock return, for the Romanian listed companies in RASDAQ section. In order to reach the objective, the study was carried on upon a sample of 70 Bucharest Stock Exchange (BSE) listed companies, between 2008 and 2014, using statistical methods like analysis of variance (ANOVA), simple linear regression and ANCOVA models. Through the obtained results, it was demonstrated the difference between financial distressed companies and performant companies and the influence of belonging to a company in the high risk category on the stock return.

Keywords: value relevance, distress risk, financial ratios, ANOVA, ANCOVA, RASDAQ

[1] *Corresponding authors*: Ioan-Bogdan Robu, Faculty of Economics and Business Administration, Alexandru Ioan Cuza University of Iasi, Romania, email addresses: bogdan.robu@feaa.uaic.ro, mihaela.robu@feaa.uaic.ro, marilena@uaic.ro; Faculty of Economics and Social Sciences, University of Geneva, Switzerland, email address: florentina.balu@unige.ch.

1. Introduction

Starting with 2007, alongside with the show up of the global financial crisis, the number of companies, both listed and unlisted, with financial difficulties or even bankrupt has grown significantly. This situation has generated shifting the focus of financial statement users to the companies' ability to continue as a going concern in a predictable future. On a capital market, a category of users that are interested in the development of distress risk is represented by investors.

Investors want to know information regarding the companies' financial position and performance based on the financial statements, in order to make the most adequate investment decisions. Information provided by the investors through the stock price regarding the anticipation of future cash flows can be used in order to determine how early the market players recognize the appearance of distress risk of the company and its financial defacement (Aharony *et al.*, 1980).

Within the decision making process, investors must take into account the macroeconomic information such as the general economic situation, the monetary policy, the price levels and international activity (Tangjitprom, 2012), and especially the factors that are specific for each country, mainly reflected by the financial statements. These represent the main communication way between companies and actual or potential investors (Vijitha & Nimalathasan, 2014). The financial information gathered from the financial statements issued according to the rules in force can be considered a credible information source on which investors can trust in the decision making process (Ragab & Omran, 2006). The main objective of the financial reporting is providing useful information to the financial statements users regarding the financial position and performance of a company (IASB, 2013).

The purpose of this study aims to test the value relevance of the appearance of distress risk on investors' decisions, with impact on stock return, for the Romanian listed companies in RASDAQ section. Stock return is quantified by the relative variation of stock prices from one period to another.

In order to reach the objective, the study was carried on upon a sample of 70 Bucharest Stock Exchange (BSE) listed companies, between 2008 and 2014, using statistical methods like analysis of variance (ANOVA), simple linear regression and ANCOVA.

Through the obtained results, it was demonstrated the difference between financial distressed companies and performant companies and the influence a company belonging to a high risk category on the stock return.

2. Literature review and hypothesis development

Alongside with Ball's and Brown's (1968), respectively Beaver's (1968) studies, the concept of value relevance of the financial statements has been developed, though it barely appeared in 1993 (Barth *et al.*, 2001). According to Beisland (2009) and El-Sayed Ebaid (2012), by analyzing the relevance of financial information, it is studied the relation between the information and the market, representing the ability of the financial information to influence the stock price or stock return, as a result, the decision making process.

Although the *value relevance* concept focuses on the information provided by financial reporting, the development of the concept implies alongside with the analysis of the information, the analysis of the influence of other non-financial factors that regard the financial statement or not, such as: the affiliation to a certain activity field (Lin & Jin, 2006; Chou *et al.,* 2012), the application of certain accounting standards (Dumontier & Raffournier, 2002; Barth *et al.,* 2008; Barth *et al.*, 2012), the existence of corporate governance (Lacker *et al.*, 2011), the report issuance and the audit opinion issuance (Gómez-Guillmón, 2008; Lee & Lee, 2013), the existence of risk and especially of the financial distress risk and bankruptcy (Katz *et al.*, 1985; Griffin & Lemmon, 2002).

Regarding the Romanian stock market, as an emerging one that offers higher growth rates and profitability (Albu & Albu, 2012), the literature is based on identifying the relevant financial information for investors in terms of earnings (Filip & Raffournier, 2010), the impact of applying IFRS on the value relevance of earnings (Filip, 2010). These studies are considered, according with Holthausen and Watts (2001), relative association studies and incremental association studies, identifying, on one side, the explanatory power of the financial information through the R^2 coefficient and, on the other side the most relevant information through regression coefficients. Studying the same problem of the influence of the financial information on stock market, Turdor (2012) and Jaba *et al.* (2013) applied event study through panel analysis, identifying a strong link between earnings and stock market. All these studies focus on the financial information, not taking into consideration other factors which can influence the decisions of investors.

2.1 The concept of financial distress risk and how it is measured

The financial distress risk concept has been referred to as various concepts. Karels and Prakas (1987) make a synthesis of several definitions of this concept according to different empirical studies from Beaver (1966) and Altman (1968) to Taffler and Tisshaw (1982): negative net assets, insolvency, bond default, overdraft, unpaid dividends for the preferred stocks, bankruptcy etc. Turetsky and McEwen (2001) also start from a series of previous studies, focusing on the meaning of economic concept characterized by various continuous inauspicious financial statuses, respectively on the moment when the assets of a company are not sufficient in order to cover its debts. Moreover, they consider that a decreasing of the cash flow corresponding to operational activities represents a signal from the beginning of the financial distress risk, subsequently characterized by dividends payment decrease, loan non-payment or debts reorganization (Turetsky & McEwen, 2001).

The specialized literature has most frequently stopped, in the analysis of the financial/business failure on the insolvency or bankruptcy meaning (Beaver, 1966; Altman, 1968; Deakin, 1972; Ohlson, 1980).

In the past, statistical methods have been mainly used by deciders in order to evaluate the insolvency and bankruptcy risk, such as: discriminant analysis (Altman, 1968; Deakin, 1972), the logistic regression analysis (Ohlson, 1980; Zavgren, 1985), the probabilistic regression analysis (Zmijewski, 1984; Theodossiou, 1991) and the surviving analysis (Lane *et al.*, 1986; Luoma & Laitinen, 1991). From the econometric approach, Aziz and Dar (2006) consider that the specialized literature is dominated by the discriminant analysis and the logistical regression analysis. Alongside these methods, other methods based on artificially intelligence have been recently added: artificial neural networks, decision trees and genetic algorithms (Olson *et al.,* 2012). These methods can be used by all financial statements users, inclusively by auditors, in order to test the going concern (Robu *et al.,* 2012).

As for Romania, the main models which have been elaborated are C. Mânecuţă and M. Nicolae model in 1996, Băileşteanu in 1998 and Ivonciu in 1998, or Anghel model in 2002 (Mironiuc, 2006) and Robu-Mironiuc model (Z_{RM}) in 20012 using multiple discriminant analysis (Robu *et al.,* 2012).

2.2 Market Reactions to financial distress risk

Most times, the financial distress risk was seen through the insolvency and the bankruptcy state. Companies that reach the insolvency or bankruptcy state are characterized by decreasing total assets, revenues and net accounting shares value and growing debts and financial expenditures (Barniv *et al.*, 2002; Mironiuc, 2006).

Regarding the influence of bankruptcy appearance probability on the market, Aharony *et al.* (1980) have emphasized a clear phenomenon, the fact that stock price significantly decreases around the moment of the announcement of the bankruptcy status. Zavgren *et al.* (1988) see bankruptcy as "bad news", and, as a result, the decrease of the stock prices is to be expected. Though, capital market actors have useful means to anticipate bankruptcy by evaluating the information corresponding to the previous period to its emergence. Chen and Church (1996) assume that the market reacts less to the announcements regarding bankruptcy

emergence when the auditor has previously issued an opinion regarding the company's activity continuity.
Barniv *et al.* (2002) suggests that investors of the companies that are heading for financial business failure loose significant values on the market sixty days before the emergence of the phenomenon. This situation is caused by the previous evaluation of the market regarding the probability of each company to become bankrupt (Green & Dawkins, 2000). Altman (1971) has, in turn, proved the emergence of an investor afferent loss of approximately 26% in a month before and after the occurrence of bankruptcy.

From the reorganization process perspective, the investors of the purchased companies or of the ones that have merged have reported significant positive yields from the emergence to the ending of the phenomenon, while investors of the liquidated companies have had significant negative yields (Green & Dawkins, 2000; Barniv *et al.*,2002).

Opinions regarding the existing relation between the probability of financial distress emergence and the capital market do not just hint at the opposite relation between them. For example, Vassalou and Xing (2004) consider that companies with a high risk of financial failure determine growing profitableness just in the case of small enterprises characterized by growing *book-to-market ratio*. This situation is explained by the shareholders' negotiating power (Apergis *et al.,* 2011).

2.3 Research hypotheses

Starting from the specialized literature regarding the influence of the financial distress risk emergence on the capital market investors' reaction, reflected through stock return, the present study aims at testing the following work hypotheses:
H_1: For the Romanian listed companies in RASDAQ, there are significant differences between the mean values of the financial ratios afferent to the performant and the financial distress companies.
H_2: For the Romanian listed companies in RASDAQ, there are significant differences between the mean values of stock return depending on the influence of the distress risk, estimated based on the financial data.
H_3: For the Romanian listed companies in RASDAQ, the financial distress risk, estimated based on financial data, has a significant influence on the investors' reaction (calculated based on the stock return), classified in performance and company's risk group affiliation categories.

3. Research methodology

The study aims at analysing the influence of the financial distress risk on the investors' decision, expressed by the stock return, quantified through the relative variation of stock price from a reporting period to another. In order to reach this objective, a positivist logical research approach is proposed, by using a deductive-inductive intercession in formulating, testing and validating the work hypotheses (Smith, 2003).

3.1 Target population and analysed sample

The target population is represented by the BSE listed companies between 2008 and 2014. A sample of RASDAQ listed companies is extracted from this population in order to be analysed, according to the principle of rational chose (Jaba, 2002). The main activity field of these companies is the industrial one.

The sample is divided in two different sub samples. The first sample includes those companies that have been initiated in the insolvency procedure (preliminary stage of bankruptcy). Out of the 123 identified companies for which the insolvency procedure has begun since 2008, 24 companies were eliminated, companies for which information provided by the financial statements have not been identified and 53 companies for which there is no information regarding the stock price in the analysed period. The number of the implied insolvent companies for the analysis is 46.

The second sub sample includes performant companies. These companies were selected from the list of the *Major Companies in Romania* study, 2013 edition, Top 300 most important companies, study that has been carried out by using an Ernst & Young developed methodology, that also takes into account the companies' performances. Out of the 33 performant RASDAQ listed companies from the field of industry, 9 companies were excluded final number of performant companies remaining at 24. The final sample is made of 46 insolvent companies and 24 performant companies.

3.2 Analysed variables and data source

The variables chosen in order to assess the objective of the research are the financial ratios that were used in the Robu-Mironiuc model (Robu *et al.*, 2012). Financial ratios can be used in order to draw conclusions on the current status of the companies (Istrate, 2007), and those that were included in Robu-Mironiuc model model are specific to the analysis of bankruptcy risk for the Romanian quoted companies and has the following form:

$$\mathbf{Z_{RM}} = 0.333 - 0.012\mathbf{FL} + 0.525\mathbf{RAF} + 0.027\mathbf{ROE} - 0.425\mathbf{DR} - 0.126\mathbf{NM} + 3.573\mathbf{ROA} - 0.663\mathbf{ITR} + 0.022\,\mathbf{CFR} \quad (1)$$

For this model, the ranges for the bankruptcy risk categories are: *high bankruptcy risk* $Z_{RM} \in (\ 5;0)$, *moderate bankruptcy risk* $Z_{RM} \in [0;0.6)$ and *low bankruptcy risk* $Z_{RM} \in [0.6;2.5]$. Variables in this model are presented in table 1 together with the formula for each variable.

Table 1. Numerical variables implicated in the analysis, taken from the Z_{RM} model

Numerical Variables	Formula
X_1=Financial Leverage Ratio (FL)	Total Debt / Shareholders Equity
X_2=The Financial Autonomy Ratio (FAR)	Shareholders Equity / Total Assets
X_3=Return on Equity (ROE)	Net Income /Shareholders Equity
X_4=Debt Ratio (DR)	Total Debt / Total Assets
X_5=Net Margin (NM)	Net Income / Turnover
X_6=Return on Assets (ROA)	Operating Income / Total Assets
X_7=Interest to Turnover Ratio (ITR)	Total interest / Turnover
X_8=Cash Ratio (CFR)	Cash / Current debts

A model of bankruptcy risk prediction was chosen on the grounds that, bankruptcy is a situation of financial distress and follow the insolvency of a company. Robu-Mironiuc model selection is primarily determined by the timeliness of this model and the specific companies that were the basis for obtaining it, to the detriment of C. Mânecuţă and M. Nicolae, Băileşteanu, Ivonciu or Altman. The information from the financial statements of these companies is for the period of crisis, period selected for study. Whatever the time when models were obtained for predicting the state of financial distress, it is necessary to review and improve them to be permanently viable. Secondly, Robu-Mironiuc model was chosen mainly due to the homogeneity of the sample (companies in the industry). Regarding Anghel model, this is characterized by diversity of activity fields of the companies analysed. Smith and Liou (2007) points out, activity fields can have sub-domains in their structure, activities of national economy characterized by differences in legislation, operating system and product life cycles with significant influence on financial conditions.

In order to test the relevance of the information regarding the distress risk, gathered based on the Robu-Mironiuc model, table 2 presents the numerical variables that were included in the analysis.

Table 2. Numerical variables implicated in the analysis, taken from The Robu-Mironiuc model

Numerical Variables	Formula
Z_{RM}	Calculated with formula (1)
CGY= Capital Gains Yield	$(Price_1-Price_0)/Price_0$*

*where P_0 = represents the stock price, after five month from the moment of the financial statements issuance previous the year the companies were initiate in insolvency;

P_1 = represents the stock price at the time of opening insolvency proceedings for companies in financial distress, after one year of registration P_0, for companies considered performant.

In order to evaluate the bankruptcy risk influence, on different risk categories calculated based on the Robu-Mironiuc model, as well as the influence of the company status on the investors' reaction, table 3 displays the main variables that have been used in the relevance analysis model.

Table 3. Categorical variables included in the relevance analysis of Robu-Mironiuc model on investors

Categorical Variables	Categories
Status	1: Distress; 2: Performante
Interval_Z_{RM}	1: high distress risk $Z_{RM} \in (\ 5;0)$: HDR 2: moderate distress risk $Z_{RM} \in [0;0.6)$: MDR 3: low distress risk $Z_{RM} \in [0.6;2.5]$: LDR

The data needed to calculate the financial ratios for each company were obtained from the annual financial statements presented on the BSE website - www.bvb.ro. The data necessary to compute the CGY were selected from the website – www.kmarket.ro.

3.3 Methods for data analysis and proposed models

In order to obtain the research results, the study proposes the use of *Analysis of variance* (ANOVA), as well as the use of simple linear regression models or ANCOVA.

ANOVA is a statistical analysis procedure of a quantitative variable variation, result type, in comparison to one or more explanatory categorical variable (Jaba, 2002). In order to verify if one factor type variable *(X)*, taken into consideration in the study, has a significant influence on the variable variation (Y), a test is carried out to see if there are significant differences between the estimated *Y* means for each group (category) defined based on the *X* factor (Jaba *et al.*, 2012). Testing the existence of significant differences between the estimated means within each group can be carried out by using multiple *post hoc* comparisons, based on *Bonferroni, Tukey*tests and *LSD* tests (Jaba *et al.*, 2012). Use of *LSD* test is proposed in this study.

In order to estimate the influence of the distress risk emergence on the variation of the stock price of the RASDAQ listed companies, the study uses the linear regression analysis. The proposed model uses the variables in table 2, as following:

$$CGY = \beta_0 + \beta_1 Z_{RM} + \varepsilon \quad (2)$$

Where, *CGY* represents the dependent variable, Z_{RM} represents the independent variable, β_0 and β_1 represent the regression model parameters, and ε a random variable. By using β_1, we are testing the influence of Z_{RM} on *CGY*. Based on the values of β_1, we can estimate the direction and the intensity of the Z_{RM} factor influence on *CGY*.

The estimation of the influence of the distress risk emergence, estimated by using the calculated Z_{RM} score on *CGY*, on companies categories (*financial distressed/performant* or presenting different bankruptcy risk degrees: *HDR, MDR* or *LDR)* is realized by using the linear regression analysis which uses ANCOVA models, such as:

$$Y = \delta_0 + \delta_1 X + \delta_2 Dummy + \delta_3 Dummy \cdot X + \varepsilon \quad (3)$$

The study proposes the analysis of two ANCOVA linear regression models. The first used model is:

$$CGY = \delta_0 + \delta_1 Z_{RM} + \delta_2 DummyDistress + \delta_3 DummyDistress \cdot Z_{RM} + \varepsilon \quad (4)$$

Where, *DummyDistress* represents an alternative variable that has value 1 for financial distress companies and 0 in the other case (of performant companies). The influence of Z_{RM} on *CGY*, for insolvent companies, is tested by using δ_3, corresponding to the *DummyDistress**Z_{RM}.

The second model used in the study is:

$$CGY = \delta_0 + \delta_1 Z_{RM} + \delta_2 DummyHDR + \delta_3 DummyMDR + \\ + \delta_4 DummyHDR \cdot Z_{RM} + \delta_5 DummyMDR \cdot Z_{RM} + \varepsilon \quad (5)$$

Where, *DummyHDR* represents an alternative value, which has value of 1 for the low financial distress risk companies. *DummyMDR* represents an alternative value which has value of 1 for medium financial distress risk companies and 0 in the opposite case. *LDR* category is set as reference point and is not included in the model. The influence of Z_{RM} on *CGY*, on companies categories with different financial distress risk levels is tested by using the estimations of δ_4 and δ_5 parameters in the equation (5), associated to the *DummyHDR**Z_{RM} and *DummyMDR**Z_{RM} products.

In order to analyse the data and obtain the results of the research, SPSS 20.0 software was used in the study.

3. Results and discussions

The objective of this study is to test the relevance of the information regarding the distress risk emergence on the investors' decisions for the Romanian stock exchange listed companies, RASDAQ section. The main objectives of the study aim at estimating the distress risk emergence for the companies in the analysed sample, calculated based on the Z_{RM} model (Robu *et al.*, 2012). Once the risk has been estimated, the study estimates and tests the influence of the risk on the variation of the stock price.

The emergency risk of the distress risk is estimated for each company in the analysed sample, considering the values of the financial ratios in the Z_{RM} model in the formula used in equation (1). Within the sample, the descriptive statistics afferent to the calculated ratios, as well as the ones of the estimated risk are displayed in table 4.

Table 4. Descriptive statistics within the analysed sample

Variables	Mean	St. Deviation	Variables	Mean	St. Deviation
FL	0.85	6.52	ROA	-0.13	0.51
FAR	0.21	0.64	ITR	0.11	0.21
ROE	-0.01	1.40	CFR	0.14	0.52
DR	0.74	0.62	Z_{RM}	-0.41	3.28
NM	-0.33	0.89	CGY	9.04	47.98

Taking into account the fact that the analysed sample contains a number of 46 insolvent companies and 23 performant companies, the descriptive statistics in table 2 must be separately estimated for each company category. Once the mean values of the analysis ratios have been estimated, it should test if there are any significant differences within the studies population between the mean values for the company categories, with financial distress and performant ones.

Testing and estimating the existence of significant differences between the mean values of the analysed ratios is made through the ANOVA, the main results being presented in table 5.

Table 5. Variation testing of the mean values of the analysed ratios depending on the company status

Variable	Mean depending on company status			Variation test	
	Distress	Performant	Difference	F Test	Sig.
(0)	(1)	(2)	(3) = (1) – (2)	(4)	(5)
FL	0.99	0.59	0.40	0.06	0.81
FAR	0.07	0.49	-0.42	7.47	0.01
ROE	-0.03	0.01	-0.04	0.01	0.92
DR	0.89	0.46	0.43	8.42	0.01
NM	-0.46	-0.07	-0.39	3.26	0.08
ROA	-0.20	0.01	-0.19	2.59	0.11
ITR	0.14	0.07	0.07	1.58	0.21
CFR	0.02	0.36	-0.34	7.43	0.01
Z_{RM}	-0.76	0.23	-0.99	1.47	0.23
CGY	5.73	15.38	-9.65	0.63	0.43

Based on the data in table 5, we can observe that, within the analysed sample, in comparison to the performant companies, the financial distress ones have on averaged a higher indebtedness degree (FL = 0.99 and DR = 0.89), a low financial autonomy (FAR = 0.07), they record loses of return on equity, net margin and return on assets (ROE = -0.03, NM = -0.46 and ROA = -0.20) and low liquidity levels (CFR = -0.02). Contrary, performant companies report on an average a lower indebtedness degree (FL = 0.59 and DR = 0.46), a high financial autonomy (FAR = 0.49), lower losses of the net margin (NM = -0.07), positive values of the return on equity and return on assets (ROE = 0.01 and ROA = 0.01) and a high liquidity level (FR = 0.36). Low values of the profitability ratios, for the performant companies, are determined by effects of financial crisis, which are still present. These all lead to the obtaining of capital gains yield that are far more higher for the performant companies (CGY = 15.38), compared with the ones with financial difficulty (CGY= 15.38).

Depending on the mean estimated values within the sample, one can estimate, within the population, if there are significant differences between the recorded values of the companies in the two considered categories (with financial distress and performant). Within the studied population, using ANOVA and *post-hoc* (LSD) tests, with a 10% degree, the existence of significant differences between the mean values corresponding to the insolvent and performant companies was estimated and tested, regarding the financial autonomy, global indebtedness, net margin and general liquidity. As for the *CGY* values, one can notice that there are no significant differences within the studied population between the mean estimated values for the insolvent and performant companies.

Depending on the distress risk emergence estimated based on the Robu-Mironiuc model and the risk categories determined through the associated intervals, means ratios were estimated in the study on different risk categories. Once the means have been calculated, the existence of differences between the average registered values for the companies in the *HDR, MDR* and *LDR* categories was estimated and tested. The obtained results after the ANOVA testing are displayed in tables 6 and 7.

Table 6. Mean values variation testing of the analysed ratios depending on the Z_{RM} risk interval

Variables	Variation Test F	Variation Test Sig.	Variables	Variation Test F	Variation Test Sig.
FL	33.36	0.00	ROA	5.37	0.00
FAR	15.08	0.00	ITR	2.07	0.13
ROE	6.51	0.00	CFR	0.63	0.54
DR	13.63	0.00	Z_{RM}	34.15	0.00
NM	8.06	0.00	CGY	1.35	0.27

The ANOVA results in table 6 show the existence of a significant influence of the company affiliation to one of the three different risk category calculated based on the Z_{RM}, on the average values of the analysed ratios. With 95% confidence, excepting ITR, CFR and CGY, the variation of the financial ratios values in table 6, is strongly influenced by the companies' affiliation to one of the three risk categories of distress risk emergence, determined based on the Z_{RM} values.

By using the *post-hoc (LSD)* tests, the groups with significant differences were identified and the values of the differences within the studied population were estimated. The results of the analysis are presented in table 7.

Table 7. Testing of the significant differences existence between the analysed ratios depending on the Z_{RM} risk interval

Variable	Average value depending on Z_{RM} risk interval								
	HDR	MDR	LDR	Difference 1	Sig	Difference 2	Sig	Difference 3	Sig
(0)	(1)	(2)	(3)	(4)=(1)-(2)	(5)	(6)=(1)-(3)	(7)	(8)=(2)-(3)	(9)
FL	-5.15	0.78	6.40	-5.93	0.0	-11.54	0.0	-5.61	0.0
FAR	-0.28	0.59	0.24	-0.87	0.0	-0.51	0.0	0.36	0.0
ROE	0.74	-0.04	-0.67	0.78	0.0	1.41	0.0	-0.62	0.1
DR	1.12	0.37	0.76	0.81	0.0	0.42	0.0	-0.39	0.0
NM	-0.92	-0.08	-0.07	-0.85	0.0	-0.85	0.0	0.00	1.0
ROA	-0.41	0.00	-0.02	-0.41	0.0	-0.40	0.0	0.02	0.9
ITR	0.19	0.09	0.07	0.11	0.1	0.12	0.1	0.01	0.9
CFR	0.03	0.19	0.18	-0.16	0.3	-0.15	0.3	0.01	1.0
Z_{RM}	-3,83	0.38	1.81	-4.21	0.0	-5.64	0.0	-1.43	0.0
CGY	-0.21	4.94	22.11	-5.15	0.7	-22.33	0.1	-17.18	0.2

Data in table 7 present the estimations of the analysed ratios means depending on the companies' affiliation to one of the three risk groups that were obtained based on the Z_{RM}.

The results of the *post-hoc* tests (namely, the *LSD* test) show that there are significant differences between the average values of the ratios that were used in the analysis for the companies with high, medium and low distress risk emergence. With 90% confidence, significant differences can be noticed between the companies in *HDR* and *MDR* categories for the *FL, FAR, ROE, DR, NM, ROA, ITR* and Z_{RM} ratios. Significant differences can be observed within the same ratios, plus *CGY*, and also in the case of companies in *HDR* and *LDR* categories. But changes appear between the companies in *MDR* and *LDR* risk groups, where the existence of significant differences was tested and estimated just for the *FL, FAR, ROE, DR* and Z_{RM} ratios.

Testing the information relevance regarding the distress risk emergence on the investors' decisions supposes the analysis of the Z_{RM} influence on the variation of the stock price *(CGY)* variation. It considers the estimation of the coefficients of the three regression models in equations (2), (4) and (5).

For each regression model the (R^2) coefficient of determination and each of them was tested using ANOVA, displaying the results in table 8.

Table 8. Test of the regression models proposed in the study

Model	R^2	ANOVA/ANCOVA	
		F test	Sig.
Model 1	0.039	2.767	0.101
Model 2	0.159	3.709	0.016
Model 3	0.150	2.258	0.059

Model 1: $CGY = \beta_0 + \beta_1 Z_{RM} + \varepsilon$
Model 2: $CGY = \delta_0 + \delta_1 Z_{RM} + \delta_2 DummyDistress + \delta_3 DummyIDistress \cdot Z_{RM} + \varepsilon$
Model 3: $CGY = \delta_0 + \delta_1 Z_{RM} + \delta_2 DummyHDR + \delta_3 DummyMDR + \delta_4 DummyHDR \cdot Z_{RM} + \delta_5 DummyMBR \cdot Z_{RM} + \varepsilon$

From table 8, the results of the analysis show an increase of the *CGY* variation as a result of the influence of the information regarding the distress risk emergence, knowing that such information come along with a company classification in performance categories (insolvent/performant or based on the risk categories resulted from the Z_{RM}). The distress risk emergence in *Model 1* has a low influence on investors' reaction regardless of the financial position and performance of the company. When willing to differentiate the companies in different performance groups, an increase of the information relevance is registered, regarding the distress risk emergence, on the investors' reaction (from *Model 2* and *Model 3).*

After processing the data, the results of the estimation and testing of the regression models coefficients are presented in tables 9, 10 and 11.

Table 9. Estimations of the regression parameters for model 1

Model 1*	β	t test	Sig.
Intercept	10.228	1.792	0.078
Z_{RM}	2.890	1.663	0.100

CGY = dependent variable

According to data in table 9, with a 90% confidence, we can notice that the information regarding the emergence of the financial distress status has a significant influence on the stock price variation. This phenomenon indicates an increased relevance of the information provided to RASDAQ investors by Z_{RM}.

Depending on the company affiliation to one of the two categories (regarding the financial distress or performance) table 10 displays the estimations of the second regression model.

Table 10. Estimations of the regression parameters for model 2

Model 2*	β	t test	Sig.
Intercept	10.904	1.175	0.244
Z_{RM}	18.269	3.370	0.001
Dummy*Insolvency*	-4.328	-0.377	0.707
Dummy*Insolvency*·Z_{RM}	-17.148	-3.010	0.004

CGY = dependent variable

Data in table 10 indicates the relevance of the information regarding the distress risk emergence reported to investors' decisions in the case of performant and non-performant companies. In the case of performant companies, one can appreciate that the Z_{RM} score significantly contributes to the investors' decision supporting and thus leads to a growth of the registered capital gains yield of the RASDAQ listed companies. In the case of companies with a significant risk of financial failure, the Z_{RM} values significantly determine the decrease of the capital gains yield of the RASDAQ listed companies. Based on the two findings, one can appreciate that the obtained values of the Z_{RM} score function are relevant for the investors especially when the performance category a company can be integrated is known.

In the case of the Romanian RASDAQ listed companies, the performance categories can be also obtained by using the Z_{RM}, based on the reference intervals associated to the calculated scores. The relevance of the information regarding the distress risk emergence, evaluated by using the Z_{RM} score, can be differently estimated on performance/risk categories. The results of the regression model 3 estimations are displayed in table 11.

Table 11. Estimations of the regression parameters for model 3

Model 3*	β	t test	Sig.
Intercept	-13.959	-0.887	0.378
Z_{RM}	19.928	2.891	0.005
Dummy*HDR*	13.986	0.664	0.509
Dummy*MDR*	20.981	0.741	0.461
Dummy*HDR*·Z_{RM}	-19.865	-2.702	0.009
Dummy*MDR*·Z_{RM}	-25.375	-0.443	0.659

**CGY = dependent variable*

In this case, for the companies that present no financial distress risk (affiliated to the *LDR* category*),* one may notice that the information provided to the investors based on the Z_{RM} score calculation are relevant and lead to a growth the profitableness of RASDAQ listed shares (evaluated by using CGY). In the case of companies that show a medium distress risk emergence, information that is provided to the investors that were calculated based on the Z_{RM} do not indicate any relevance within RASDAQ. But, for the companies with a high degree reaching the failure status, one can appreciate that the calculated Z_{RM} score determines a significant decrease in the share profitableness of the RASDAQ listed companies. Thus, we can appreciate that the calculated values of the Z_{RM} model are relevant for the investors only in the case of companies that present a high or very low probability to reach the failure status.

5. Conclusions

After processing the data using analysis of variance (ANOVA), simple linear regression and ANCOVA, the results led to the validation of the proposed working hypothesis regarding the existence of significant differences between the mean values of financial ratios of the performant companies and insolvent, and according to the influence of the distress risk estimated based on financial data (computed on the stock return basis). Validation of these assumptions determine to achieve the goal proposed of testing the relevance of information on the distress risk on the investors decisions, regarding the purchase or sale of shares, with impact on stock return, for Romanian listed companies on RASDAQ.

The results are consistent with the views expressed by Aharony *et al.* (1980) and Zavgren *et al.* (1988) that considers the phenomenon of financial distress as a "bad sign", which act in reverse. Although adverse event is the occurrence of insolvency, which can be completed either by reorganizing companies, either through bankruptcy and liquidation, investors who act on the Romanian capital

market, notes rather the unfavourable state of insolvency often followed by bankruptcy.
From the variables presented in Robu-Mironiuc model, the variables analysed differ from the point of view of performant companies and financial distress companies, as well as from the point of view of the three risk categories. These results again validate the model Robu-Mironiuc. Regarding the econometric models obtained, Z_{RM} score and membership of a company in the high risk category influence CGY and therefore investors' decisions CGY, result considered to be somewhat expected. No investor, no matter how rational is, will accept the possibility of disappearance of the company.

The necessity of such a study is determined by the existence in the Romanian literature, especially statistical models that can be applied to determine the state of difficulty, without taking into account their impact on stock return. For a potential investor, knowing the probability distress risk, characterized by insolvency, bankruptcy or significant losses is important, always reflecting their decisions.
The limits of this study relate mainly to the size and nature of the sample which contains 46 companies with financial difficulties, from industry, in the period 2008-2014. At the same time, the study was focused only on the analysis of the influence of financial factors on investors' decisions without taking into question a number of non-financial factors as control variables. However, future research directions aimed precisely at reducing or eliminating these limitations, focusing on the influence of audit opinion on going concern.

Acknowledgements

This work was co-financed from the European Social Fund through Sectoral Operational Programme Human Resources Development 2007-2013, project number POSDRU/159/1.5/S/142115 „Performance and excellence in doctoral and postdoctoral research in Romanian economics science domain" and through the grant POSDRU/159/1.5/S/133652, and it was presented on the 9th edition of the International Conference on Accounting and Management Information Systems which was held at the Bucharest University of Economic Studies, on June 11-12, 2014. The authors would like to thank to the Editor Nadia Albu for their comments on the paper, to Robert Faff and Allan Hodgson for their precious recommendations and to the anonymous reviewers.

References

Aharony, J., Jones, C. P. & Swary, I (1980) "An Analysis of Risk and Return Characteristics of Corporate Bankruptcy Using Capital Market Data", *The Journal of Finance*, vol. 35, no. 4: 1001-1016

Albu, N. & Albu, C. (2012) "International Financial Reporting Standards in an Emerging Economy: Lessons from Romania", *Australian Accounting Review*, vol. 22, no. 63: 341-352

Allison, P. D. (2010) *Survival Analysis Using SAS: a Practical Guide*, 2nd edition, North Carolina: SAS Publishing

Altman, E. I. (1968) "Financial ratios, discriminant analysis and the prediction of corporate bankruptcy", *Journal of Finance*, vol. XXIII, no. 4: 589-609

Altman, E. I. (1971) *Corporate Bankruptcy in America (Lexington Books)*, Massachusetts: Heath Lexington Books cited in Clark, A., Weinstein, M. I. (1982) "The Behavior of the Common Stock of Bankrupt Firms", *The Journal of Finance*, vol. 32, no. 2: 489-504

Apergis, N., Sorros, J., Artikis, P. & Zisis, V. (2011) "Bankruptcy Probability and Stock Prices: The Effect of Altman Z-Score Information on Stock Prices Through Panel Data", *Journal of Modern Accounting and Auditing*, vol. 7, no. 7: 689-696

Aziz, A. M. & Dar, H. A. (2006) "Predicting corporate bankruptcy: where we stand?", *Corporate Governance*, vol. 6, no. 1: 18-33

Ball, R. & Brown, P. (1968) "An empirical evaluation of accounting income numbers", *Journal of Accounting Research*, vol. 6, no. 2: 159-177

Barniv, R., Agarwal, A. & Leach, R. (2002) "Predicting Bankruptcy Resolution", *Journal of Business Finance & Accounting*, 29(3): 497-520

Barth, M. E., Beaver, W. H. & Landsman, W. R. (2001) "The relevance of the value relevance literature for financial accounting standard setting: another view", *Journal of Accounting and Economics*, vol/ 31, no. 1-3: 77-104

Barth, M. E., Landsman, W. R. & Lang, M. H. (2008) "International Accounting Standards and Accounting Quality", *Journal of Accounting Research*, vol. 46, no. 3: 467-498

Barth, M. E., Landsman, E. R. Lang, M. & Williams, C. (2012) "Are IFRS-based and US GAAP-based accounting amounts comparable?", *Journal of Accounting and Economics*, vol. 54, issue 1: 68-93

Beaver, W. H. (1966) "Financial ratios as predictors of failure", *Journal of Accounting Research*, Vol. 4, Empirical Research in Accounting: Selected Studies: 71-111

Beaver, W. H. (1968) "The Information Content of Annual Earnings Announcements", *Empirical Research in Accounting: Selected Studies*, vol. 6: 67-92

Carretta, A., Farina, V., Martelli, D., Fiordelisi, F. & Schwizer, P. (2011) "The Impact of Corporate Governance Press News on Stock Market Returns", *European Financial Management*, vol. 17, no. 1: 100-119

Chen, K. C. W. & Church, B. K. (1996) "Going Concern Opinions and the Market's Reaction to Bankruptcy Filings", *The Accounting Review*, vol. 71, no. 1: 117-128

Chou, P.-H., Ho., P.-H. & Ko, K.-C. (2012) "Do industries matter in explaining stock returns and asset-pricing anomalies?", *Journal of Banking and Finance*, vol. 36, issue 2: 355-370

Deakin, E. (1972) "A Discriminant Analysis of Predictors of Business Failure", *Journal of Accounting Research*, vol. 10, no. 1: 167-179

Dumontier, P. & Raffournier, B. (2002) "Accounting and capital markets: a survey of the European evidence", The European Accounting Review, vol. 11, no. 1: 119-151

Filip, A. (2010) "IFRS and the value relevance of earnings: evidence from the emerging market of Romania", *International Journal of Accounting, Auditing and Performance Evaluation,* vol. 6, no. 2/3: 191-223

Filip, A. & Raffournier B. (2010) "The value relevance of earnings in a transition economy: The case of Romania", *The International Journey of Accounting*, vol. 45, issue 1: 77-103

Gómez-Guillmón, A. D. (2008) "The usefulness of the audit report in investement and financing decisions', *Managerial Auditing Journal*, vol. 18, no. 6-7: 549-559

Green, E. R. & Dawkins, M. C. (2000) "The Association between Bankruptcy Outcome and Price Reactions to Bankruptcy Filings", *Journal of Accounting, Auditing & Finance*, 15: 425-438

Griffin, J. M. & Lemmon, M. L. (2002) "Book-to-Market Equity, Distress Risk, and Stock Returns", *The Journal of Finance*, vol. LVII, no. 5: 2317-2336

Holthausen, R. W., and Watts, R. L. (2001) "The relevance of the value-relevance literature for financial accounting standard setting', *Journal of Accounting and Economics*, vol. 31, issue 1-3: 3-75

International Accounting Standard Board (2013) *Standardele Internaţionale de Raportare Financiară*, translated by CECCAR, Bucureşti: CECCAR

Jaba, E. (2002) *Statistica*, 3rd ed., Bucureşti: Editura Economică

Istrate, C (2007) "Appreciation on the debt ratio of some companies of Iaşi county", *Analele Ştiinţifice ale Universităţii "Alexandru Ioan Cuza" din Iaşi*, Tomul LIV, Ştiinţe Economice: 9-14

Jaba, E., Robu, I.-B., Balan, C.B. & Robu, M.-A. (2012) "Folosirea ANOVA pentru obţinerea probelor de audit cu privire la efectul domeniului de activitate asupra variaţiei indicatorilor poziţiei şi performanţei financiare", *Audit Financiar*, 10(8): 3-12

Jaba, E., Mironiuc, M., Roman, M., Robu, I-B. & Robu, M-A. (2013) "The Statistical Assessment of an Emerging Capital Market Using the Panel Data Analysis of the Financial Information", *Economic Computation and Economic Cybernetics Studies and Research*, 47(2): 21-36

Katz, S. & Lilien, S., Nelson, B. (1985) "Stock Market Behavior around Bankruptcy Model Distress and Recovery Predictions", vol. 41, no. 1: 70-74

Karels, G. V. & Prakash, A. J. (1987) "Multivariate normality and forecasting of business bankruptcy", *Journal of Business Finance & Accounting*, 14(4): 573-593

Lane, W., Looney, S. & Wansley, J. (1986) "An application of the Cox proportional hazards model to bank failure", *Journal of Banking and Finance*, 10: 511-531

Larcker, D. F., Ormazabal, G. & Taylor, D. J. (2011) "The market reaction to corporate governance regulation", *Journal of Financial Economics*, vol. 101, issue 2: 431-448

Lee, H.-L. & Lee, H. (2013) "Do big 4 audit firms improve the value relevance of earnings and equity?", *Managerial Auditing Journal*, vol. 28, no. 7: 628-646

Li, D. & Jin, J. (2006) "The effect of diversification on firm returns in chemical and oil industries", *Review of Accounting and Finance*, vol 5, no. 1: 20-29

Luoma, M. & Laitinen, E. (1991) "Survival analysis as a tool for company failure prediction", *Omega International Journal of Management Science*, vol. 19, no. 6: 673–678

Mironiuc, M. (2006) *Analiză economico-financiară: Elemente teoretico-metodologice şi aplicaţii*, Iaşi: Sedcom Libris

Ohlson, J. A. (1980) "Financial Ratios and the Probabilistic Prediction of Bankruptcy", *Journal of Accounting Research*, vol. 12, no. 1: 109-119

Olson, D. L., Delen, D. & Meng, Y. (2012) "Comparative analysis of data mining methods for bankruptcy prediction", *Decision Support Systems*, vol. 52, issue 2: 464-473

Ragab, A. A. & Omran, M. M. (2006) "Accounting information, value relevance, and investors' behavior in the Egyptian equity market", *Review of Accounting and Finance*, 5(3): 279-297

Robu, M.-A., Mironiuc, M. & Robu, I.-B. (2012) "Un model practic pentru testarea ipotezei de "going-concern" în cadrul misiunii de audit financiar pentru firmele româneşti cotate", *Audit financiar*, anul X, nr. 86-2: 13-24

Smith, M. (2003) *Research Methods in Accounting*, London: SAGE Publications

Smith, M. & Liou, D.-K. (2007) "Industrial sector and financial distress", *Managerial Auditing Journal*, vol. 22, no. 4: 376-391

Taffler, R. J. & Tisshaw, H. (1977) "Going, going, gone–four factors which predict", *Accountancy*, 88(1083): 50-54 cited in Karels, G. V., Prakash, A. J. (1987) "Multivariate normality and forecasting of business bankruptcy", *Journal of Business Finance & Accounting*, 14(4): 573-593

Tangjitprom, N. (2012) "The Review of Macroeconomic Factors and Stock Returns", *International Business Research*, vol. 5, no. 8: 107-115

Theodossiou, P. (1991) "Alternative Models for Assessing the Financial Condition of Business in Grece", *Journal of Business Finance & Accounting*, vol. 18, no. 5: 697-720

Tudor, C. (2012), "Information asymmetry and risk factors for stock returns in a post-communist transition economy: Empirical proof of the inefficiency of the Romanian stock market", *African Journal of Business Management*, vol. 6, no. 16: 5648-5656

Turetsky, H. & McEwn, R. A. (2001) "An Empirical Investigation of Firm Longevity: A Model of the *Ex Ante* Predictors of Financial Distress", *Review of Quantitative Finance and Accounting*, vol. 16: 323-343

Vassalou, M., Xing, Y. (2004) "Default risk in equity returns", *Journal of Finance*, vol. 59, issue 2: 831-868

Vijitha, P. & Nimalathasan, B. (2014) "Value Relevance of accounting information and share price: A study of listed manufacturing companies in Sri Lanka", *Merit Research Journal of Business and Management*, vol. 2(1): 1-6

Zavgren, C. V. (1985) "Assessing the Vulnerability to Failure of American Industrial Firms: A Logistic Analysis", *Journal of Business Finance & Accounting*, vol. 12, no. 1: 19-45

Zmijewski, M. E. (1984) "Methodological Issues Related to the Estimation of Financial Distress Prediction Models", *Journal of Accounting Research*, vol. 22, Studies on Current Econometric Issues in Accounting Research: 59-82

4

Credit risk prediction: A comparative study between discriminant analysis and the neural network approach

Sihem Khemakhem [a,1] and Younés Boujelbène[a]

[a] *University of Sfax, Tunisia*

Abstract: Banks are concerned with the assessment of the risk of financial distress before giving out a loan. Many researchers proposed the use of models based on the Neural Networks in order to help the banker better make a decision. The objective of this paper is to explore a new practical way based on the Neural Networks that would help the banker to predict the non payment risk the companies asking for a loan. This work is motivated by the insufficiency of traditional prevision models. The sample consists of 86 Tunisian companies and 15 financial ratios were calculated, over the period from 2005 to 2007. The results were compared with those of discriminant analysis. They show that the neural networks technique is more accurate in term of predictability.

Keywords: credit risk, prediction, discriminant analysis, artificial neural networks

1. Introduction

The evolution of banking in recent decades also led to the appearance of new risks and deepening of existing ones. Thus, risk management in the field of credit is an important issue; it has significantly improved and helped to strengthen the financial reliability of credit institutions: it is the central theme of the new Basel II. The Basel II is a step towards international harmonization of banking regulations. It

---

[1] *Corresponding address:* Sihem Khemakhem, University of Sfax (Tunisia), 1, Rue de l'aéroport Km 4 P14, Sfax, Tunisia; email address:sihemkhemakhem@yahoo.fr

allows among others to correct some obvious weaknesses of Basel I. The evolution of prudential Cooke ratio to the Mc Donough ratio is mainly aimed at maintaining the financial stability and reliability of the banking system. This way the new guidelines of the three fundamental pillars of Basel II: credit, market and operational risks encourage the intensification of effective and sound risk management, taking into account the rapid evolution of financial markets. But to what extent will the new rules actually ensure the safety and stability of the international financial system?

Several types of risks can affect a bank. However, the counterparty risk, or credit risk, is simultaneously the first, the most dangerous and the common risk that face a financial institution. Generally, credit risk is defined as the risk that a borrower will default: they are unable to keep their promise to pay interest payments on time or repay the principal at maturity.

Banks are competitive financial institutions of vital importance that seek profit by providing various financial services to households and businesses while managing different types of risk. Therefore, risk-taking is often regarded as the basic driver of financial performance and profitability (Bekhet & Eletter, 2014). From this fact, and because risk taking is a synonym for profitability, banks make a large part of their profits out of their lending activities and are therefore very interested in developing credit risk assessment models always more accurate to optimize the performance of granted loans .

Several methods have been proposed to predict the risk of credit. The most used technique is the credit scoring from discriminates analysis. This operation is completed by the engagement of a score function which helps decision making in granting credit to companies that borrow. Many researches were based on discriminant analysis (Altman, 1968; Altman *et al.*, 1977; Conan & Holder, 1979).

However, the method of discriminates analysis has been criticized by several authors (Eisenbeis, 1977; Deakin, 1976; Joy & Tollefson , 1975) because the validity of the results found by this technique depends on their restrictive assumptions in case of the assumption of normality of the distribution of each of the variables used and the assumption of independence between them .

To overcome the shortcomings of the discriminant analysis method, other models of risk analysis have emerged. Neural networks are powerful nonlinear data processing techniques, which have proven their reliability in many areas. The neural network is a new approximation method of complex systems, especially useful when these systems are difficult to model by means of conventional statistical methods.

The first implementation of neural networks to estimate the risk of financial failure was conducted by Bell & Alii (1990). The use of this technique was then intensified with work by Tam (1991) and Altman *et al.* (1994). Several studies have shown that the neural approach offers improved predictive accuracy compared to discriminant analysis (Odom & Sharda, 1990; Abdou *et al.*, 2008). However, Altman *et al.* (1994) recommended using both methods (neural approach and discriminant analysis).

In this context, this paper's main objective is to determine a discrimination model to detect financial distress of companies requesting credit from banks by means of a new approach based on artificial neural networks and compare the method to discriminant analysis to improve decision support for Tunisian bankers.

2. Literature review

2.1. The Discriminant analysis

Discriminant analysis is a statistical technique used to discriminate between observations given their individual characteristics. It is used to classify and / or predict a phenomenon and make the dependent variable qualitative. Its empirical application started since the 1930s with the work of Fisher (1936) and Mahalanobis (1936).

The discriminant analysis is to find a weighted average of several ratios (discriminate function), calculated for each company, which best ensures the distinction between firms in financial distress and successful ones. This is a method used by banks especially for Scoring.

The discriminant analysis requires that data are independent and normally distributed. Therefore, the general equation is as follows (Jackson & Wood, 2013)

$$Z_i = \propto + \beta_1 X_{i1} + \beta_2 X_{i2} + \cdots + \beta_n X_{in}$$

Where Z represents the score of firm i, α is the constant, X_{i1} are the attributes (ratios, categorical or qualitative variables) of firm i and βi represents the coefficients of the linear combination of explanatory variables.

The pioneer of the Credit Scoring method is Beaver (1966). He used univariate analysis to distinguish between efficient firms and firms in difficulty up to 5 years before bankruptcy. This allows assigning companies to the group of healthy companies or those in difficulty with the lowest error rate. Although this method provides effective results, it was greatly criticized. On the one hand, this approach does not provide a comprehensive assessment of the situation of the company.

Treating ratio each separately does not simultaneously take into account the existing interdependence between the different financial ratios. On the other hand, the financial situation of a firm cannot be fully described through a single ratio regardless of the importance of this ratio. Despite all these criticisms, this method has been the starting point for the development of other models such as the z-score model published by Altman (1968) which brought about the prediction model of the most popular defects in literature. It calculates a score function Z is a linear combination of n financial ratios and whether the score of any business is above or below a certain threshold. It checks if the company is healthy or in distress.

However, the major problem in the application of these methods is that the validity of the results found by these techniques is dependent on their restrictive assumptions that are rarely met in real life, in this case the assumption of normality distribution of each of the variables used and the assumption of independence between them which can make these theoretically invalid methods (Huang *et al.*, 2004; Sustersic *et al.*, 2009).

Therefore, the constraint of the basic assumptions necessary for effective implementation of the discriminant analysis has led some researchers to test the effectiveness of other statistical tools.

2.2. Artificial Neural Networks (ANNs)

ANNs are flexible and non-parametric tools inspired from biological neural systems. The field of artificial neural networks appeared in the 1940s with the work of Warren McCulloch and Walter Pitts who showed that with such networks we could, in principle, compute any arithmetic or logic function. The first practical application of artificial neural networks occurred in the late 1950s with the work of Frank Rosenblatt (1958) on the perceptron. ANN is a tool of artificial intelligence, commonly used in applied sciences (biology, physics, etc.), that was firstly used in finance at the early 1990s, in addition to the classic statistical methods, as a quantitative forecasting method.

ANN is based on learning, that is to say, these systems learn by themselves the relationships between different variables from a data sample, simulating human reasoning. They allow us to connect the inputs (the database) and the outputs (results) under the assumption that the relationship is nonlinear. In our case, we forecast the presence of credit risk or not, according to the diagram below:

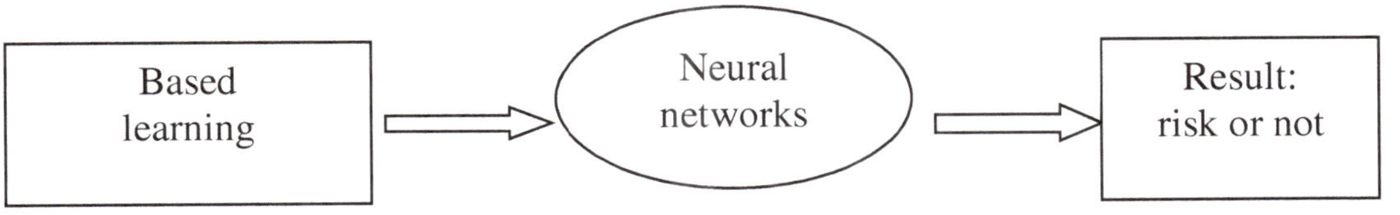

Figure 1 General scheme of treatment

ANN usually consisting of an input layer representing input neurons (input variables), an output layer with the vector of output variables that transfer information outside the network, and one or more hidden layers having all hidden nodes with connections incoming from the input neurons.

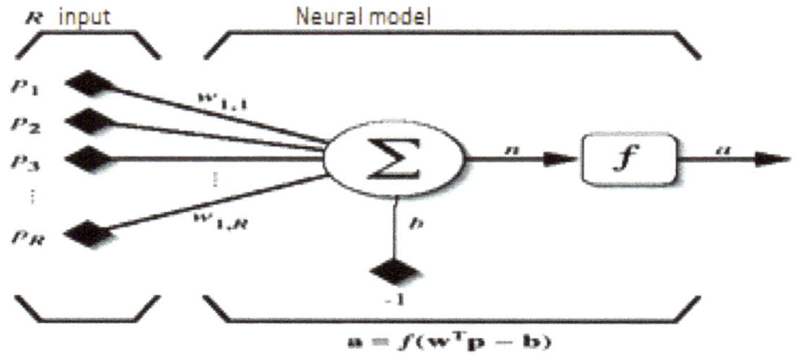

Figure 2 Model of artificial neural networks

The figure above has R inputs; each entry is assigned a $P_i$synaptic weight$w_{1,i}$. The neuron will start to make the weighted sum is the input function, which will give its internal state. The result n of this sum is transformed by a transfer function (also called activation function) f which produces the output $a$of neuron. This transfer function is very important and determines the operation of the neuron network. It can take different forms; it can be a linear or sigmoid function threshold. It can be considered a model neuron as a black box with inputs and outputs. In the case of McCulloch - Pitts neurons (1943), the transfer function is the "all or nothing" (bipolar threshold function) if the activation of the neuron is above the threshold , the final status will be one , if it is below the threshold, the final status will be -1 . Bipolar threshold functions are hardly used anymore. Generally, we use those sigmoid. Parameters (weight of arcs) of ANN need to be estimated before the model is used for predictive purposes. The process of determining these weights is the period of training or learning. For classification problems, learning is said supervised in the sense that the input-output combinations are known desired. Supervised learning is much faster than the other two existing algorithms (unsupervised or reinforcement) as the weight adjustment is made directly from the error, the difference between the output obtained by the ANN and desired output or observed. A popular supervised learning algorithm is the process error back propagation (back propagation of errors).

The ANNs were examined by Arminger *et al.* (1997), Desai *et al.* (1996), Lee *et al.* (2002), West (2000), Khashman (2010), Tsai *et al.* (2009), and Oreski *et al.* (2012) in the treatment of credit Scoring problems. The majority of studies have shown that neural networks are more accurate, flexible and robust than conventional statistical methods for the assessment of credit risk (Oreski *et al.*, 2012).

2.3. Comparison between discriminant analysis and the neural approach

The comparison of these two methods is presented through the results of several works. Numerous studies have attempted to demonstrate the effectiveness of one rather than the other.

Based on the importance of the neural approach in detecting problems in several areas, Paquet (1997) mentions that there are two main reasons why researchers became interested in this tool. First, this method is more flexible than some conventional statistical methods since no assumptions are required about the functional form of the relationship between the characteristics and the probability of default or about the distribution of the error terms and variables. Second, it is a suitable instrument for dealing with unstructured complex issues, making it impossible to specify a priori the shape of the relationship between the variables studied.

Angelini *et al.* (2007) find that the neural approach differs from the conventional method of credit scoring mainly in the nature of the black box and its ability to handle non-linear relationships between variables. In general, according to these authors, the neural networks are considered as a black box because of the inability to extract symbolic information from their internal configuration.

Studies by Odom & Sharda (1990) reported that neural networks are more efficient than conventional statistical methods. The network used in this study gives better results than discriminant analysis on the test sample. Indeed, it correctly classifies 81.81 % against 74.28 % companies for discriminant analysis.

Coats & Fant (1993), in the context of the prediction of business failures, recommend using both the discriminant analysis and neural networks method if the user problem is simply a correct classification. Meanwhile, neural networks perform better than the discriminant analysis method in terms of the type of error and associated cost.

The results obtained by Altman *et al.* (1994), making their study of 1000 Italian industrial companies between 1982 and 1992, concluded that achieving the best results require the use of both methods of neural networks and the technique of discriminant analysis.

However, Swales & Yoon (1992) confirm that the simultaneous use of methods of neural networks and discriminant analysis would be quite difficult to implement in the current tests, since both methods are based on different theoretical backgrounds.

Hoang (2000) , in his doctoral thesis , says the methods of discriminant analysis can achieve better performance than the methods of neural networks when linear patterns are involved in the classification task , but the methods by neuron networks are more likely to detect non-linear patterns in the classification task .

As part of the credit risk prediction, Abdou *et al.* (2008) conducted a comparative analysis between the neural network and discriminant analysis. The sample for the study that was provided by a commercial bank in Egypt consisted of 581 management credit records. Individuals in the sample were classified into two groups: group of companies in good financial health (1) and companies in financial distress group (0). An initial batch composed of 20 independent variables was selected by the bank, but some variables were identical for all the samples, thus they were excluded, such as the duration of the loan that was four years in all cases and all the clients had a credit card. Therefore, the selected variables were reduced to 12. Thus, these variables were used in the discriminant analysis. The number of highly ranked companies in this model is equal to 86.75 %. From this batch of 12 variables, the authors applied the method of stepwise regression. The results of this method showed that only nine variables showed a significant discrimination power. Variables found are then used in the discriminant analysis. This method allowed having a good ranking rate of about 86.92 %. Abdou *et al.* (2008) kept the 12 variables to build the neural model. The results of this approach show good classification rates of about 93.98 % using the neural network with 4 hidden nodes, and a correct classification rate of about 94.84 % using the neural network with 5 hidden nodes. These authors concluded that the neural approach dominates the technique of discriminant analysis because neural networks have the highest right ranking.

3. Methodology: presentation of the sample, selected variables and approach to score model constructing

3.1. Presentation of the sample

The database was composed of 86 Tunisian client companies of a Tunisian commercial bank from various sectors over three years from 2005 to 2006 and 2007. To test the predictive power of the discrimination method, the sample was divided into two sub-samples called base sample and test sample comprising information about 2005 - 2006 and 2007 respectively.

Companies were classified according to two groups with reference to the opinion of the lending operations manager at the bank: efficient companies group (class 1) and inefficient companies group (class 0).

The base sample comprised 60 efficient companies and 26 inefficient companies over 2005 and 2006 with a total of 120 efficient and 52 inefficient observations. Data from 2007 included 60 efficient and 26 inefficient companies used for the test sample.

The choice to analyze situations of Tunisian firms is explained by the fact that in Tunisia, according to financial statistics conducted by the central bank in 2013, the credit risk has increased given the growth of credit to the economy. Indeed, the overall volume of credit increased from 14,451.221 MTD in 1998 to 53,127 MTD in 2012, with an increase of about 267.630%. In addition, a general problem identified by all Tunisian banks is the constant increase of the number of non performing loans.

3. 2. Selected variables

An initial batch containing ratios 15, encoded R01 to R15, was selected. These ratios were used by the bank and considered relevant in explaining the financial situation of enterprises.

Table 1. The variables of the study

	Title variables	Measure variables
R01	Added value rate	Added value / Turnover
R02	Operating profitability	EBITDA / Turnover
R03	Operating margin	EBIT / Turnover
R04	Debt ratio	Financial expenses / Turnover
R05	Profit Margin Ratio	Net profit / Turnover
R06	Financial profitability	Net income / Net Equity
R07	Solvency ratio	Net equity / Total assets
R08	Financial dependence	Long-and medium-term loan / Permanent Capital
R09	Repayment capacity	Long-and medium-term debt/ Net cash flow
R10	Economic profitability	Net income / Total assets
R11	Ratio of capital assets	Capital assets / Total assets
R12	Financial autonomy	Equity / Permanent capital
R13	Cash flow from operations	Cash flow/ Turnover
R14	Change in working capital	Working capital / Turnover
R15	Synthesis ratio	Permanent capital/ Net capital

3.3. Approach to score model construction

We applied an approach to study the variables and select the most discriminating one to determine score equations using the conventional scoring method i.e. discriminant analysis and the artificial intelligence techniques based on neural networks that identify companies in difficulty and non-difficulty ones.

To do so, we first considered the variables dependence according to a correlation test and then developed the variable selection aspect.

3.3.1. Correlation analysis

We define the intensity of binding between the different variables, relying on the correlation measure. To detect whether two variables are collinear, we examined the Pearson coefficients according to the correlation matrix.

Table 2. Matrix of correlation

	R01	R02	R03	R04	R05	R06	R07	R08	R09	R10	R11	R12	R13	R14	R15
R01	1														
R02	0,977	1													
R03	0,959	0,986	1												
R04	0,979	0,984	0,978	1											
R05	0,319	0,362	0,359	0,255	1										
R06	-0,002	0,010	0,017	0,001	0,091	1									
R07	-0,028	-0,026	-0,026	-0,068	0,280	0,117	1								
R08	-0,015	-0,015	-0,011	-0,009	-0,042	0,013	-0,132	1							
R09	-0,013	-0,011	-0,010	-0,007	-0,003	0,004	-0,051	-0,010	1						
R10	-0,002	0,032	0,029	-0,024	0,428	0,131	0,120	-0,059	-0,028	1					
R11	-0,026	-0,038	-0,043	-0,040	-0,025	0,016	0,029	-0,013	0,017	0,445	1				
R12	0,015	0,015	0,011	0,009	0,043	-0,012	0,132	-1,000	0,010	0,060	0,013	1			
R13	0,106	0,100	0,098	0,094	0,046	-0,031	-0,069	-0,017	-0,015	-0,044	-0,064	0,017	1		
R14	0,827	0,786	0,755	0,791	0,213	0,006	0,009	-0,012	-0,018	-0,023	-0,060	0,012	0,111	1	
R15	0,105	0,092	0,095	0,091	0,096	0,061	0,260	-0,020	-0,023	0,047	-0,122	0,020	0,029	0,227	1

Presence of collinearity

If the absolute value of the Pearson coefficient between two variables exceeds 0.8, which is the boundary drawn by Kennedy (1985) (cited by Marrakchi, 2000), we suspect collinearity.

Under this rule, and from table 2, we may suspect a problem of collinearity between variables R01 and R02, R01 and R03, R02 and R03, R01 and R04, R02 and R04, as well as R03 et R04.

3.3.2. Automatic variable selection

To construct a score for the early detection of the company's difficulties, the choice of explanatory variables is an important step that determines the effectiveness of the score function. For this reason, we used a stepwise selection analysis of the most relevant ratios to discriminate between the two company groups defined by the respective values of the indicator of financial hardship.

The objective of the "Stepwise" method is to choose the model with the best predictive value, and retain the most discriminating variables.
It first calculates the empty model, consisting solely of the constant and then the variables are introduced one by one. The process stops when it is no longer possible to enter a variable capable of improving the model performance in a "statistically significant" way.

The selection variables to be used later in this work are as follows: R02, R03, R04, R05, R06, R08, R09, R10 and R12.

4. Results

4.1. Results of the discriminant analysis

Test of equality of group means is necessary to check the existence of a strong relationship between the ratios used and their belonging to a group. Moreover, the most discriminating variables in the analysis should have high values in the Fisher test and, of course, a significance which tends towards zero.

Table 2. Test of equality of group means

	Wilks' Lambda	F	ddl1	ddl2	Signification
R02	0,992	1,36	1	170	0,245
R03	0,993	1,15	1	170	0,285
R04	0,989	1,87	1	170	0,174
R05	0,979	3,64	1	170	0,058
R06	0,999	0,16	1	170	0,693
R08	0,952	8,57	1	170	0,004
R09	0,984	2,7	1	170	0,102
R10	0,986	2,34	1	170	0,128
R12	0,953	8,38	1	170	0,004

Table 2 shows the relevance of the R08 ratio "Long-and medium-term debt / Permanent capital" with the highest discriminate power (F 8, 57 Fisher), which shows that this variable deeply influences the situation of the company and allows to differentiate between the two categories of firms (efficient and inefficient). Debt plays an important role in assessing the current and future financial situation of a company. This result is confirmed by the works of St. Cyr & Pinsonneault (1997). These authors argue that the more a company's debt, there is more risk that it would experience solvency problems over time. According to these authors, the use of debt induces risks relating to the variability of performance and increases the probability of insolvency. R12 ratio "Equity / Permanent Capital" also have a high discriminative power. According to the bank standard, this ratio must be greater than or equal to 0.5. Otherwise, we say that the long-term debt capacity of the company is saturated. In financial terms, companies in distress suffer from high debt burden in the short term and low financial autonomy (Lelogeais, 2003). From the results, we note that some variables had a very low discriminatory power and a significance level of error that exceeded 0.05. Indeed, the ratio R06 "Net income / Net Equity" had the lowest discriminate power. The study by Vernimmen (2002) confirms this result. According to this author, this criterion although attractive in terms of simplicity of calculation, is not perfect. Indeed, and in contrast to other indicators, it does not take account of the risk. It is often limited to one year. Moreover, it should be compared to the rates required to be significant. The R02 ratio "EBITDA /turnover" has a low discriminatory power. However, Stili (2002) mentioned that the EBITDA is the first balance obtained at the end of the production process and marketing. This concept is the main component in the calculation of the ratio of operating profitability. It is the first direct measurement of the industrial and commercial performance of the company and an indicator, usually significant, about its earnings capacity.

To make the discriminate equation and determine a score, discriminate function coefficients were estimated from Table 3.

Table 3. Coefficients of canonical discriminate functions

	Function
	1
R02	1,671
R03	-0,779
R04	-0,566
R05	-6,151
R06	0,087
R08	1,364
R09	0,008
R10	0,005
R12	0,037
(Constant)	-0,188

This establishes the following discriminant function:
D1 (i0) = - 0,188+ 1,671R02 - 0,779R03 - 0,566R04 - 6,151R05 + 0,087R06+ + 1,364R08+ 0,008R09+ 0,005R10+ 0,037R12

One of the discriminating power measures is the rate of right classification. It is equal to the number of companies well classified in two groups divided by the total number of companies.

Table 4. Classification results of the base sample

			Class (es) of expected allocation (s)	Total
Y		**0**	**1**	
Original Number	0	10	42	52
	1	2	118	120
%	0	19,231	80,769	100
	1	1,667	98,333	100

at 74.4% of the original correctly classified observations.

As the table shows, the rate of correct classification of inefficient firms is equal to 19.231 % and the rate of correct classification of successful companies is equal to 98.33 %. Thus, the number of companies classified by the model is equal to 74.4 %.

4.2. Results of artificial neural networks

To create, manipulate and visualize results of neural networks, we used the Matlab 7.1 software that contains an application of "neural network toolbox", which allows the modeling of artificial neural networks.

The architecture of the multilayer perceptron neural network is used to build models for predicting financial distress. To determine the best architecture, we used the function "trainrp" as a learning function. In our case, the selected algorithm was the back gradient propagation algorithm trained through the entire learningdataset. In addition, the activation function selected for our application was the sigmoid "logsig" function for the hidden neurons in the hidden layers and the linear function "purelin" for the output neuron. The function of creating a network was "newff" for feedforward neural inputs which were not connected with those of output. This command creates the network and initializes its weight. Finally, we selected as a function of performance the meansquared error (MSE):

$$E = \frac{1}{2}\sum_{i=1}^{n}(d_i - y_i)^2$$

With d_i: desired value of output, y_i: calculated value of the output and n: number of observations in the sample

This equation determines the mean square error of the neural model. It is from this indicator that the network decides whether to continue to seek the desired solution or not. The ideal result is to have a very low or even zero error. Function "sim" is used to calculate the MSE of the test sample. We took as input of the learning function the 9 identified relevant variables and one output variable that takes a value 1 or 0 depending on whether the company is considered healthy or struggling during the learning process.

Therefore, in this work, we tried to do several tests on the network by varying the number of hidden layers and the number of hidden neurons in each layer in order to choose the best architecture that provides a minimal error rate since there is no rule, or theorem that would determine the number of hidden layers and the number of neurons to place in the hidden layer to get an optimal network of neurons. Indeed, in our program, we set a number of iterations equal to 500 and a minimum number of hidden layers equal to 1 to 5. The following table summarizes the results we reached:

Table 5. Summary of results of neural networks

Multilayer networks: Feed forward architecture	Number of layers	Number of hidden layers	Total Number of hidden layers MSE[1]	MSE learning sample test
Net1_1 [9 1 1]	3	1	0,1485	0,16038
Net1_2 [9 3 1]	3	1	0,1249	0,14437
Net1_3 [9 4 1]	3	1	0,1013	0,1053
Net1_4 [9 6 1]	3	1	0,1046	0,11895
Net1_5 [9 7 1]	3	1	0,0807	0,1257
Net1_6 [9 4 6 1]	4	2	0,0569	0,09744
Net1_7 [9 6 8 1]	**4**	**2**	**0,0086**	**0,0608**
Net1_8 [9 2 4 5 1]	5	3	0,1298	0,14756
Net1_9 [9 5 6 7 1]	5	3	0,0671	0,08604
Net1_10 [9 2 3 4 3 1]	6	4	0,1384	0,1523
Net1_11 [9 3 4 4 4 1]	6	4	0,0846	0,11891
Net1_12 [9 1 2 3 4 1 1]	7	5	0,1106	0,16454

From this table, we notice that the optimal number of layers is 4, including 2 intermediate. This network enabled us to get a least high MSE for the training sample and the test sample which are respectively 0.00868 and 0.0608 mean square error.

In this work, the correct classification rate of the test sample of the best architecture is determined using a threshold value of 0.5 for the business holding (Khashman, 2011). If the output result of the neural network is greater than or equal to 0.5, the case is assigned to a class (good, acceptance); otherwise, it is assigned to the other category (bad, rejection). Thus, the network output y_i is interpreted as follows:

Seeker$_i$ ∈ Good credit class if: $y_i \geq 0.5$

Seeker$_i$ ∈ Bad credit class if: y_i <0.5

Table 6. Results of ranking the best architecture

	1	**2**	**3**	**4**	**5**	**6**	**7**	**8**	**9**	**10**	**11**	**12**
desired **d_i**	1	1	1	1	1	1	1	1	1	1	1	1
real **y_i**	0,852	0,785	0,798	0,795	0,791	0,85	0,808	0,896	0,799	0,008	0,892	0,865
	1	1	1	1	1	1	1	1	1	0	1	1
	13	**14**	**15**	**16**	**17**	**18**	**19**	**20**	**21**	**22**	**23**	**24**
desired **d_i**	1	1	1	1	1	1	1	1	1	1	1	1
real **y_i**	0,516	0,873	0,848	0,008	0,785	0,882	0,818	0,803	0,785	0,791	0,785	0,852
	1	1	1	0	1	1	1	1	1	1	1	1
	25	**26**	**27**	**28**	**29**	**30**	**31**	**32**	**33**	**34**	**35**	**36**
desired **d_i**	1	1	1	1	1	1	1	1	1	1	1	1
real **y_i**	0,884	0,809	0,832	0,828	0,785	0,743	0,304	0,864	0,873	0,887	0,785	0,876
	1	1	1	1	1	1	0	1	1	1	1	1
	37	**38**	**39**	**40**	**41**	**42**	**43**	**44**	**45**	**46**	**47**	**48**
desired **d_i**	1	1	1	1	1	1	1	1	1	1	1	1
real **y_i**	0,262	0,151	0,899	0,039	0,872	0,191	0,817	0,617	0,785	0,859	0,869	0,54
	0	0	1	0	1	0	1	1	1	1	1	1
	49	**50**	**51**	**52**	**53**	**54**	**55**	**56**	**57**	**58**	**59**	**60**
desired **d_i**	1	1	1	1	1	1	1	1	1	1	1	1
real **y_i**	0,833	0,926	0,95	0,835	0,85	0,877	0,785	0,563	0,862	0,897	0,868	0,041
	1	1	1	1	1	1	1	1	1	1	1	0
	61	**62**	**63**	**64**	**65**	**66**	**67**	**68**	**69**	**70**	**71**	**72**
desired **d_i**	0	0	0	0	0	0	0	0	0	0	0	0
real **y_i**	0,523	0,333	0,325	0,466	0,788	0,072	0,27	0,069	0,433	0,192	0,366	0,371

	1	**2**	**3**	**4**	**5**	**6**	**7**	**8**	**9**	**10**	**11**	**12**
	1	0	0	0	1	0	0	0	0	0	0	0
	73	**74**	**75**	**76**	**77**	**78**	**79**	**80**	**81**	**82**	**83**	**84**
desired $\mathbf{d_i}$	0	0	0	0	0	0	0	0	0	0	0	0
real $\mathbf{y_i}$	0,162	0,111	0,132	0,878	0,287	0,008	0,558	0,441	0,445	0,812	0,821	0,611
	0	0	0	1	0	0	1	0	0	1	1	1
	85	**86**										
desired $\mathbf{d_i}$	0	0										
real $\mathbf{y_i}$	0,008	0,24										
	0	0										

Misclassified Company

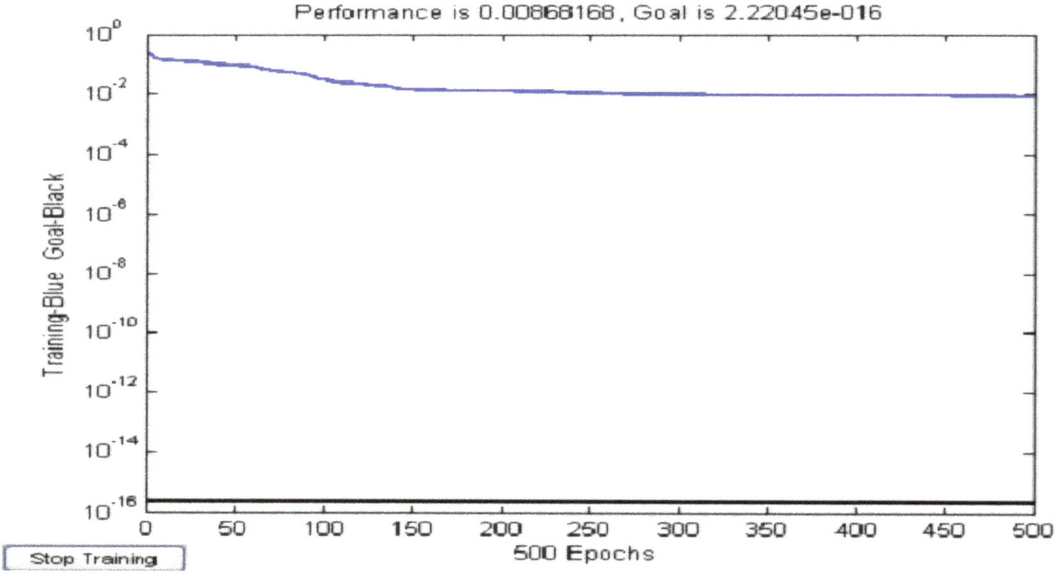

Figure 3. Learning curve of the optimal network with two hidden layers and one output

4.3. Comparison of model performance

The comparison of the two models (discriminates analysis and neural approaches) in terms of predictability shows to the efficiency of neural technique as compared to discriminates analysis. Indeed, the percentage of correct classification, resulting from the application of artificial neural networks is better than discriminates analysis.

Result of the discriminates analysis	results of neural networks
74,4%	82,55%

Thus, artificial neural networks appear to be a powerful tool for the prediction of the financial distress of companies. This work goes hand in hand with the empirical studies already established (Kerling & Podding, 1994; Oden & Sharada, 1990; Abdou *et al.*, 2008; Khashman, 2011).

Artificial neural network models are increasingly used in scoring with varying success. According to some statisticians, although these new methods are interesting and sometimes more efficient than traditional statistical techniques, they are also less robust and less well founded. Furthermore, neural networks are unable to explain the results they provide. Finally, they are as black boxes with unknown operating rules. They create their own representation in learning. In terms of interpretation of weights, discriminates analysis seems to be more efficient. Indeed, in an artificial neural network, internal links do not have any economic significance. Weight ratios appearing in the discriminates functions are rather transparent and easily interpretable in terms of the financial analysis.

To conclude, it is clear that the neural approach and discriminant analysis are two complementary techniques. Discriminates analysis allows us to select the most relevant variables and the neural network can resume variables and calculates the lowest error rate.

5. Conclusion

At this level, we can say that the neural approach outperforms discriminant analysis in terms of credit risk prediction. According to the results of this study, we can make the following major criticisms:

- The present work could be extended by taking into account a larger number and greater variety of variables, including qualitative ones. Bauer *et al* (1998) note that the financial ratios analysis is not an exact science because the priorities in terms of calculation vary from one examination to another. These authors refer to the use of quantitative factors as a guide for the orientation of institutions face to credit risk, which remains unequivocally partially unpredictable.
- The assessment of the Tunisian bank's lending is biased. First, the ratios used by the bank to assess the companies do not give a comprehensive view of the financial situation as there are other variables that are not operated by the bank even though they may reflect the reality of financial situation of companies. Second, Tunisian bank actually grants loans without theoretical or scientific solid

reference. Sometimes, there are records of credits that are accepted even if they have financial difficulties either because the client has relations with the bank staff or because they are custodian customers which lead to problems of insolvency. Finally, banks in Tunisia assess their clients only through the criteria of its financial situation. However, Coats & Fant (1993) took the opinion of the auditors on the financial position of companies as a criterion to identify companies in distress. But this advice may lead to misleading results, since according to Altman *et al.* (1994); this criterion is very subjective and prone to misunderstanding.

Several extensions to the discriminant analysis and artificial neural networks are considered. They are likely to improve prediction and to overcome the drawbacks of the latter. This includes genetic algorithms and large margin separators which are also applied to the prediction of financial distress of companies.

References

Altman, E.I., Haldeman, R. & Narayaman, P. (1977) "Zeta Analysis: A New Model To Identify Bankruptcy Risk of Corporations", *Journal of Banking and Finance*, vol. 1, no. 1: 29-54

Altman.E.I., Marco, G. & Varetto, F. (1994) "Corporate Distress Diagnosis: Comparisons Using Linear Discriminant Analysis and Neural Networks", *Journal of Banking and Finance*, vol. 18, no. 3:505-529

Angelini-Tollo, E.G. & Roli, A. (2008) "A Neural Network Approach for Credit Risk Evaluation", *The Quarterly Review of Economics and Finance*, vol. 48, no. 4: 733-755

Arminger, G., Enache, D. & Bonne, T. (1997) "Analyzing Credit Risk Data: A Comparison of Logistic Discriminant Classification Tree Analysis and Feedforward Networks", *Computational Statistics*, vol. 12, no. 2: 93-310

Bauer, G. (1998) "Ratios and Bank Ratings - What's the Connection?", *Moody 's Investors Service Global Credit Research*, August

Beaver, W.H. (1966) "Financial Ratios as Predictors of Failure", *Journal of Accounting Research*, vol. 4: 71-111

Bekhet, H. A. & Eletter, S. F. K. (2014) "Credit Risk Assessment Model for Jordanian Commercial Banks: Neural Scoring Approach", *Review of Development Finance*, vol. 4, no. 1:20-28

Coats, P.K. & Fant, L.F. (1993) "Recognizing Financial Distress Patterns Using a Neural Network Tool", *Financial Management*, vol. 22, no. 3:142-154

Conan, J. &Holder, M. (1979) "Variables explicatives de performance et de contrôle de gestion dans les PMI", *Thèse de Doctorat d'Etat*, Université Paris

Deakin, E.B. (1976) "Distributions of Financial Accounting Ratios: Some Empirical Evidence", *Accounting Review*, vol. 51, no. 1: 90-96

Desai, V.S., Crook, J.N., George, A. & Overstreet, Jr. (1996) "A Comparison of Neural Networks and Linear Scoring Models in the Credit Union Environment", *European journal operational*, vol. 95, no. 1: 24-37

Eisenbeis, R.A. (1977) "Pitfalls in the Application of Discriminant Analysis in Business, Finance, and Economics", *Journal of Finance*, vol. 32, no. 3: 875-900

Fisher, R.A. (1936) "The Use of Multiple Measurements in Taxonomic Problems", *Annals of Eugenics*, vol. 7, no. 2:179-188

Hoang, E.H. (2000) "Evaluation stratégique d'entreprises par méthodes neuronales", *Thèse de Doctorat en Sciences de Gestion*, Université Panthéon

Huang, Z., Chen, H., Hsu, C.J., Chen, W.H. & Wu, S. (2004) "Credit Rating Analysis with Support Vector Machines and Neural Networks: A Market Comparative Study", *Decision Support Systems*, vol. 37, no. 4: 543-558

Jackson, R.H.G. &Wood, A. (2013) "The Performance of Insolvency Prediction and Credit Risk Models in the UK: A Comparative Study", *The British Accounting Review,* vol. 45, no. 3: 183-202

Joy, O. &Tollefson, J. O. (1975) "On the Financial Applications of Discriminant Analysis", *Journal of Financial and Quantitative Analysis*, vol. 10, no. 5: 723-739

Khashman, A. (2010) "Neural Networks for Credit Risk Evaluation: Investigation of Different Neural Models and Learning Schemes", *Expert Systems with Applications*, vol. 37, no. 9: 6233-6239

Khashman, A. (2011) "Credit risk evaluation using neural networks: Emotional versus conventional models", *Applied Soft Computing*, vol. 11, no. 8: 5477-5484

Lelogeais, L. (2003) "Un score sur variables qualitatives pour la détection précoce des défaillances d'entreprise", *Bulletin de la Banque de France*, no. 114: 29-46

Mahalanobis, P.C. (1936) "On the Generalized Distance in Statistics", *National Institute of Sciences*, vol. 2, no. 1: 49-55

Marrakchi, S. (2000) "Gestion de bénéfice et gouvernement d'entreprise : une étude empirique", *Thèse de doctorat*, Faculté des Sciences de l'Administration, Université Laval

McCulloch, W. &Pitts W. (1943) "A Logical Calculus of the Ideas Immanent in Nervous Activity", *Bulletin of Mathematical Biology*, vol. 5, no. 4: 115-133

Odom, M. & Sharda, R. (1990) "A neural network for bankruptcy prediction", *inProceedings of the international joint conference on neural network*, IJCNN International Joint Conference on, San Diego, vol. 2: 163-168

Oreski,S.,Oreski, D. & Oreski, G. (2012) "Hybrid System with Genetic Algorithm and Artificial Neural Networks and Its Application to Retail Credit Risk Assessment", *Expert Systems with Applications*, vol. 39, no. 16: 12605-12617

Paquet, P. (1997) "L'utilisation des réseaux de neurones artificiels en finance ", *document de recherche n° 1-1997*, Laboratoire Orléanais de Gestion, 26 p

Rosenblatt, F. (1958) "The Perceptron: A Probabilistic Model for Information Storage and Organization in the Brain", *Psychological Review*, vol. 65, no. 6: 386-408

St-Cyr, L. & Pinsonneault, D. (1997) "Mesure et analyse du risque d'insolvabilité", *Ecole des hautes études commerciales*, Montréal

Stili, D. (2002) "La détection précoce des défaillances d'entreprises dans le secteur de construction score BDFB", *Cahiers d'études et recherches de l'observatoire des entreprises*

Šušteršic, M., Mramor, D. & Zupan, J. (2009) "Consumer Credit Scoring Models with Limited Data", *Expert Systems with Applications*, vol. 36, no. 3: 4736-4744

Swales, G.J. & Yoon, Y. (1992) "Applying Artificial Neural Networks to Investment Analysis: Comparison with Multiple Discriminant Analysis Approach", *Financial Analysts Journal*, vol. 48, no. 5: 78-80

Tam, K. (1991) "Neural Network Models and the Prediction of Bank Bankruptcy", *Omega*, vol. 19, no. 2: 429-445

Tsai, M.C., Lin S.P., Cheng, C.C. & Lin, Y.P. (2009) "The Consumer Loan Default Predicting Model – An Application of DEA–DA and Neural Network", Expert Systems with applications, vol. 36, no. 9: 11682-11690

Vernimmen, P. (2002) "Finance d'entreprise", *Edition Dalloz*, 5ème édition, Paris, 2002

West, D. (2000) "Neural Network Credit Scoring Models", *Computers and Operations Research*, vol. 27, no. 11-12:1131-1152

---

[1] Mean square error in the classification of companies of the training sample
Mean square error in the classification of companies in the test sample

5

The value of discretionary accruals computed using both national and international standards

Florin Dobre, Laura Brad and Radu Ciobanu [a, 1]

[a] *Bucharest University of Economic Studies, Romania*

Abstract: The present research provide information about the value of discretionary accruals considering the fact that a switch from Romanian Accounting Standards to International Financial Reporting Standards was compulsory, from 2012, for the entities that have securities admitted on trading. The value of discretionary accruals has been estimated using two methods, but either of them has provided pertinent information about a difference in the value of discretionary accruals. A comparison between the mean, the median and the variance of discretionary accruals computed under the two accounting regimes has been conducted, but not a statistically significant difference could be detected. Moreover, no influence of specific factors could be observed on the value of discretionary accrual.

Keywords: discretionary accruals, IFRS, transition period, Romania

1. Introduction

Considering the 881/2012 and 1286/2012 Orders of the Romanian Ministry of Finance, the entities that are listed in the stock exchange have to report their individual financial statements using the International Financial Reporting Standards (IFRS) starting with 2012. These entities had the possibility to construct before 2012, a distinct set of financial statements according to the IFRS approach, but they were used only by other users different from the public institutions. The implementation of the 881/2012 order is based on the fact that a shift from voluntary adoption of IFRS to mandatory adoption of IFRS is done. Moreover, this

---

[1] *Corresponding authors*: Laura Brad, Bucharest University of Economic Studies, 6 Piata Romana, Sector 1, Bucharest, E-mail: laura.brad@fin.ase.ro

regulation repeals the article 4 from 1121/2006 Order, which requested that entities that use the IFRS as accounting method have also to prepare their financial statements using the Romanian Accounting Standards (RAS). The entities for which the adoption of IFRS is compulsory, starting from 2012, have to provide the accounting information for their individual financial statements under IFRS, considering that the adoption of IFRS standards and their interpretation is in accordance with the procedure laid down in article 6 of Regulation 1606/2002 of EC of the European Parliament and Council from July 19, 2002. These entities have to construct their financial statements in Romanian and have to use the Romanian RON. The entities have also to ensure the comparability of their data and of the IFRS accounting method, even if their securities are no longer admitted on trading on a regulated market.

From the entities' perspective, in 2012, an harmonization of the accounting procedures was done due to the fact that the entities that had their securities admitted on trading in a regulated market have to report their consolidated financial statements according to IFRS accounting measure from 2006 (Order 1121/2006 of the Ministry of Finance).

The order is in accordance with the development of the implementation of the IFRS accounting standards in Romania. As a fact, starting from 2012, the financial institutions from Romania adopted as compulsory the IFRS approach, as an accounting measure for their individual financial statements. The financial institutions could have provided IFRS financial statements before 2012, but these documents had only an informative purpose and could only be own used.

The adoption of the IFRS is considered that is going to bring significant improvements in the accounting quality, which is going to create more confidence for the users of the financial statements.

Taking these elements into consideration, the present research is conducted on the entities that have their securities admitted on trading in the Bucharest Stock of Exchange (BSE) and that have to report their financial statements under IFRS. The idea of research is to provide evidence about the value of accruals and the value of discretionary accruals these companies had before and after the implementation of the IFRS accounting measure.

The rest of the paper is structured as follow: the first part presents a short literature review regarding the implementation of the IFRS standards, the way the accounting quality had improved or not after their adoption and several models that were used for establishing the value of discretionary accruals. The next section presents the methodology of research, data sampling and the models developed, while the forth section emphasizes and discusses the results of the research. The article ends with conclusions and provides information about future research.

2. Literature review

A wide literature in the accounting field is concern with the implementation of the IFRS as accounting measures and it deals with their impact on the earnings management process. The earnings management is viewed as the ability of manager to influence the external financial reporting process with the purpose to gain private benefit either by influencing the entity's contractual outcomes or by influencing the investors' perception about the economic situation of the entity and its ability to create future benefits for them (Schipper, 1989 ; Healy & Wahlen, 1999).

It is considered that the transition from the national accounting standards to the international accounting standards – IFRS - can reduce the likelihood that managers present disclosure information in order to obtained private benefit (Leuz *et al.*, 2003) or can increase the earnings management considering the flexibility that was given to prepares (Barth *et al.*, 2008).

The adoption of the IFRS, as an accounting measure, enquires the preparation and the presentation of the financial statements under this accounting regime. As a fact, a cost benefit analysis is required. Brown (2011) provides evidence about the fact that the results of IFRS implementation are mixed due to the fact that the samples on which the accounting quality is tested are different in terms of size and characteristics. Moreover, there is a wide range of proxies used for underlying the same idea. It seems that that the shift to IFRS has brought significant improvements in the valuation of equity process and the entire equity markets. Improvements in the accounting quality have also been frequently observed.

Considering these features, the adoption of the IFRS can provide additional information to stakeholders, as specific measurement and recognition rules can positively influence the quality of accounting numbers. Thus, the financial reporting becomes more transparent (Daske, 2006). While Barth *et al.* (2008) observed a positive influence of the adoption of the IFRS, for the countries that have adopted them, when earnings management process, timely loss recognition and value relevance elements are analyzed, Lin *et al* (2012) pointed out that a significant decrease was observed in terms of accounting quality as the value of earnings management had increased and the value of timely loss recognition and of value relevance had decreased after the adoption of the IFRS accounting measures. In Romania, to our knowledge an analysis on the effect of IFRS was conducted by Brad *et al* (2014) who concluded that an improvement in earnings management have been observed in the post – IFRS period, while Munteanu *et al.* (2014) provide evidence about several differences between the values of financial indicators and of financial ratios measured by RAS and IFRS accounting regime.

Mixed results were also obtained when the value relevance element is analyzed. Oliveira *et al.* (2010) detected that the adoption of IFRS do create improvements in the value relevance for Portuguese entities, while Morais & Curto (2008) found opposite results. Paglietti (2009) consider that the impact of the IFRS accounting measures generates an improvement of the accounting quality in the value relevance for Italian Companies, while Iatridis (2010) found no relevant effect on UK firms.

Considering the discretionary accruals as a measure of earnings management, Ahmed *et al.* (2013) conducted a review analysis on the effects of IFRS adoption. They provided evidence not only about the methods and the samples used in estimating the value of discretionary accruals, but also information about other techniques according to which an evaluation of earnings management has been done. In accordance with the results that have been already obtained on the earnings management, using either value relevance models or earnings smoothing techniques, mixed results were also identified for the discretionary accruals elements. The results are in this form due to the fact that several estimation techniques where used in the literature.

The models on which the estimation of discretionary accruals can be done where developed by Jones (1991), Larcker and Richardson (2004), Ball and Shivakumar (2005), Kothari *et al.* (2005), Barth *et al.* (2008) or Jeanjean and Stolowy (2008). These models present the influence of the IFRS accounting measures' implementation considering both the voluntary and the mandatory adoption of them. Van Tendeloo and Vanstraelen (2005) provide evidence about the fact that that voluntary adoption of IFRS does not create less earnings management for the societies that have adopted them. Similar results were obtain for South Africa entities compared with US entities that used GAAP standards by Prather-Kinsey & Shelton (2005), while same authors provide evidence about the fact that the discretionary accruals do indeed decrease for UK entities that applied the IFRS approach. Guenther *et al.* (2009) found that discretionary accruals decrease only for the entities that mandatory have adopted the IFRS approach and not for the companies that engaged in voluntary adoption of them.

When this indicator is analyzed for mandatory adopters, Callao and Jarne (2010) emphasize the effect of transition of EU countries to IFRS and compare the value of discretionary accruals before and after the implementation of the IFRS accounting measures. They found evidence that discretionary accruals do indeed increase after the adoption of IFRS standards. Similar conclusions were obtained by Houqe *et al.* (2012) who used data from 46 countries and demonstrated that the discretionary accruals were not mitigated considering the mandatory adoption of the IFRS. Manzano and Conesa (2014) revealed that the adoption of IFRS is not associated with lower levels of discretionary accruals in Mexico. Similar results were obtained by Yosr (2013) as the magnitude of discretionary accruals is higher after the transition period.

Opposite to their conclusion, Chen *et al.* (2010) consider that the value of discretionary accruals for 15 European countries has significantly decreased after the entities have used the IFRS accounting approach. Sellami and Fakhfakh (2013) provide evidence about the fact that the value of discretionary accruals is significantly reduced in France after 6 year period from the mandatory adoption of the IFRS.

Considering these elements, we wonder if the value of discretionary accruals of Romanian entities that have to report their individual financial statements using the IFRS approach suffer or not an increase after the implementation of the new accounting standard. Based on our knowledge, few studies were conducted on Romanian market and no relevance of the change of the value of discretionary accruals has been provided.

3. Methodology of research

In order to identify if any significant improvement has been observed in Romania in the value of discretionary accruals since the adoption of IFRS accounting approach, we conducted an analysis on the entities that have to report their individual financial statements using the IFRS regulation.

Considering the 881/2012 Order, 68, respectively 71, entities have to provide their individual financial statements using the IFRS approach. From this sample, the entities that were in their insolvency procedure during 2010-2012 were excluded (CGC, UZT, COFI, UCM, SRT). Other entities that were excluded, were the companies that have a negative value of own capital in the period 2010-2012. These entities are: RRC, OLT, COS, MJM.

In order to detect if an improvement in the value of discretionary accruals has been realized, some financial information has been collected, both from the Bucharest Stock of Exchange site (www.bvb.ro) and from the individual site of each company. For each entity, data regarding the value of net profit, the value of cash flow from operations, the value of current assets, the value of current liabilities, the value of total debts, the value of income tax payable during the financial year, the value of cash, the value of amortization and depreciation, the value of revenues, the value of accounts receivable, the value of gross property, plant and equipment, the value of total assets, the value of own capital and the value of sales has been collected. This information was manually collected as no proper database regarding it exists in Romania. The information was collected for two periods of time: one period refers to 2010-2011 and the data is reported using the RAS approach and the second period refers to 2011-2012 and the data is reported using the IFRS accounting approach. The data has been collected for these two periods as the difference between several indicators is needed for quantifying the value of discretionary accruals. We used other qualitative information such as the quality of audit and the separation between the CEO and the board of directors. As a fact, both variables were quantified using dummy variables. For the auditor variable, the value one was conferred if the auditor is a company from Big 4 and zero otherwise. It is considered that a higher quality of accounting reporting should be detected if the entity is audited by a Big 4 company. For the second dummy variable, value one was conferred if the position of executive manager and the position of company's president is hold by two different persons. Otherwise, the variable received zero value.

In order to estimate the evolution of discretionary accruals, the value of total accruals had to be estimated. For calculating the value of total accruals, we used two methods. The first one is based on presenting the value of total accruals as a difference between net profit and cash flow from operation. The formula that we used is presented in equation (1).The formula is similar with the one used in other research papers, such as Teoh *et al* (1998) or Xie (2001). There are also research papers where the authors used the value of net income before extraordinary items (Keung & Shih, 2014). As we have no extraordinary items, we used the value of net income.

$$TA_i = NP_i - CFO_i \tag{1}$$

Where:

TA_i is total accruals for company i;

NP_i is the value of net profit for company i;

CFO_i is the value of cash flow from operations for company i.

For the entities that have not provided their cash flow from operation, we have calculated it, using the formula presented in equation (2). The formula is used considering the approach met in Dumitrescu *et al.* (2002, p. 42). It is presented in equation (2).

$$\begin{aligned} CFO_i &= NP_i + Amortization_i + Assest's\ sales\ result_i - \\ &- Financial\ result_i - \Delta The\ need\ of\ floating\ capital_i \end{aligned} \tag{2}$$

Where:

CFO_i is the value of cash flow from operations for company i;

NP_i is the value of net profit for company i;

$Amortization_i$ is the value of amortization for company i;

$Assets' \; sales \; results_i$ is the value of the difference between revenues of the assets transferred and the expenses of the assets transferred for company i;

$Financial \; result_i$ is the value of the difference between financial revenues and financial expenses;

$\Delta The \; need \; of \; floating \; capital_i$ is the value computed using the elements presented in equation (3).

$$\Delta Invent + \Delta Accounts \;\; rec - \Delta Operating \;\; liabil(no \, cash \;\; liabilities) \qquad (3)$$

Where:

$\Delta Inventories$ is the value computed considering the inventories that the entity has in two different period of time;

$\Delta Accounts \; rec$ is the value computed considering the value of accounts receivables that the entity has in two different period of time;

$\Delta Operating \;\; liabil$ is the computed considering the liabilities that the entity has in two different period of time.

The second way of computing the total accruals was realized by using the earnings components, as they were proposed by Leuz *et al* (2003). The formula is provided in equation (4).

$$TA_i = \Delta CA_i - \Delta Cash_{\,i} - (\Delta CL_i - \Delta STD_i - \Delta TP_i) - Dep_i \qquad (4)$$

Where:

TA_i is total accruals for company i;

ΔCA_i is the change in current assets computed for company i;

$\Delta Cash_{\,i}$ is the change in cash components computed for company i;

ΔCL_i is the change in current liabilities computed for company i;

ΔSTD_i is the change current debt for company i;

ΔTP_i is the change in income tax payable for company i;

Dep_i is the current value of depreciation and amortization for company i in the year of reporting.

In order to establish the value of discretionary accruals, a regression model was calculated for total accruals using Kothari *et al* (2005) technique. This model has been widely used in most recent studies for discretionary accruals estimation. No reliable data for other models' estimation was available.

The Kothari *et al* (2005) model has the expression presented in equation (5).

$$TA_{it} = \alpha_{0t} + \alpha_{1t} \times (\Delta \mathrm{Re}v_{it} - \Delta AR_{it}) + \alpha_{2t} \times PPE_{it} + \alpha_{3t} \times ROA_{it} + \varepsilon_i \qquad (5)$$

Where:

TA_{it} is the total accruals for company i in year t;

$\Delta \mathrm{Re}v_{it}$ is the change in revenues for company i between year t and t -1;

ΔAR_{it} is the change in accounts receivable for company i between year t and t-1;

PPE_{it} is the gross property, plant, and equipment for company i in year t;

ROA_{it} is the return on assets for company i in year t;

ε_i is the error term of the equation.

All variables are divided by lagged total assets. The variables are scaled by total assets in order to reduce the correlation that exists between them. The scaling procedure is found in several studies, such as DeAngelo (1986), Jones (1991), Teoh *et al.* (1998), Leuz *et al.* (2003), Chen *et al.* (2010) or Houqe *et al.* (2012).

Considering the fact that there is no possibility to estimate the value of accruals on each type of industry, as we have areas where the number of companies is under 10, we develop an analysis by including all entities into it. In order to establish the value of discretionary accruals, the fitted values for total accruals were estimated. They are used in order to compute the value of non-discretionary accruals. Consequently, the value of discretionary accruals is represented by the residual obtained from the estimation of the model (the residuals are used as they provide evidence about the difference between total accruals and non- discretionary accruals). In order to detect if a decrease in the value of discretionary accruals has been realized on Romanian market, we compare the individual elements of the residuals calculated in the pre-adoption period and in the post adoption period of time. As a fact, estimation was conducted on the years 2010-2011 and an estimation of the residuals was conducted on 2011-2012 period of time.

In the last part of our analysis, we try to identify the factors that can influence the value of discretionary accruals. We also tested the influence of the IFRS accounting approach. As individual elements, we included the size of the company (considering Burgstahler and Dichev (1997) results, small firms and large firms tend to manage earnings), measured as the natural logarithm of total assets, the debt ratio calculated between total debts and own capital (firms with high debt ratio tend to have higher discretionary accruals (Gul *et al*, 2000), the change in total sales (firms with high growth can generate information asymmetry, which can lead to higher earnings management Llukani, 2013), the auditor type, the CEO variable (according to Idowu, 2014: 292 firms where CEO is also the president of the company have higher values of discretionary accruals, but this effect can be mitigated by an auditor form BIG 4) as it can be seen in equation (6). Equation (6) is own research.

$$DA_{it} = \alpha_{0t} + \alpha_{1t} \times size_{it} + \alpha_{2t} \times levier_{it} + \alpha_{3t} \times \Delta Sales_{it} + \alpha_{4t} \times DCEO + \\ + \alpha_{5t} \times DAUD + + \alpha_{6t} * DIFRS_{it} + \varepsilon_{i} \quad (6)$$

Where:

DA_{it} is the value of discretionary accruals for company i in year t;

$size_{it}$ is the value of firm express by natural logarithm of total assets for company i in year t;

$levier_{it}$ is the value of debts divided by own capital for company i in year t;

$\Delta Sales_{it}$ is the change in sales between company i sales form year t to year t-1 $DCEO$ is the variables that reflects the if the CEO of the company is different form the president of the company i in year t;

$DAUD$ is the variable that reflects the type of auditor for company i in year t (if the auditor is from BIG 4 or not);

$DIFRS$ is a dummy variable that has value one for the period where the IFRS approach was used;

ε_{i} is the error term of the equation.

Considering these, we based our analysis on the hypotheses:

H1: Larger the company is, larger the value of discretionary accruals is.

H2. Larger the indebtedness ratio is, larger the value of discretionary accruals is.

H3. The change in sales can influence positively the value of discretionary accruals.

H4. The existence of CEO and of the president of the company as two different persons should influence negatively the value of discretionary accruals.

H5. The existence of the financial auditor from BIG 4 should mitigate the value of discretionary accruals.

H6. The adoption of the IFRS should mitigate the value of discretionary accruals.

4. Results and discussions

The purpose of the analysis was to determine if a change occurred in the value of discretionary accruals and what is the influence of the IFRS accounting approach on it. In order to provide this kind of information, the value of total accruals was firstly estimated using two different approaches. As a consequence, the summary statistics for it is presented in Table 1.

Table 1. Summary statistic for total accruals

Element	Values for 2011 RAS approach		Values for 2012 IFRS approach	
	Method 1	Method 2	Method 1	Method 2
Mean	-56952505	-74239626	-57310562	-1.20E+08
Median	-4326918	-722534.5	-2113365.0	-3251775.0
Standard deviation	3.07E+08	4.39E+08	3.89E+08	6.89E+08
Skewness	-6.814999	-5.949448	-6.504996	-6.911222
Kurtosis	38.68414	49.18538	47.05901	50.26036

As it can be seen in Table 1, the values of the mean and median are closer in period one and period two, while a change can be observed in the value of standard deviation. In order to reveal if this difference is statistically significantly, test of equality of mean, median and variance was conducted. The results are provided in Table 2.

Table 2. Test of equality

Mean		Median		Variance	
T test	P- Value	Wilcoxon	Probability	Levene Test	Probability
0.005413	0.9957	1.085281	0.2778	0.128421	0.7208

As it can be observed in Table 2, no significant differences between the mean, median and the variance of total accruals computed using both the national and the international approach can be detected. Either the probability of p-value, the probability of Wilcoxon rank or the one associated with Levene' test is under the threshold of significance of 1%, 5% or 10%. For the variance the Levene test was used and not the Barlett's one, as there is a probability for the Barlett test to provide information only about the distribution of elements, which in this case is not a Gaussian one. As a fact, no reliable assumption about the total accruals variable calculated in the pre-adoption and the post-adoption period of IFRS accounting approach can be generated. The difference in the variance of Levene test can be considered statistically significant if we assume a risk of 72.08% of rejecting the null hypothesis, which is extremely high.

The next step was to realize the estimation for the total accruals and to determine the value of discretionary accruals using the fitted values of total accruals. The results are presented in Table 3.

Table 3. Results on non-discretional accruals

Element	RAS approach		IFRS approach	
	Dependent variable DA estimated through first approach		Dependent variable DA estimated through first approach	
	Value	p-value	Value	p-value
Constant	-0.044480	0.0748*	-0.038454	0.1720
$\Delta \text{Re}v_{it} - \Delta AR_{it}$	0.020782	0.4899	-0.010611	0.7199
PPE_{it}	0.008383	0.8188	0.008918	0.8343
ROA_{it}	0.125582	0.3950	0.737881	0.0000***
F	0.549995	0.650399	12.30294	0.000003***
R squared	0.030755		0.415131	
	Dependent variable DA estimated through second approach		Dependent variable DA estimated through second approach	
	Value	p-value	Value	p-value
Constant	-0.083900	0.0722*	0.028806	0.5578
$\Delta \text{Re}v_{it} - \Delta AR_{it}$	0.008364	0.8815	0.037529	0.4715
PPE_{it}	0.128032	0.0655*	-0.065127	0.3865
ROA_{it}	0.135643	0.6222	0.224646	0.2999
F	1.234404	0.306621	0.830579	0.483111
R squared	0.0664		0.045727	

Where ***, * denotes significance at 1% and 10 %

As it can be revealed in Table 3, the equation does not provide statistically significant information for the value of non-discretionary accruals. It can be observed that the value of non-discretionary accruals is influenced by the value of gross property, plant and equipment when the total accruals are calculated by Leuz *et al.* (2003) method. On the other hand, regarding the first approach of total accruals, only a positive correlation between the value of non-discretionary accruals and the value of return on assets exists when the RAS accounting regime is considered. The problems are that the models are not statistically significant, with the exception being the scenario where the return on assets is statistically significant different from zero and it's correlated with the value of total accruals. The idea of research was to provide evidence about the existence or not of a difference in the value of discretionary accruals considering the fact that two different accounting regimes are used. The literature in the field emphasizes that not the relevance of the model is the element that interests us, but the characteristics of the obtained residuals (see the research conducted by Chen *et al.* (2010), Houqe *et al.* (2012)). Thus, we have analyzed the properties of the residual that we had obtained and we have performed the test of equality as it has been done with the value of total accruals. These characteristics are presented in Table 4.

Table 4. Test of equality of discretional accruals

TA-First Approach			TA- Leuz *et al* Method		
	T test	P- Value		T test	P- Value
Mean	7.35E-16	1.0000	Mean	2.14E-15	1.0000
	Wilcoxon	Probability		Wilcoxon	Probability
Median	0.165847	0.8383	Median	0.9339	0.3503
	Levene Test	Probability		Levene Test	Probability
Variance	1.1140	0.6903	Variance	0.5933	0.4428

According to the results presented in Table 4, no proper assumption about the value of discretionary accruals can be formed. There is no significant difference either in the mean of them, the median or at least in the variance (their variability). Due to this situation, it can be concluded that there is no difference in the value of discretionary accruals when the IFRS or the RAS accounting measures are used, so no reliable improvement in the value of discretionary accruals were observed.

In order to shed the robustness of the results, we realized a regression model where both quantitative and qualitative variables were used considering equation (6). This model consists both of RAS and of IFRS measures and is trying to provide information about the evolution of discretionary accruals. The results are presented in Table 5.

Table 5. Results of the model estimation

Element	TA-first approach		TA- Leuz *et al* method	
	Value	**P-value**	**Value**	**P-value**
Constant	0.0551	0.5968	0.1468	0.4325
$size_{it}$	-0.003	0.5893	-0.008	0.4128
$levier_{it}$	-0.0003	0.5016	-0.0006	0.3947
$\Delta Sales_{it}$	-0.0182	0.4735	-0.0139	0.7595
DCEO	0.0078	0.5858	0.0311	0.2297
DAUD	-0.003	0.8486	-0.0281	0.8962
DIFRS	-0.0001	0.9025	-0.003	0.8962

From Table 5, it can be observed that, in case the model was statistically significant, H1, H2 and H3 are not valid. Consequently, the size, the indebtedness ratio and the increase in sales does not influence positively the value of discretionary accruals, rather negatively. The independence of CEO influences positively the value of discretionary accruals, which is opposite to our assumption (H4). When the auditor type and the accounting regime are analyzed, we observed that higher the auditor quality is lower the value of discretionary accruals is (H5 would be valid) and the adoption of the IFRS influence negatively the value of discretionary accruals (H6 would be valid- higher transparency of financial data).

Overall, due to the lack of significance of the modes, the conclusion is that there is no difference between the value of discretionary accruals computed using RAS and the value of discretionary accruals computed under IFRS accounting measure. Even though the variables included in the model are nearly not correlated, the regression model that was developed is not statistically significant as all coefficients are not significantly different from zero.

Considering the research conducted, there is no pertinent information according to which an increase/decrease in the value of discretionary accruals could be observed.

5. Conclusions

The present research tried to detect a difference between the value of discretionary accruals reported under IFRS and the value of discretionary accruals computed under RAS accounting measure. The idea was to provide information about an increase/decrease of the value of discretionary accruals considering that the companies that have securities admitted on trading have to report their individual financial statement using the IFRS accounting measure from 2012.

In the research, the value of total accruals was firstly computed as a difference between net profit and cash flow from operation (Teoh *et al.*, 1998)) and secondly, by using Leuz *et al.* (2003) model. The value of non-discretionary accruals was estimated using Kothari *et al.* (2005) technique (the fitted values for total accruals). The difference between total accruals and non-discretionary accruals represented the value of discretionary accruals. An analysis on their characteristic was conducted. As a fact, a comparison between the mean, median and variance was tested, but no proper difference was detected. Consequently, it can be said that there is no difference between the value of discretionary accruals reported under RAS and under IFRS. The results are similar with the results obtained by Houqe *et al.* (2012). An explanation of these results could be the fact that the analysis is conducted on the first year of adoption of the IFRS when higher costs of using the IFRS approach are encountered.

The problems of the research are related with manually collecting the data and the fact that we have a small sample on which the analysis was conducted. Another problem is related with the fact that the analysis focuses on the transition year. In fact, according to Houqe *et al.* (2012) the switch from national to international accounting measures can encounter higher costs and thus, the benefits of IFRS adoption can be observed with a delay. As the entities have to report the data using the IFRS a year before the adoption, several entities could have already adjusted their financial information and thus, this could be the reason why we found not a significant difference in the value of discretionary accruals. Further research might provide evidence about the value of discretionary accruals using a panel data model.

Acknowledgements

Florin Dobre was cofinanced from the European Social Fund through Sectoral Operational Programme Human Resources Development 2007-2013, project number POSDRU/159/1.5/S/142115 „Performance and excellence in doctoral and postdoctoral research in Romanian economics science domain".
Laura Brad was co-financed from the European Social Fund, through the Sectoral Operational Programme Human Resources Development 2007-2013, project number POSDRU/159/1.5/S/138907 "Excellence in scientific interdisciplinary research, doctoral and postdoctoral, in the economic, social and medical fields - EXCELIS", coordinator The Bucharest University of Economic Studies.
Radu Ciobanu was cofinanced from the European Social Fund through Sectoral Operational Programme Human Resources Development 2007-2013, project number POSDRU/159/1.5/S/134197 „Performance and excellence in doctoral and postdoctoral research in Romanian economics science domain".

References

Ahmed, K., Chalmers, K. & Khlif, H. (2013) „A Meta-analysis of IFRS Adoption Effects", *The International Journal of Accounting*, vol. 48, no. 2: 173-217

Ball, R. & Shivakumar, L. (2005) "Earnings quality in UK private firms: Comparative loss recognition timeliness", *Journal of Accounting and Economics*, vol. 39, no.1: 83-128

Barth, M. E., Landsman, W. R. & Lang, M. H. (2008) "International Accounting Standards and accounting quality", *Journal of Accounting Research*, vol. 46, no.3: 467-498

Brad, L., Dobre. F, Turlea, C., Brasoveanu, I. V. (2014) "The impact of IFRS adoption in Romania upon the earnings management of the Bucharest Stock Exchange entities", *Procedia Economics and Finance*, vol.15: 871-876

Brown, P. (2011) "International financial reporting standards: What are the benefits?", *Accounting and Business Research*, vol. 41, no.3: 269-285.

Burgstahler, D. & Dichev, I. (1997) "Earnings management to avoid earnings decreases and losses", *Journal of Accounting and Economics*, vol. 24: 99-126

Callao, S. & Jarne, J. I. (2010) "Have IFRS affected earnings management in the European Union?", *Accounting in Europe*, vol. 7, no.2: 159-189

Chen, H., Tang, Q., Jiang, Y. & Lin, Z. (2010) "The role of International Financial Reporting Standards inaccounting quality: Evidence from the European Union", *Journal of International Financial Management and Accounting*, vol. 21, no. 3: 220-278

Daske, H. (2006) „Economic benefits of adopting IFRS or US-GAAP: Have the expected cost of equity capital really decreased?", *Journal of Business Finance & Accounting*, vol. 33, no. 3&4: 329-373

De Angelo, L. E. (1981) "Auditor Size and Auditor Quality", *Journal of Accounting and Economics*, vol.3, no.3: 183-199

Dumitrescu, D. Dragotă V. & Ciobanu, A. (2002) *Evaluarea întreprinderilor*, Bucureşti: Ed. Economică

Guenther, N., Gegenfurtner, B., Kaserer, C. & Achleitner, A. (2009) "International Financial Reporting Standards and earnings quality: The myth of voluntary vs. mandatory adoption", Working paper: Center for Entrepreneurial and Financial Studies (Available at http://papers.ssrn.com/sol3/papers.cfm?abstract_id=1413145)

Gul, F., A., Leung, S., & Srinidhi, B. (2000) "The Effect of Investment Opportunity Set and Debt Level on Earnings-Returns Relationship and the Pricing of Discretionary Accruals", available at http://papers.ssrn.com/sol3/papers.cfm?abstract_id=236080

Healy, P. M. & Wahlen, J. (1999) „A review of the earnings management literature and its implications for standard setting", *Accounting Horizons*, vol. 13, no.4: 365–384

Houqe, M., K., Van Zijl, T. Dunstan, K. & Waresul Karim, A.K.M. (2012). „The effect of investor protection and IFRS adoption on earnings quality around the World", *The International Journal of Accounting*, vol. 47, no. 3:333-355

Iatridis, G. (2010) „International Financial Reporting Standards and the quality of financial statement information", *International Review of Financial Analysis*, vol. 19, no. 3: 193-204.

Idowu,S., O. (2014) *Corporate governance: an international perspective*, Berlin: Springer Publishing

Jeanjean, T. & Stolowy, H. (2008) "Do accounting standards matter? An exploratory analysis of earnings management before and after IFRS adoption", *Journal of Accounting and Public Policy*, vol. 27, no. 6: 480-494

Jones, J. J. (1991) "Earnings management during import relief investigations", *Journal of Accounting Research*, vol. 29, no.2: 193-228.

Keung, E. & Shih, M. S. H. (2014) "Measuring discretionary accruals: are ROA-matched models better than the original Jones-type models?", *Review of Accounting Studies*, vol. 19, no. 2:736-768

Kothari, S.P., Leone, A.J. & Wasley, C.E. (2005) „Performance matched discretionary accrual measures", *Journal of Accounting and Economics*, vol. 39, no. 1: 163-197

Larcker, D. F. & Richardson, S. A. (2004) "Fees paid to audit firms, accrual choices, and corporate governance", *Journal of Accounting Research*, vol. 42, no. 3: 625-658

Leuz, C., Nanda, D. & Wysocki, P. D. (2003) „Earnings management and investor protection: An international comparison", *Journal of Financial Economics*, vol. 69, no.3: 505-527.

Lin, S., Ricardi, W. & Wang, C. (2012) „Does accounting quality change following a switch from U.S. GAAP to IFRS? Evidence from Germany", *Journal of Accounting and Public Policy*, vol. 31: 641-657

Llukani, T. (2013) "Earnings management and firm size: an empirical analyze in Albanian market", *European Scientific Journal*, vol. 9, no. 16: 135-143

Manzano, M. P. & Conesa, I. M. (2014) „Assessing the impact of IFRS adaptation on earnings management: an emerging market perspective", *Transformations in Business & Economics*, vol. 13, no. 1(31): 21-40

Morais, A. I. & Curto, J. D. (2008) „ Accounting quality and the adoption of IASB standards: Portuguese evidence", *Revista Contabilidade & Finanças*, USP, São Paulo., vol. 19, no. 48: 103-111

Munteanu, A., Brad, L. Ciobanu, R. & Dobre, E. (2014) "IFRS Adoption in Romania: The Effects upon Financial Information and its Relevance", *Procedia Economics and Finance*, vol. 15: 288-293

Oliveira, L., Rodrigues, L. L . & Craig, R. (2010) „Intangible assets and value relevance: Evidence from the Portuguese stock exchange", *The British Accounting Review*, vol. 42, no. 4: 241-252

Paglietti, P. (2009) „Investigating the effects of the EU mandatory adoption of IFRS on accounting quality: Evidence from Italy", *International Journal of Business and Management*, vol. 4, no. 12: 3-18.

Prather-Kinsey, J. & Shelton, S. W. (2005) "IAS versus U.S. GAAP: Assessing the quality of financial reporting in South Africa, the United Kingdom, and the United States", *Advances in International Accounting*, vol. 18: 153-168

Selami, M.& Fakhfakh, H. (2013) „The effects of mandatory adoption of IFRS on the earning management: An analysis of 100 French companies", *International Journal of Accounting and Economics Studies*, vol. 2, no. 1: 22-33

Schipper, K. (1989) "Earnings management", *Accounting Horizons*, vol. 3, no. 4: 91-103

Teoh, S. H., Welch, I. & Wong, T.,J. (1998) "Earnings management and the underperformance of seasoned equity offerings", *Journal of Financial Economics*, vol. 50:63-99

Van Tendeloo, B. & Vanstraelen, A. (2005) "Earnings management under German GAAP versus IFRS", *European Accounting Review*, vol. 14, no. 1: 155-180

Yosr, H. (2013) „The effects of mandatory adoption of IFRS on the earning management : An analysis of 100 French companies", *Revue des Sciences de Gestion*, vol. 48, no. 263/264: 12

Xie, H. (2001) "The mispricing of abnormal accruals", *The Accounting Review*, vol. 76, no. 3: 357-373

*** Order 1286/2012 of the Ministry of Finance for approving the Accounting regulations in accordance with International Financial Reporting Standards applicable to companies whose securities are admitted for trading on a regulated market published in 687 The official Journal from 4 October 2012

*** Order 881 from June 25, 2012 of the Ministry of Finance on the application of IFRS approach by companies whose securities are admitted for trading on a regulated market published in 424 The official Journal from 26 June 2012*** Order no. 1121/2006 of the Ministry of Finance on the application of International Financial Reporting Standards, published in 602 The official Journal from 12 July 2006

*** Regulation (EC) No 1606/2002 of the European Parliament and of the Council from19 July 2002 on the application of international accounting

6

The current status of management accounting in Romania: the accountants' perception

Corina Grosu[a], Alina Almăşan[a] and Cristina Circa[a,1]

[a] *West University of Timişoara, Romania*

Abstract: The purpose of this paper is to investigate the accountants' perceptions as providers of accounting information, regarding the status of the management accounting in the Romanian business environment. In this respect we conducted a questionnaire-based study among accounting professionals from the Timis County. The study shows that the accountants' perception on management accounting is strongly influenced by factors like: the taylorian mentality, lack of interest, motivation and initiative, as well as the excessive focus on the financial and fiscal reporting, making us doubt the usefulness of the management accounting in the Romanian business accounting. This paper fills a current gap in the management accounting literature, as the existing papers focus rather on the managers' perception than on the accountants' perception. It is an interesting topic in the Romanian context because the atypical evolution of the accounting led to the neglection of the management accounting field, with its enormous informative potential.

Keywords: management accounting, accountants' perception, mentalities, attitudes

1. Introduction

The manner in which management accounting is perceived in the Romanian business environment is deeply disappointing, in terms both of the managers' attitude and of the accountants' interest in providing useful information for the

---

[1] *Corresponding author*: Department of Accounting and Audit, West University of Timişoara; J.H. Pestalozzi no.16, 300115 Timisoara; email addresses: maria.grosu@e-uvt.ro

decision making process. The developments over the last twenty-five years in the Romanian accounting field had a huge contribution to this situation.

The management accounting field is just slightly covered by the studies conducted in Romania. Most of the published papers are oriented towards the identification of the existing management accounting tools and techniques and their use in practice (Almăşan and Grosu, 2009; Volkan, 2007; Volkan, 2008; Albu, 2008; Albu, 2003). None of these papers approaches the behavior of the accounting information providers and users.

The adoption of the French accounting system in 1993/1994, which replaced the accounting system used in the communist period, led to a separation between the financial and the management accounting. This disruption was exacerbated, on the one hand, by the existing regulations which made companies focus more on the tax compliance and, on the other hand, by the attitude of accountants and managers, who left the management accounting in the background.

Almăşan and Grosu (2008) note that the providers and the users of accounting information have different motivations and attitudes which lead to highly different perceptions. In time, a gap appeared between managers and accountants regarding their perceptions about the collaboration which should exist between them. Shields (1995) identified a potential source of the difference between these perceptions. He argued that the changes of the accounting system are simple administrative innovations, their success depending on the manner in which the behavioral and organizational implications are managed.

The way these implications are managed influences the relevance of the accounting system for those interested in the information provided. Most of the studies focused rather on the perception of the managers (as users of the information), than on the perception of the accountants (Pierce and O'Dea, 2003). In this context, our paper investigates the accountants' perception – as providers of the accounting information – regarding the role of management accounting in the Romanian organizations. In fact, it resumes the topic approached by Almăşan and Grosu (2008), which identified the accountants and managers' perceptions regarding the management accounting information, but it deepens the analysis, by investigating the accountants' attitude regarding a decision-oriented accounting.

This paper is of interest both to researchers and to practitioners from several reasons. *First*, because Romania had an atypical evolution in the accounting field, and this evolution influenced the attitude of practitioners and managers regarding the information provided by the management accounting, i.e. they neglected a field with an enormous information potential. *Secondly*, there are few studies conducted in Romania, in the field of management accounting and they are limited in terms of their connection with the business realities. However, this paper seeks to discuss the status of the management accounting just from the perspective of accounting professionals. *Thirdly*, most papers focus more on the perception of managers and less on the perception of information providers. Although there is enough evidence in the literature on the discrepancies between managers' and accountants' perception regarding the content and relevance of the information provided by the accounting system (Pierce and O'Dea, 2003), to the best of our knowledge, there are no papers that deepened the analysis on the accountants' perception. Therefore, we believe that this study fills a current gap in the field of management accounting in Romania.

The reminder of the paper is structured as follows. The first section provides a short literature review, describing the management accounting evolution from the centralized to the market economy, as well as the management accounting research in Romania. The second section discusses the research design, also presenting the hypothesis evolved from the literature review section. The third section presents the main results of this study, together with our comments and analysis. The paper ends with a conclusion section, which refers to the limits of our study and future research directions.

2. Literature review

2.1. A brief description of the management accounting evolution

The management accounting changes have always proved to be of great interest for researchers (Scapens, 2006; Jarvenpaa, 2007; Falconer, 2002). Over time, the management accounting crossed more or less auspicious periods, i.e. periods of searches and attempts to find its identity, not only in Romania, but also in developed countries. The International Federation of Accountants (1998) identified four stages in the evolution of the management accounting, at international level, namely:

Stage 1 – prior to 1950 – the management accounting was seen as "*a technical activity necessary for the pursuit of organizational objectives*" (paragraph 19). It was particularly oriented towards the calculation of the product costs and less frequently towards the use of budgets and the controlling of the production processes.

Stage 2 – by 1965 – the management accounting became „*a management activity, but in a staff role*" (paragraph 19). Therefore, the focus was on providing the information for planning and control, but it was a focus on the production and internal administration system and less on the strategic and environmental considerations.

Stage 3 – by 1985 – the management accounting was challenged to find new managerial and production techniques and, at the same time, to control its costs for the „*reduction of waste in resources used in business processes*" (paragraph 7). It became obvious that there was a need to disseminate the information and the decision making within the organization (delegating the responsibilities). The management accounting had to provide adequate information to managers and employees at all levels of the organization.

Stage 4 – by 1995 – the management accounting pursues „*the use of technologies which examine the drivers of customer value, shareholder value and organizational innovation*" (paragraph 7). There is a shift towards the value creation through an efficient use of resources.

The main difference between the second, third and fourth stage is the change of orientation from providing the information, to the resource management for the waste reduction (stage 3) and for the value creation (stage 4). However, providing the information, specific to stage 2, does not disappear; it is redirected. In fact, the information itself is a resource which contributes to the value creation. Thus, the management accounting becomes „*an integral part of the management process, as real time information becomes available to management directly and as distinction between staff and line management becomes blurred*" (IFAC, 1998, paragraph 19).

The evolution of the management accounting was also influenced by the responsibilities delegated to the managers at lower levels of the organization, which made the distinction between the financial and management accounting information blur.

In Romania, the management accounting had a different evolution from the one described above. This evolution was strongly influenced by the political and social regimes, as well as by the development of the economic and business environment (Cardos and Pete, 2011). The previously identified stages are not as well outlined in Romania, because the economical and political context was very different. Romania is a former communist country, nowadays member of the European Union. The important changes that occurred after the fall of communism in 1989 influenced the accounting system, and the adoption of internationally accepted practices is still undergoing (Albu, 2013).

2.2. The Romanian accounting – from the centralized to the market economy

Between 1948 and 1989 the accounting system was used in order to provide information for statistical reasons and forecasts at the national level. It was not a useful management tool in order to facilitate the decision making process, but it served only for reporting the fulfillment (or over-fulfillment) of the plans (Albu *et al.*, 2011a)

In a socialist economy, where the evaluation and fulfillment of the information requirements were less developed, the design of the accounting system in one or two cycles (monist or dualist model) did not have the significance it had after the 1990. Although the one-cycle accounting system (monist) was "*imposed and uncommented*" (Feleaga, 1996: 61) there were authors who advocated even then a two-cycle accounting system, drawing the attention to the advantages it offered to "modern enterprises" (Olariu *et al.*, 1974; Ristea *et al.*, 1980).

After the fall of communism, in early nineties, the accounting in Romania was reconsidered in order to connect it to the European realities. In this context, Romania adopted the French accounting system, which replaced the centralized planning system, leading to a clear separation between the financial and the management accounting. The accounting was organized into two separate cycles: one concerned with preparing and reporting the information to external users (financial accounting) and the other one aiming at supporting the management in the decision making process (management accounting).

After the adoption of the Accounting Law no. 82 / 1991, the companies turned their attention more to the proper organization of their financial accounting system (Almăşan, 2008). Between 1994 and 1999 the accounting was seen as a control tool, the Government playing a dual role: accounting regulator and privileged user of the accounting information (Jianu and Jianu, 2012). Under these circumstances, the management accounting played the "Cinderella" part (Almăşan, 2008). The regulation for the implementation of the Accounting Law (Regulation no. 704 / 1993) stated that *the manner in which management accounting was organized* was up to each entity, according to its particularities and specific needs. However, most managers understood by this that the management accounting was optional. Probably, the economic environment and the legal framework at the time accepted this situation.

The 90s were the years of adjustment and development of an accounting system required by the transition to the market economy. Although there were inconsistencies and deficiencies in the accounting legislation, Jianu and Jianu (2012) believe that these are probably natural, if judged in the context of that time.

With the approval in 1999 of the Order of the Minister of Public Finances no. 403, the Romanian accounting entered a new stage, through the harmonization of the national accounting system with the international one. Initially, it was an experimental stage for 13 national companies. Following this phase, the accounting legislation was revised, adopting several regulatory documents designed to support the alignment of the Romanian accounting legislation with the European and international regulations (Order no. 94 / 2001, Order no. 306 / 2002, Order no. 1752 / 2005 and Order no. 3055 / 2009).

In 2003, the Minister of Public Finance issued the Order no. 1826 for the approval of some measures regarding the implementation of management accounting. In our opinion, this Order created more confusion among practitioners by its approach, which was still "frozen" in the past. These are regulations only on the costing structure, characterized by a limitative view, based on the traditional value added concept and not on the value chain and holistic view associated with the continuous progress and the prioritization of the customer. These procedures show the lack of vision which induces a short term view to the accountants, without any correlation with the long term impact, critical for the exploitation of the opportunities to increase the organizational value. The "classical" costing principles are explained, not those underlying the implementation of an appropriate management accounting system for issues which managers face: the cost-advantages principle, the individuals' involvement and different costs for different purposes.

In these circumstances, it should not be surprising that the accounting research, as well as the concerns of the practitioners, focused excessively on the financial reporting (Barbu *et al.*, 2010; Mustaţă *et al.*, 2012; Albu and Albu, 2012a; Megan 2006; Albu *et al.*, 2011b). In this context, the management accounting continued to suffer, both conceptually, through the researches conducted, and especially within the companies.

First of all, the management accounting has to comply with the managers' information needs regarding the internal performance, without having as main purpose a close relationship with the financial accounting. However, this relationship exists because the two cycles are the components of the same accounting system.

The separation between financial and management accounting was initially considered logical and necessary; however, the current trend is to develop these two parts of the accounting system together (Almăşan and Grosu, 2008). Their harmonization is driven and caused by the strong orientation towards international accounting regulation. The global standardization of accounting, through the application of the international financial reporting standards, represents the basis for the accounting harmonization.

The alignment to the international regulations creates the premises for a closeness between management and financial accounting. The information and decision support functions gain relevance in the financial accounting, the management accounting pursuing the same objectives. The information needed by the external reporting indicates that management accounting information "is more required" to be transferred to the financial accounting. This reflects the increasing importance of management accounting.

2.3. Management accounting research in Romania

A study conducted by Hooper *et al.* (2009) shows that the management accounting literature in the less developed countries is still very poor. Albu and Albu (2012b) identify two trends in the management accounting research in these countries: one that aims the effects of the economic development on the use of management accounting techniques and one that aims the use of these techniques in different countries, distinguishing between “traditional” and “modern” techniques.

These trends were also observed in studies conducted for Romania. The 90s were the most difficult years from this point of view, as the management accounting was searching for its identity, so that the studies from that period present practical alternatives for designing the management accounting system. After 2000, the management accounting started to be more present in papers which followed a modern approach. Although the papers published discussed the “modern” management accounting techniques (Almăşan and Grosu, 2009; Volkan, 2007; Volkan, 2008; Albu, 2008; Albu, 2003; Jinga *et al.*, 2010), following the international trends, they were completely decoupled from practice.

Dumitru *et al.* (2011) observed that most articles published in Romania offer some generic “recipes”, while the number of articles which discuss a specific issue is considerably reduced. Obviously, this kind of papers does not have any relevance for the practitioners, so that the gap between research and practice deepens increasingly. Malmi and Granlund (2009) suggest that the studies should give importance to the managerial and accounting practices within successful organizations. Moreover, at international level, there is a trend to use the case studies as a research tool, with the purpose of helping the practitioners. Dumitru *et al.* (2011) found that the case study represented the most frequently used method for the papers published in the Management Accounting Research Journal (40%), while in Romania this method was not found.

Most published papers discuss the costing techniques because in Romania management accounting is still seen as a cost accounting, aiming at the calculation of product costs, based on traditional tools and techniques (Almăşan, 2008; Cardos and Pete, 2011). The purpose of the costing system is not to support the decision making process, but to use the cost information for assets valuation (Albu *et al.*, 2011a). The traditional costing systems simplify the reality, offering a one-dimensional model for the representation of the company’s performance and ending as an “easy to manipulate” model (Grosu *et al.*, 2005). The cost calculated in these terms loses its relevance as a management control tool, as it is characterized by subjectivity and arbitrary.

Dumitru and Calu (2008: 32) believe that the current status of management accounting is marked, on the one hand, by the lack of a specialized professional body and, on the other hand, by the lack of specific legal regulations. Moreover, Dumitru *et al.* (2011) argue that "*the absence of legal constraints has resulted in a diversity of methods of organization of the management accounting, whereas many of these organization methods present gaps from the standpoint of the informational potential*". Albu (2013) observes that it is difficult for the national professional body (CECCAR) to provide an adequate training to its members, who work in various fields. In our opinion, it is necessary to have a specialized professional body, able to offer training and certification in the field of management accounting. But the purpose of this body should not be the regulation/ standardization of the management accounting, but the training of the accountants, so that they can become business partners, active in the decision making process. This change of the management accountant role is supported by several authors in the field (Jarvenpaa, 2007; Kaplan, 1995; Granlund and Lukka, 1998; Burns and Baldvinsdottir, 2005)

The changes that affected the management accounting field have "contributed" in creating a distorted perception of management accounting among practitioners. Generally, the accountants tend to overestimate the usefulness of the information they produce and which support the decision making process. In this paper we try to capture the accountants' perceptions regarding the role of management accounting, but also their attitude regarding this area.

3. Research design

In order to "capture" the accountants' perceptions regarding the role of management accounting in Romania, we designed our study based on following assumptions:

A1. The accountants neglect the management accounting, focusing on the financial reporting and tax compliance

The changes that the Romanian accounting system has undergone turned the practitioners' attention to that accounting cycle which reflects the relationships of the organization with third parties (i.e. financial accounting). If in the early 90s the Government was seen as the main "user" of the accounting information, gradually, the later regulations gave priority to shareholders. However, in practice, things did not evolve as expected, the focus remaining on the reports required by the fiscal authorities. Under these circumstances, the management accounting failed to emerge from the shadow it came with separation of the two cycles. The reasons are diverse and they are related to the attitudes and perceptions of both accountants and managers.

A2. The informative potential of the management accounting is not sufficiently exploited

As Johnson and Kaplan (1987) remarked, the relevance loss of management accounting was determined by its excessive focus on assets valuation and financial reporting needs. The current model of management accounting pays an excessive attention to short term financial objectives for assessing the organizational performance. The focus on the short term result is justified by the managers' speculative interests. They seek to "invent" means to reach the assigned financial indicators on which their activity is assessed and they are paid.

The managers' motivations, as main users of the accounting information, become more complicated, taking into account the evolutions of the social and economic environment, in general, and of the company, in particular, which enhance the role of management accounting. In order to be useful, it must be able to assess the economic consequences of the decision regarding the operating conditions, emphasizing the economic and managerial dimension of the informational system.

A3. The attitude of the Romanian accountants is characterized by lack of involvement and remanent behavior

Most accountants believe that they should not get involved in the decision making process, because it is the exclusive prerogative of managers (Almăşan and Grosu, 2008). The accounting is primarily a "language" which facilitates the communication and dialogue between internal and external "actors". It involves a constant education and training. It proves more necessary nowadays when the economic and social environment is transforming and the effective management requires more and more the information control.

Despite the changes in the economic environment, the management accounting still uses the same traditional tools and techniques, thus having less relevance for the decision making process. The main issues of the accounting system for management are not of a technical or structural nature, but they concern the need of an effective accounting for management (Almăşan and Grosu, 2008). The communication system, which provides the information to the managers, underlies this process. Ensuring a real communication between the factors involved requires an effort, sustained with patience and perseverance.

Granlund and Lukka (1998) described the role of the accountant changing from "historian" and "watchdog" to business consultant, the subsequent roles involving also the "watchdog" one. Sathe (1983) characterized the two responsibilities in terms of independence (required for ensuring the integrity of the financial information and control procedures efficiency) and involvement (essential for the management servant role and active involvement in the decision making process). Sathe (1983) concludes that only "strong" controllers, with personal qualities and abilities can overcome the inherent tension between these two responsibilities.

In order to test the above mentioned assumptions, we conducted a questionnaire-based study addressed to the certified accountants from Timis County. We chose this region because it is considered "the economic driving force" from the Western side of Romania. The GDP per capita (10.011 euro) ranks the Timis County on the 2nd place in Romania, after Bucharest. In an Econtext ranking of Counties, based on their contribution to the Romanian economy, the Timis County ranks 2 (2012 – 29.3 billion RON, 2013 – 31.3 billion RON). It is the county with the highest standard of living based on indicators from the National Institute of Statistics, the National Agency for Workforce Employment and the National Commission for Prognosis. All these, plus the attractiveness for foreign multinational companies, indicate an active business environment.

The study was conducted from October 2013 to January 2014. The questionnaire uses different types of questions (multiple choice, yes/no questions, scaled questions, open ended questions), because we wanted rather to capture the accountants' perceptions and opinions, than to get a statistical measurement of their answers. 114 accountants responded out of 484 to whom the questionnaire was (electronically) sent, i.e. 23.55%.

The questionnaire consisted of two parts: the first one containing information about the respondent (its experience and the type of company where he/she is employed) and the second one with questions that capture the perceptions of the certified accountants, regarding the status of management accounting.

4. Results and discussions

Our study addressed accountants with heterogeneous professional experience, acting in different types of companies. The majority of the respondents (82) came from accounting firms. We got 10 responses from multinational companies, while in other types of organizations (manufacturing, services, public institutions, non-for-profit etc.) we obtained 22 responses. In terms of their experience, we mostly got answers from accountants with over 15 years of experience (58 respondents – 51%), but also 43 responses from accountants with an experience of 5 to 15 years and 13 responses from less experienced practitioners (up to 5 years). Hereinafter we will present the results of our study, along with our comments and observations.

4.1. The accountants neglect the management accounting, focusing on the financial reporting and tax compliance

In our opinion, the "delicate" relationship between financial and management accounting during the last two decades has fully contributed to the fact that management accounting has been ignored in Romania, while a special attention has been paid to the tax compliance. The accountants limited themselves to responding to the Government authorities' requirements (through the regulations). The preparation of information to this purpose was made at the expense of the preparation and reporting of information regarding the internal process of resource allocation and their transformation into results.

The focus on issues like financial reporting and tax compliance was confirmed by our study, because the respondents estimated a considerable time allocated for processing the data and preparing financial and fiscal reports (52.28%). The allocation of the activity time is shown in table no.1.

Table 1. The allocation of the activity time

ACTIVITY	AVERAGE ALLOCATED TIME
Data processing	25,44%
Cost analysis and control	16,67%
Preparation of financial reports	15,09%
Preparation of fiscal reports	11,75%
Ensuring the relationship with banks	6,31%
Legislation study	15,09%
Other activities	9,65%
TOTAL	**100,00%**

It is noted that the cost analysis and control is not a priority for the majority of the accountants. A higher percentage for this activity (44%) was noted in case of practitioners from multinational companies. However, this result was an expected one, given the existing control system within these organizations. Moreover, these entities have a particular structure of the allocation of the activity time. They emphasize on cost analysis and control (44%) and preparation of financial and performance reports (38%).

We also noticed that accounting firms dedicate a considerable time for processing the data (26.83%) and studying the accounting and fiscal legislation (16.59%). Preparing the financial and fiscal reports "consumes" 26.34% of the accountants' time. This means that preparing the information for external users represents the main objective of the accountants within these organizations, while issues as cost analysis and control are neglected. A further aspect that came into notice was the high percentage of the time allocated for other activities. In this category the respondents mentioned activities related to employees records and relationships with fiscal authorities.

An analysis of the activities performed according to the respondents' experience revealed a paradoxical situation – the data processing activity increases as the accountants' experience increases. Also, in case of experienced accountants, an increase of activities like the study of legislation and preparation of fiscal reports is noted. As expected, the share for other activities is higher for less experienced accountants.

77% of respondents stated that lately the management accounting was overshadowed by the financial accounting. They mainly aimed at tax compliance (86%) and the Government was seen as the main user of the accounting information. The study shows that the cost calculation and analysis is mainly oriented towards planning activities and budget preparation, as well as for pricing decisions. Regarding the budgets, our study does not provide evidence that the preparation logic is accurate or the results and variances are determined, analyzed and properly solved.

For most Romanian companies, the cost calculation is used only for assets valuation (eventually, for tax purposes), rather than being a real support for decision making process. The study confirmed it, the Romanian organizations often forego the strategic responsibilities which aim sustainable effects (increase company's value, abandon unprofitable products, motivate managers, customer loyalty etc.), thus threatening their adaptability and even their survival.

In order to ensure a balance between the short term performance and the contribution to the overall progress of the company, aiming its competitive objectives (quality, services, time etc.) it is necessary to design a management accounting system better adapted to the strategy. The legitimacy of a modern management accounting involves a less technical approach, adopting a global view of the economic reality of the company.

4.2. The informative potential of the management accounting is not sufficiently exploited

The competitive environment has profound implications on the management accounting system. In this context, the importance of the management accounting increases considerably because, through its tools, it allows obtaining relevant information for making appropriate decisions in order to support the value creation and achieving notable performances, according with the company's goals. The challenge in a competitive environment is to adopt a flexible approach in designing an effective management accounting system, a cost control system, as well as a performance measurement system.

Through our study, we tried to find out to what extent the management accounting is capitalized in the Romanian accounting practice as a privileged source of information for the managerial system. The respondents appreciated that the informative potential of management accounting is poorly exploited within Romanian companies (2.25 on a 1 to 5 scale). As we noticed previously, within accounting firms the focus is on fiscal reporting and the preparation of financial reports, so naturally the respondents ignored this field. Only the accountants from multinational companies appreciated a proper use of management accounting (3.4 on a 1 to 5 scale), based on the activities they perform. Given the well-defined controlling system within these organizations, we consider that multinationals could become a "driving force" in promoting the management accounting in the Romanian economic environment.

We asked the participants in this study to point out the main advantages that they believe the management accounting offers. It was on open-ended question and the responses received are summarized in table 2.

Table 2. Advantages of management accounting

IDENTIFIED ADVANTAGES	NUMBER OF RESPONSES
Profitability analysis	39
Knowing the company's situation	24
Better cost control	17
Providing correct information to managers	15
Pricing	12
Asset valuation	11
Improving business activities	10
Performance measurement	2

It is noted that in the Romanian economic environment, the focus is on achieving and explaining short term results. The advantages of management accounting are oriented towards the profitability analysis of products and services, while the strategic advantages are completely ignored.

From the evolution of management accounting at international level, we noticed that the view changed from providing information to the resource management (including information) and value creation, using a strategic approach. The new tools and techniques left marks on the entire managerial process (planning, control, decision making and communication) in the first place, but also on the accounting system, forced to "come close to" the strategy. This involves focusing on future, on long term, outside the company, on the entire value chain, as well as providing nonfinancial information.

The advantages of management accounting, perceived by our respondents, are particularly oriented towards the analysis of short term results, by maximizing the results and observing situations after the events. They do not consider a permanent collaboration with the management in order to achieve strategic goals of the organization, constantly coordinating and controlling daily actions.

In order to support the decision making process, the management accounting requires a set of useful tools for managers' information. In this respect, we asked the accountants to list the tools they used. The synthesis of the answers received is shown in table 3.

Table 3. The management accounting tools used

TOOLS	NUMBER OF RESPONSES
Budgets	84
Actual costs (job order costing, process costing)	67
Activity based costing	57
Standard costs, variance analysis	34
Dashboards, balanced scorecard	31
Cost-volume-profit analysis	23
Costs of quality	21
Life cycle costing	10
Environment costs	7

Analyzing these results, we see that the budget is the preferred tool in most organizations, but the share of those who use the standard costs and variance analysis is quite small. In this case, we wonder if there is a real budgetary management within Romanian companies that could help finding the causes of variances, but also identifying the responsibilities.

We note that the traditional costing systems (process costing, job order costing) are preferred by the Romanian companies, the practices being oriented towards the simple calculation of cost, considered as a "fatality" (Horngren *et al.*, 2003: 383). The costs are not necessarily oriented towards the investigation of the relationships between resources, activities and product, like activity based costing (ABC) does. The large number of those who used the activity based costing makes us wonder if the respondents correctly understood the logic of designing ABC or they are considering a simple delimitation of expenses on major business activities.

We found that there is a conservatism regarding the use of the same tools and techniques, which most of the accountants consider relevant, without capitalizing the potential of some news tools, better adapted to current requirements. In addition, there is a trend for all the events and transactions to be monetary quantified, ignoring a number of nonfinancial indicators which are more useful in the decision making process.

The strategic tools, like costs of quality and life cycle costing are less frequent in practice, which emphasize once again the focus on tools which provide useful information for the short term decision making process. Strategically, the cost information should be used for developing strategies and gaining a sustainable competitive advantage.

We should not forget that these are simple tools which should "shape" the managers behavior. It's up to the accountant, as an "information provider", how he/she uses these tools and to what extent they are involved in the decision making. Referring to the partnership between accountants and managers, in a study conducted by Almăşan and Grosu (2008) one manager stated: "*the accountants must become managers; I believe that they should change and, if they do not do that, they will become like auditors appearing once a year and presenting a reporting on what you did*". The accountants' interest, motivation and attitude are essential in the evolution of management accounting, in order to be adapted to the changing needs of the organizations.

4.3. The attitude of the Romanian accountants is characterized by lack of involvement and remanent behavior

Hilton (2005: 17) stated that "*the better a managerial accountant's understanding of human behavior is, the more effective he or she will be as a provider of information*". A study of The Chartered Institute of Management Accountants conducted within the Irish companies found that what management accountants believe it is useful to managers, underestimated in fact their information needs (Dempsey and Vance, 2006). In order to be a real support in the decision making process, the accountants are forced "to guess" the managers information needs. It is said that "*an accountant should tell, not ask managers what they need*".

Our study finds that the accountants perceive the managers' interest for management accounting as being low (2.77 on a 1 to 5 scale). For this reason, there is a certain convenience and lack of motivation on accountants' part in developing this field. As expected, within the multinational companies, the management interest for the management accounting is slightly higher (4.0 on a 1 to 5 scale).

The lack of initiative from accountants, induced by their perception regarding the managers' interest, leads them to neglect their training in the field of management accounting. In this context, it is not surprising that they are aware of the fact that they do not have enough knowledge in this field (2.26 on a 1 to 5 scale). Moreover, 84.21% of the accountants feel the need for training programs in management accounting. But, their remanent behavior makes them search for "recipes" within these programs, instead of developing a judgment that offers them the adaptability to the situations which managers confront with.

It also seemed interesting that 60% of accountants consider that the lack of regulation in management accounting is the reason why this field is neglected. Their arguments in this respect vary from expressing the imperative need for regulations which would be the solution to this problem:

(a) *Models which can be used in practice must be developed and shaped according to each company's needs;*
(b) *Everything is presented generally; there are no monographs as a rough guide; each of us does it in the own manner.*
(c) *Some practical procedures, applicable to various fields, would be required.*
(d) *I believe that minimum mandatory rules or a guideline would contribute to the increase of the management accounting role within a company.*

to becoming aware of the fact that the companies neglect anything that is not mandatory:

(a) *Since there are no reporting requirements, the managers' interest is considerably reduced.*
(b) *The lack of unitary standards and the lack of importance given to this field lead to a lack of interest from those involved in management accounting and a carelessness of accountants.*
(c) *Due to the multiple legislative fiscal changes, both accountants and managers focus on tax legislation, thus neglecting the management accounting.*

There are also accountants who recognize that the regulations do not represent a solution to this problem and the interest for management accounting should come from the information users, namely managers.

(a) *Accounting professionals and managers have the mentality of doing what is imposed by some regulations, while they forget the internal tools, specific for each entity.*
(b) *The regulation is useless in this case. The managers' willingness and understanding is crucial.*
(c) *If this does not come from their own conviction I do not believe that a detailed regulation can solve the problem.*
(d) *This field is neglected due to the managers' lack of interest.*
(e) *Managers' education should be more important than imposing regulations in this regard.*

It is interesting that the respondents underlined the managers' lack of interest, but they do not discuss the accountant's role in solving this situation. However, a response we received refers to the judgments called by such a field.

The regulations cannot help in a field where approximate information prevails over accuracy as well as judgment-based modeling prevails over legal or strict regulations.

The accounting system is "fed" by the information it provides, the individuals' activities and perceptions regarding the business evolution, as well as their performances. It facilitates the interactions and communication between actors who belong to different professions, with different cultures and languages within the organization.

As long as the accountants are seen as conservative, past oriented, with an attitude of sufficiency, their image will seriously suffer. They have "earned" the reputation of solving the problems from a primarily financial perspective, having a too rigid and closed spirit, less willing to take the risks (Mersereau, 2006). Their mission is to understand, analyze and report the key aspects of the business processes.

A study sponsored by CIMA and conducted by Burns and Yazdifar (2001) asked the management accountants to rank the 10 most important tasks that they have to fulfill. The most important ones included performance measurement, cost control, preparing and presenting financial reports, profit improvement, budget preparation. Among the least important (to them), they mentioned strategic planning, decision making and strategy implementation, value creation, design and implementation of new informational systems. The study found that these last tasks are exactly what managers expected from accountants.

5. Conclusions

The management accounting should be an important tool in motivating the employees to be "in harmony" with the long term goals of the organization. It must "create" the future and not necessarily "quantify" the current performance of the company. This points out that the continuous progress and improvement is more important than the result itself, so the management accounting should rather influence than inform.

The results of the study reveal that the accountants' perceptions on management accounting are strongly influenced by factors like: their mentality (taylorian type, without an integrated view, and less involved), the managers' lack of interest regarding the accounting information, as well as the overwhelming activities in the financial and fiscal reporting field. Under these circumstances, the accountants' attitudes, together with the attitude of the managers, makes us doubt the usefulness of the management accounting in the Romanian business accounting.

Our study is limited out of two reasons. First, it addressed the accounting professionals from the Timis County, which does not allow us to uniform the perceptions at national level because of the cultural differences between different areas in Romania. Secondly, most responses were collected from accountants working in relatively small companies, where it is difficult to find a rigorous management accounting system.

Based on the results of this study, we can identify two directions for future research: (a) to investigate the managers' perceptions and the information usefulness for them, in terms of communication between accountants and managers and (b) to investigate how the closeness between the business and academic environment can positively influence the practitioners' (both accountants and managers) mentality regarding management accounting.

Acknowledgement

The paper was presented at the 9th edition of the International Conference on Accounting and Management Information Systems (AMIS 2014), organized by the Bucharest University of Economic Studies. We are grateful for the helpful comments and suggestions provided by the AMIS 2014 anonymous reviewer, the AMIS 2014 chairs and participants, as well as by the participants of the IAAER and ACCA Early Career Researchers Workshop associated with the AMIS 2014 Conference.

References

Albu, C.N., Albu, N., Faff, R. & Hodgson, A. (2011a) "Accounting competencies and the changing role of accountants in emerging economies: The case of Romania", *Accounting in Europe*, vol. 8, no. 2: 153-182

Albu, N. (2008) "Metoda Activity Based Costing – pentru cine, pentru ce?" (Activity-based costing system – for whom, for what?), *Contabilitatea, Expertiza si Auditul Afacerilor,* no. 9: 59-64.

Albu, N. (2013) "Exploring the recent evolution of the accounting profession in Romania – an institutional approach", *Journal of Accounting and Management Information Systems*, vol. 12, no. 4: 537–552

Albu, N. (2003) "Continuitate, evolutie si inovatie in contabilitatea de gestiune prin metoda ABC" (Permanence, evolution and innovation in management accounting through ABC), *Journal of Accounting and Management Information Systems*, no. 4: 50-57

Albu, N. & Albu, C.N. (2012a) "International Financial Reporting Standards in an emerging economy: Lessons from Romania", *Australian Accounting Review*, vol. 22, nr. 4: 341-352

Albu, N. & Albu, C.N. (2012b) "Factors associated with the adoption and use of management accounting techniques in developing countries: The case of Romania", *Journal of International Financial Management and Accounting*, vol. 23, no. 3: 245-276

Albu, N., Albu, C.N., Bunea, S., Calu, D.A. & Girbina, M.M. (2011b) „A story about IAS/IFRS implementation in Romania", *Journal of Accounting in Emerging Economies*, vol. 1, issue 1: 76-100

Almăşan, A. (2008) "Challenges of a dynamic and complex environment on management accounting", *The Annals of the University of Oradea. Economic Sciences*, vol. XVII, issue 3: 913-917

Almăşan, A. & Grosu, C. (2008) "Managers' awareness of the accounting information usefulness", *Journal of Accounting and Management Information Systems*, no. 24: 57-71

Almăşan, A. & Grosu, C. (2009) "The usefulness of the process approach for value creation in the telecom sector", *Journal of Accounting and Management Information Systems*, Vol. 8, Nr. 4: 521–537

Barbu, E., Farcane, N. & Popa, A. (2010) "Looking for an Accounting Identity: The Case of Romania during the 20th Century", *Cahier de recherche no 2010-03 E2*, CERAG CNRS 5820, available online at http://hal.inria.fr/docs/00/53/47/41/PDF/cr_2010 _03_E2.pdf

Burns, J. & Baldvinsdottir, G. (2005) "An institutional perspective of accountants' new roles – the interplay of contradictions and praxis", *European Accounting Review*, vol. 14, no. 4: 725–757.

Burns, J. & Yazdifar, H. (2001) "Tricks or Treats?", *Financial Management*, March: 33-35.

Cardos, I.R. & Pete, S. (2011) "Managerial and cost accounting practices: a Romanian overview", *The Annals of the University of Oradea. Economic Sciences*, vol. XX, Issue 2: 484-490

Dempsey, S. & Vance, R. (2006) "Management accountants: leading the agenda, not just supporting it", *Accountancy Ireland*, vol. 38, no. 6: 13-16

Dumitru, M. & Calu, D.A. (2008) *Contabilitatea de gestiune si calculatia costurilor* (Management and cost accounting), Bucuresti: Contaplus

Dumitru, M., Calu, D.A., Gorgan, C. & Calu, A. (2011) "A historical approach of change in management accounting topics published in Romania", *Journal of Accounting and Management Information Systems*, Vol. 10, No. 3: 375–396

Falconer, M. (2002) "Research and practice in management accounting: improving integration and communication", *The European Accounting Review*, vol. 11, no. 2: 277-289

Feleaga, N. (1996) *Controverse contabile. Dificultati conceptuale si credibilitatea contabilitatii* (Accounting controversies. Conceptual difficulties and accounting credibility), Bucuresti: Economica

Granlund, M. & Lukka, K. (1998) "Towards increasing business orientation: Finnish management accountants in a changing cultural context", *Management Accounting Research*, no. 9: 185-211

Grosu, C., Almăşan, A. & Mariut, L. (2005) "Contabilitatea de gestiune – intre recunoastere si deziluzie" (Management accounting between recognition and disappointment), *Journal of Accounting and Management Information Systems*, no. 13-14: 116-121

Hilton, R.W. (2005) *Managerial Accounting - Creating value in a dynamic business environment, 6th edition*, Boston: McGraw Hill

Hopper, T., Tsameny, M., Uddin, S. & Wickramasinghe, D. (2009) "Management accounting in less developed countries: what is known and needs knowing", *Accounting, Auditing & Accountability Journal,* vol. 22, no. 3: 469-514

Horngren, C., Bhimani, A., Datar, S. & Foster, G. (2003) *Comptabilité de gestion (adaptation française de G. Langlois)*, Paris: Pearson Education

IFAC (1998) *Management Accounting Concepts*, available online at http://www.mia.org.my/handbook/guide/IMAP/imap_1.htm

Jarvenpaa, M. (2007) "Making business partners: a case study on how management accounting culture was changed", *European Accounting Review*, vol. 16, no. 1: 99-142

Jianu, I. & Jianu, I. (2012) "The told and retold story of Romanian accounting", *Journal of Accounting and Management Information Systems*, vol. 11, no. 3: 391-423

Jinga, G., Dumitru, M., Dumitrana, M. & Vulpoi, M. (2010) "Accounting systems for cost management used in the Romanian economic entities", *Journal of Accounting and Management Information Systems*, vol. 9, no. 2: 242-267

Johnson, H.T. & Kaplan, R.S. (1987) *Relevance lost: The rise and fall of management accounting*, Boston: Harvard Business School

Kaplan, R. S. (1995) "New roles for management accountants", *Journal of Cost Management*, Fall: 6–13

Legea contabilitatii nr. 82 / 1991, republicata in Monitorul Oficial al Romaniei nr. 454 / 2008 (Accounting Law no. 82 / 1991, revised, *Official Journal of Romania* no.454 / 2008)

Malmi, T. & Granlund, M. (2009) "In search of management accounting theory", *European Accounting Review*, vol. 18, no. 3: 597-620

Megan, O. (2006) "Adopting European Union accounting directives: A new challenge for Romanian managers", *Strategijski menadzment*, no. 11(3): 61-65.

Mersereau, A. (2006) "Perfectionner l'art de la comptabilité de management", CMA, FCMA / février, vol. 79, no. 9: 17-22, available on-line at http://www.hec.ca/cicma/communications/documentations/articles/fevrier2006_alexandermersereau_perfectionner_art_comptabilite_de_management.pdf

Mustata, R.V., Matis, D. & Bonaci, C.G. (2012) "Integrated financial reporting: from international experiences to perspectives at national level", *Review of Business Research*, vol. 12, issue 2: 144-150

Olariu, C., Epuran, M. & Cara, Al. (1974) *Contabilitatea intreprinderii moderne* (The accounting of modern enterprises), Timisoara: Facla

Ordinul Ministrului Finanţelor Publice nr. 1752/2005 pentru aprobarea Reglementarilor contabile conforme cu Directivele Europene, Monitorul Oficial al României nr. 1080 bis/2005 (Order of the Minister of Public Finances no. 1752/2005 for the approval of accounting regulations in accordance with the European Directives, Official Journal of Romania no. 1080 bis/2005)

Ordinul Ministrului Finanţelor Publice nr. 1826/2003 pentru aprobarea Precizarilor privind unele masuri referitoare la organizarea si conducerea contabilitatii de gestiune, Monitorul Oficial al României nr. 23/2004 (Order of the Minister of Public Finances no. 1826/2003 for the approval of some measures regarding the implementation of management accounting, *Official Journal of Romania* no. 23/ 2004)

Ordinul Ministrului Finanţelor Publice nr. 3055/2009 pentru aprobarea Reglementarilor contabile conforme cu Directivele Europene, Monitorul Oficial al României nr. 766 bis/2009 (Order of the Minister of Public Finances no. 3055/2009 for the approval of accounting regulations in accordance with the European Directives, *Official Journal of Romania* no. 766 bis/ 2009)

Ordinul Ministrului Finanţelor Publice nr. 306/2002 pentru aprobarea Reglementarilor contabile simplificate, armonizate cu Directivele Europene, Monitorul Oficial al României, nr. 279/2003 (Order of the Minister of Public Finances no. 306/2002 for the approval of simplified accounting regulations harmonized with the European Directives, *Official Journal of Romania* no. 279/2003)

Ordinul Ministrului Finanţelor Publice nr. 403/1999 pentru aprobarea Reglementarilor contabile armonizate cu Directiva a IV-a a Comunităţilor Economice Europene si cu Standardele Internationale de Contabilitate, Monitorul Oficial al României nr. 480/1999 (Order of the Minister of Public Finances no. 403/1999 for the approval of accounting regulations harmonized with the European Directives and the International Accounting Standards, *Official Journal of Romania*, no. 480/1999)

Ordinul Ministrului Finanţelor Publice nr. 94/2001 pentru aprobarea Reglementarilor contabile armonizate cu Directiva a IV-a a Comunitatilor Economice Europene si cu Standardele Internationale de Contabilitate, Monitorul Oficial al României nr. 85/2001 (Order of the Minister of Public Finances no. 94/2001 for the approval of accounting regulations harmonized with the Fourth European Directive and the International Accounting Standards, *Official Journal of Romania* no. 85/2001)

Pierce, B. & O'Dea, T. (2003) "Management accounting information and the needs of managers: Perceptions of accountants and managers compared", *The British Accounting Review*, vol. 35, no. 3: 257-290

Regulamentul nr. 704/1993 pentru aplicarea legii contabilitatii, Monitorul Oficial al României, nr. 303 bis /1993 (Regulation no. 704/1993 for the implementation of the *Accounting Law Official Journal of Romania*, no. 303bis /1993)

Ristea, M., Otoiu, A., Ciucur, E. & Vaslan, A. (1980) *Contabilitate* (Accounting), Bucureşti: Didactica si Pedagogica

Sathe, V. (1983) "The controller's role in management", *Organizational Dynamics*, no. 11: 31-48

Scapens, R.W. (2006) "Understanding management accounting practices: a personal journey", *The British Accounting Review*, vol. 38, no. 1: 1-30.

Shields, M.D. (1995) "An empirical analysis of firms' implementation experiences with activity-based costing", *Journal of Management Accounting Research*, no. 7: 148-166

Volkan, I.R. (2007) "ABC & ABM – The couple which prevails cost calculation and modern administration for performance", *Journal of Accounting and Management Information Systems*, supplement: 284-292

Volkan, I.R. (2008) "New perspectives regarding cost calculation", *Journal of Accounting and Management Information Systems*, supplement: 509-519

7

The generalizability of financial distress prediction models: Evidence from Turkey

Ibrahim Onur Oz[a,1] and Tezer Yelkenci[b]

[a] *Central Connecticut State University, United States*
[b] *Izmir University of Economics, Turkey*

Abstract: This study analyzes five of the well-known and most cited distress prediction models in the literature. The models are implemented to continuous publicly listed industrial firms in Turkey through their original and re-estimated coefficients in a comparative way to examine their generalizability in different time periods and samples. The effect of 2008 financial crisis is also assessed to conduct a fuller analysis of the models' prediction accuracies. The results emphasize that Ohlson (1980), Taffler (1983), Zmijewski (1984), and Shumway (2001) provide highly accurate distress classification results through their original coefficients for Turkish industrial market. On the other hand, the re-estimation of the models (other than Ohlson's [1980]) fails to improve the prediction accuracies which are also found insignificant by considering the pre and post crisis periods.

Keywords: Financial distress prediction, emerging markets, model comparison, financial crisis, multiple discriminant analysis, logit, probit, hazard model, financial ratios

1. Introduction

The business capability of a firm is affected by distinct factors. These factors, grouped as managerial, economic, political, and environmental, should be identified to sustain the value creation and survival of firms. Although there are many external factors that are difficult to analyze due to measurement concerns,

[1] *Corresponding authors*: Ibrahim Onur Oz, Department of Accounting, School of Business; email addresses: ozi@ccsu.edu, tezer.yelkenci@ieu.edu.tr

one way to assist firms in planning for future operations is to conduct an elaborate financial analysis based on the financial statements and the financial ratios.

The information provided by the financial statements not only presents the current condition of the firm, but also shed lights on its future (Beaver, 1966), and the ratios calculated from distinct accounts represent a simplified interpretation of the information with a predictive ability (Horrigan, 1968). Therefore, analyzing the financial statements through financial ratios as indicators for the future of the firm would allow the estimation of the risk of failure. On the other hand, considering each financial ratio in isolation may not help understanding the condition of the firm as a whole. Since each ratio accommodates information from distinct sections, these should be conceded simultaneously in order to understand the entire operating ability of the firm. In particular, the studies after 1960s are statistically more sophisticated, enabling the prediction of firm bankruptcy/distress (the term distress will be used throughout of the manuscript) constituting the basis of the current study. The concurrent analysis of the ratios in distress models aims to determine the accuracy of the failure prediction vital due to its high cost for the stakeholders.

There are numerous bankruptcy studies in the accounting and finance literature, applied to both developed and developing markets. In most of these studies, the main concern is to establish a distress classification model, without clearly establishing the need or purpose of the model. The main purpose of these studies is to acknowledge the distress, or even the failure, in advance, so the contribution is on the *"obvious practical interest"* as indicated by Ohlson (1980). In addition to this, the absence of a theoretical base or the so called "*common ground*" for prediction model studies (Grice & Dugan, 2003) does not necessarily imply that these models cannot be generalized in terms of the accuracy levels in which they provide for distinct samples and time periods. Thus, the motivation of the current study is to produce a comparative measure of the accuracy levels of the five well known distress prediction models described in the literature for an emerging economy. The questions that are asked: 1) Is applying these prediction models, derived for developed markets, to an emerging market sample enable the generalizability of these models for different market samples and time periods?; 2) Is there a significant change in terms of the prediction accuracies before and after the financial crisis of 2008?

In order to show evidence of generalizability, the prediction accuracies are measured, and each model is initially applied over its original coefficients and then re-estimated by adhering to its original variables to each of the industrial firms in the sample. In the event that one or more of these models is generalizable, depending on prediction accuracies, it will be conceded that the related model(s) are plausible to use as a benchmark for the establishment of a new prediction model, which would strengthen the so called "*common ground*" for distress prediction studies.

The models of the present study are mainly developed on the US sample by Altman (1968), Ohlson (1980), Zmijewski (1984) and Shumway (2001), and on the UK sample by Taffler (1983) to classify bankrupt and healthy firms. To the authors' knowledge, the current study is the pioneer to conduct a comparative analysis of these five models on a continuing firm sample. The prediction models are implemented to continuous firms, following Altman (1968), for his sub-sample for the period of 1958 to 1961, and Tinoco and Wilson (2013). The continuous firm sample measures the predictive ability of the models on ongoing firms which enables practitioners to understand whether the industrial firms would report negative income in the following consecutive years. Any of the firms reporting negative income for two consecutive fiscal years are considered as distressed (Li and Sun, 2008; Xie *et al.* 2011). Furthermore, analyzing ongoing firms helps researchers overcome some vital concerns mentioned in the literature regarding the incompleteness and the limited number of bankruptcy data (Ohlson, 1980; Zmijewski, 1984).

Few studies have compared the prediction models over their original and the re-estimated versions only for the developed market samples. These were the models of Altman by Grice and Ingram (2001), Altman vs Ohlson by Begley *et al.* (1996), and Zmijewski vs Ohlson by Grice and Dugan (2003). Thus, this study contributes to the literature in three ways: i) The five best known and most cited prediction models used in this study are initially applied over original coefficients and then through their re-estimated versions in order to compare the results in an emerging market sample for their generalizability. ii) Both the original and the re-estimated models are applied to continuous firms in an emerging market sample, rather than those that have failed or are in the bankruptcy process. iii) The original and the re-estimated versions of the prediction models are exercised in a comparative way regarding the effects of the financial crisis of 2008.

2. Literature review

The very first steps in financial distress modeling were taken by Beaver (1966). Beaver's study introduced a univariate analysis of financial ratios to explore whether financial ratios had predictive ability for the financial failure of individual firms; the claim of the study is that the financial ratios are composed of numbers taken from the financial statements that represent both important and non-important events related to the firm. Moreover, Beaver indicated the usefulness of financial ratios in their predictive ability; in other words, the predictive ability of accounting numbers in financial statements were indirectly measured in his study, and were found to be significant. The sample included 79 failed firms and 79 non-failed firms. Non-corporate, privately held and non-industrial firms were not included in the sample. The sample firms were gathered from Moody's Industrial Manual, the only database available. The firms were grouped according to industry and asset size; thus, the method used was to match pair of firms from the sample. Moreover, the sample of the study represented 90% of the invested capital of all industrial firms, and thus had the potential to affect a substantial number of stakeholders. The high level of descriptive detail of the study was important; an in-depth analysis of the six chosen ratios showed that the mean differences of the financial ratios increased as firms approached failure. As a result, Beaver emphasized the importance of financial ratio analysis in warning financially unhealthy firms and preventing becoming bankrupt.

The following study by Altman (1968), one of the most cited studies in the field of financial distress modeling, indicated the importance of financial ratio analysis over bivariate analysis when using the ratios in his model. Bivariate analysis is suitable for measuring the simultaneous contribution of the ratios to the explanatory power of the model, which makes Altman's study innovative because it measures the individual effect of each selected ratio on predicting failure, an approach which he named "traditional". Altman developed a model composed of distinct ratios. The presented model aimed to classify bankrupt and non-bankrupt manufacturing firms by using multi-discriminant analysis (MDA). The ratios used in the model were expected to explain the bankruptcy of a firm by their simultaneous contribution to the model. This approach was necessary because earlier studies on univariate analysis indicated contradictory results due to the different effects of individual ratios. For instance, a firm could be classified as bankrupt because of its high debt ratio, whereas its performance indicators encouraged a non-bankrupt categorization of the same firm. The sample of the study consisted of 66 manufacturing firms divided equally into two groups, and matched in accordance with their asset sizes, as in Beaver's 1966 study. The study indicated the importance of a multivariate analysis of the financial ratios to achieve 95% accuracy in the prediction of bankruptcy within two years, compared to an individual comparison of each financial ratio in a sequence.

Altman's (1973) study employed a linear discriminant analysis in the estimation of the bankruptcy of the US railroads between 1946 and 1969. The results of his model indicated a 97.7% accurate prediction of failure one or two years in advance. A study by Blum (1974) established the "Failing Company Model" using MDA to study the period from 1954 to 1968, using a sample of 115 failed and 115 non-failed industrial firms, and a model consisting of 12 variables. The failed firms were chosen as having a liability over one million dollars, while the matching criteria included the industry, sales, number of employees, and fiscal year. The results of the study indicated the power of the MDA analysis, which produced a 94% accurate classification of failed and non-failed firms in the year before failure.

The accuracy levels decreased as the period to failure increased: 80% for two to three years before failure, and 70% for the third year before failure: Nevertheless, Blum's results highlighted the robustness of the MDA results.

Altman *et al.*'s (1979) study on Brazilian firms in the textile, furniture, pulp and paper, plastics, and metallurgy industries, retail stores, and other firms considered whether problematic and non-problematic firms could be differentiated in advance through linear discriminant analysis. The period of the study spanned from January 1975 to June 1977. The accuracy level of the model was 88% for the 58 firms considered, indicating that the information content of an emerging market is important.

In his 1980 study, Ohlson represented his early prediction model using a logistic regression method. Ohlson's research differed from previous studies in terms of the statistical model and the chosen sample. The conditional logit model, a maximum likelihood estimator, was used to analyze the data, which included 105 bankrupt firms and 2058 non-bankrupt firms from 1970 to 1976. The sample was also unique; rather than Moody's Manual, the year-end 10-K financial statements were used to select bankrupt firms; these have the potential to indicate whether a company will fall into bankruptcy before or after the release of the related data to public. In other words, the timing of bankruptcy could be captured more effectively than in studies using a given sample of bankrupt firms. The predictions of bankruptcy within one year were also improved compared to previous studies, with an accuracy of 96.12%.

Taffler (1983) explored the predictability of the bankruptcy of UK firms using a linear discriminant analysis. The sample was composed of 46 publicly listed firms from 1969 to 1976. The model sample was matched for failed and non-failed firms. The accuracy level was 95.7% for the bankrupt firms and 100% for the non-bankrupt firms. The models have changed over time, and statistical approaches other than MDA have been used.

In 1984, Zmijewski applied a probit analysis to 129 bankrupt industrial firms from a total of 2241 firms in the NYSE and AMEX. Zmijewski found that accuracy levels for the sample varied according to different approaches, including matched sample, non-matched sample, and weighted exogenous sample maximum likelihood (WESML) probit analyses. The accuracy of this study changed depending on the sample. The results for the accuracy of classification for matched sample were 92.5% for failed firms and 100% for non-failed firms, whereas the accuracy of the classification decreased when the sample was non-matched; the accuracy levels were 62.5% for failed firms and 99.5% for non-failed firms. The results of using WESML further decreased the accuracy for failed firms to 52.5% for the matched sample and to 42.5% for the non-matched sample.

Bhatia (1988) measured the classification accuracy of 18 distressed firms and 18 non-distressed firms with an MDA model for the 1976-1985 period, and found 87% accuracy for predicting type I errors and 86.6% for type II. Another study by Ramana *et al.* (2012) in India, using Altman's Z score, indicated that for the 2001-2010 period, the classification accuracy of the MDA model represented the estimation results for three cement companies.

Bidin's (1988) study represents the evaluation of companies owned by an investment trust fund of the government of Malaysia. The related firms in the portfolio of the entity were measured by a multivariate discriminant analysis distress model that was primarily focused on the manufacturing, transportation and service sectors. The sample was composed of 21 distressed companies and an unknown number of non-distressed companies. It was indicated that the government used the revised version of the same model to analyze data covering the period until 1997. Another study was conducted in Singapore in 1981 using multi-discriminant analysis to consider 24 failed and 21 non-failed firms for the period from 1975 to 1983. The companies in the sample were manufacturing and commercial firms. 77.3% accuracy was achieved in the prediction of a type I error one year prior to the failure, and 93.5% for a type II error.

Gilbert *et al.* (1990) measured the prediction accuracy of a logistic regression model and multivariate discriminant analysis for non-financial US firms to determine which method was more accurate. To determine the prediction results of the two models, the sample was divided into two groups, each separated into two sub-groups. The variables were chosen from the models of Casey and Bartczak (1985) and Altman (1968). The sub-samples were composed of bankrupt-to-non-bankrupt, and bankrupt-to-distressed firms to determine the accuracy of the classifications. A logistic regression model was used to measure the separation of bankrupt firms from non-bankrupt ones, and the Altman model was used to measure the separation of bankrupt firms from distressed ones. Bankrupt and non-bankrupt group data were collected through Compustat Annual Industrial or Research Files. The bankrupt group was composed of 76 firms, and the non-bankrupt group included 304 firms. It was found that the accuracy level decreased when the model was processed for the classification of bankrupt and distressed firms. The study highlighted the poor performance of the logistic regression model in the classification of bankrupt and distressed firms.

Shumway (2001) established a dynamic model, a binary logit model, to calculate the financial bankruptcy of firms. The sample was composed of 300 bankrupt firms for the period from 1962 to 1992. Bankrupt firms were defined as those bankrupt within 5 years of delisting. Shumway differentiated his model from the others in the literature through the calculation of firms' trading years, in order to reduce the loss of firms from the sample over time. His simple hazard model was a type of survival analysis that allowed the inclusion of market-driven variables in his model to predict corporate bankruptcy. To emphasize the accuracy power of his model, he adjusted Altman's and Zmijewski's models by adding new market-driven variables. There were two model estimates: one consisted only of market-driven variables, while the other included accounting variables, as a result of considering the studies of Altman and Zmijewski. Altman's and Zmijewski's models were improved through the inclusion of the trading age of the corporations, and following this development, the market models were considered in the sample used by Shumway for the years 1962-1992. Shumway's emphasis was that Altman's model decreased the number of observations, and working capital divided by the total assets variable decreased simply due to the omission of the variables, which also deteriorated the results of statistical significance tests. The model developed another point of view on risk adjustment over the life of the corporations in the sample, by correcting the risk at distinct periods. The model developed through accounting- and market-based variables indicated the most accurate results, as emphasized by Shumway's 95% accuracy rate for market-driven variables.

Ugurlu (2006) measured the prediction accuracy of Turkish manufacturing firms between 1996 and 2003 with multi-discriminant and logit analysis. The logistic regression was found to be more accurate, and the model results indicated that logit regression results provided 95.6% accuracy for the overall fit of the model. The model classified non-failed and failed firms with 97.5% and 91.4% accuracy, respectively. Moreover, the predictive results of the logit model were 94.3%, 91% and 87.1% accuracy from year one to year four, respectively.

Xie *et al.* (2011) compared the accuracy results of MDA and Support Vector Machine (SVM) estimation methods for Chinese listed companies. The study considered the classification of ongoing firms over financial, macroeconomic and internal governance ratios in the prediction model and concluded that SVM provided improved accuracy rates for distress classification due to its non-parametric structure conceding the sample distribution as non-linear. A study by Bauer and Agarwal (2014) indicated that Taffler (1983) Z-score and hazard models have the clear bankruptcy classification abilities while hazard models were more cost efficient in terms of their prediction performances over risk weighted assets.

Although bankruptcy estimation model studies have a long history in the accounting and finance literature, studies so far have primarily focused on developing new models using different financial statement variables. Moreover, the literature has generally focused on the accuracy levels of the bankruptcy models applied to bankrupt firms in a matched sample of bankrupt to non-bankrupt firms, even though the models can be applied to distinguish financially healthy firms from the firms that were not bankrupt but were called financially weak and distressed firms by Altman (1968) and Gilbert *et al.* (1990).

3. Research design

Following the models of Altman (1968), Ohlson (1980), Zmijewski (1984), Taffler (1983), and Shumway (2001), the current study considers the original coefficients to examine whether these models provide significantly accurate prediction results through their original coefficients for publicly listed Turkish industrial firms. Then, each of the models is re-estimated and the coefficients are calculated to analyze if the prediction accuracies are improved. Additionally, the models are processed in their original and re-estimated versions, considering the financial crisis of 2008 as a cut-off year for the comparison of prediction results. The comparison analysis is conducted through the use of accuracy rates calculated by the rate of the correct classification of the financially distressed or non-distressed firm observations to total sample observations.

3.1 Data

The study sample is composed of publicly listed industrial firms for the validity of the prediction results, as the models are derived from publicly listed industrial firms of the developed markets. In addition to that the sample is also plausible due to Turkey's well regulated market structure in comparison to other developing markets and the Borsa Istanbul's high trading volume, the fourth largest among emerging markets.

The study covers the period from 2000 to 2012. The dataset is collected from two reliable sources, the Bloomberg Professional and the Thomson Reuters Eikon data terminals. Besides being an industrial firm, another condition is to be listed in the stock market between the years 2000 to 2012, otherwise the dataset would have been failed in terms of consistency. The maximum industrial firm number is observed between the years 2000 and 2012. Therefore the dataset is composed of 45 publicly listed industrial firms, with 585 observations for the full sample in the Borsa Istanbul with 140 financially distressed (FD) and 445 non-distressed firms. The sample period also satisfies the relative observation distribution for pre and post financial crisis which enables the analysis of the related prediction accuracies. Industrial firms were selected in order to sustain the validity of the models established for this type of firms in developed markets. The sample was also divided into two sub-samples in order to analyze the models' level of accuracy before and after the financial crisis of 2008, with 360 pre-crisis and 225 post-crisis observations. After the data collection, outliers within the dataset were extracted based on a 95% confidence level. Two important conditions for inclusion in the sample were to be an industrial firm and to be listed in the stock market between 2000 and 2012; this was to prevent the dataset being biased and failing in terms of consistency.

After the data collection, descriptive statistics were produced to check whether the variables were appropriate for estimation. Table 1 represents the descriptive statistics for all firms.

Table 1. Descriptive statistics for the variables

	Mean	Standard Error	Median	Mode	Standard Deviation	Kurtosis	Skewness
CL/CA	1.51	0.10	1.16	0.96	2.49	6.20	340.69
WC/TA	0.01	0.03	0.07	2.53	0.71	0.51	116.88
RE/TA	0.00	0.03	0.11	2.38	0.74	0.55	105.53
$EBIT/TA$	0.08	0.00	0.07	0.09	0.12	0.01	11.79
$SALES/TA$	0.98	0.03	0.90	0.91	0.69	0.48	5.08
MVE/TL	4.57	0.50	1.15	0.00	12.85	165.18	48.91
TL/TA	0.60	0.03	0.53	0.45	0.69	0.47	140.69
$OENEG$	0.04	0.01	0.00	0.00	0.20	0.04	19.19
ROA	5.68	0.54	5.20	28.61	14.02	196.43	18.06
$CHIN$	0.07	0.02	0.05	0.00	0.53	0.28	0.16
$SIZE$	3.07	0.01	3.02	3.04	0.29	0.08	0.92
$RETURN$	0.06	0.02	0.00	0.00	0.47	0.22	6.48
$SIGMA$	0.04	0.00	0.03	0.04	0.02	0.00	10.17
PBT/ACL	0.32	0.04	0.19	0.03	1.02	1.05	35.44
CA/TL	1.08	0.05	0.84	0.21	1.30	1.70	143.48
CA/CL	0.42	0.03	0.35	0.15	0.66	0.43	174.71
$(CA - INV - CL)/(SALES - NIBT + DEPR)$	2.88	1.10	0.13	29.80	28.61	818.58	217.75

The descriptive statistics show that the median values for all variables are close to the mean values, indicating that the data seem to be evenly distributed around the mean.

3.2. Methodology

Altman's Methodology

Estimation Method: Discriminant Analysis

Discriminant analysis allows the simultaneous examination of differences between two or more groups of objects with respect to several variables. In the social sciences, there are a wide variety of situations in which this technique may be useful (Huberty & Olejnik, 2006). Discriminant analysis aims to determine:

1. Which variables within the equation, if any, are effective in predicting the ultimate outcome
2. How these variables might be combined into a mathematical equation to predict the most likely outcome, and
3. The accuracy of the derived equation.

The basic prerequisites are the existence of two or more groups, which are presumed to differ in terms of several variables, and that those variables can be measured at the interval level or ratio level. Discriminant analysis will then enable the analysis of the differences between the groups and provide a means to assign a particular case into the group it most closely resembles.

Ohlson's Methodology

Estimation Method: Logit Model

The logit model is similar to the probit model because it is a binary model, but it has a number of features that make it more convenient than the probit model (Gujarati, 2004). For the logit model, the function $F(x)$ is the logistic function

$$\Lambda(x) \equiv (1+e^{-x})^{-1} = \frac{e^x}{1+e^x}$$

which has a first derivative

$$\lambda(x) \equiv \frac{e^x}{(1+e^x)^2} = \Lambda(x)\Lambda(-x)$$

The second equality will later prove to be useful. The logit model is most easily derived by assuming that

$$\log\left(\frac{P_t}{1-P_t}\right) = X_t\beta$$

which says that the logarithm of the odds is equal to $X_t\beta$. Solving for P_t,

$$P_t = \frac{\exp(X_t\beta)}{1+\exp(X_t\beta)} = (1+\exp(-X_t\beta))^{-1} = \Lambda(X_t\beta)$$

It is also possible to derive the logit model from a latent variable model, but with errors that follow extreme rather than normal value distributions; see, among others, Domencich and McFadden (1975), McFadden (1984), and Train (1986).

Shumway's Methodology

Estimation Method: Simple Hazard Model

The logit and hazard models have the same likelihood functions, and therefore the same asymptotic variance-covariance matrices (Amemiya, 1985). However, the test statistics produced by a logit program is incorrect for the hazard model because the assumption is that the number of independent observations used to estimate the model is equal to the number of years for each firm within the data sample. Calculating correct test statistics requires an adjustment of the sample size assumed by the logit program to account for the lack of independence between firm-year observations.

Zmijewski's Methodology

Estimation Method: Probit Model

For the probit model, the transformation function $F(x)$ is the cumulative standard normal distribution function

$$\Phi(x) \equiv \int_{-\infty}^{x} \frac{1}{\sqrt{2\pi}} \exp\left(-\frac{1}{2}X^2\right) dX$$

Because $\Phi(x)$ is a cumulative distribution function, it automatically satisfies the condition above. The probit model can be written as

$$P_t \equiv E(y_t|\Omega_t) = \Phi(X_t\beta)$$

Although there exists no closed-form expression for $\Phi(x)$, the variable is easily evaluated numerically, and its first derivative is simply the standard normal density function

$$\phi(x) = \frac{1}{\sqrt{2\pi}} \exp\left(-\frac{1}{2}x^2\right)$$

The probit model can be derived from a model that involves an unobserved or latent variable y_t^*.

$$y_t^* = X_t\beta + u_t, \qquad u_t \sim NID(0,1)$$

Only the sign of y_t^*, is observed which determines the value of the observed binary variable y_t according to the relationship

$$y_t = 1 \; if \; y_t^* > 0 \; and \; y_t = 0 \; if \; y_t^* \leq 0$$

The variance of u_t is normalized for unity. If u_t actually had some other variance, such as σ^2, dividing y_t^*, β, and u_t by σ would yield a model observationally identical to the one with is started.

Now it can be asked what the probability is that $y_t = 1$. Some straightforward manipulations yield

$$\begin{aligned}\Pr(y_t = 1) = pr(y_t^* > 0) = \Pr(X_t\beta + u_t > 0) = 1 - \Pr(u_t \leq -X_t\beta) \\ = 1 - \Phi(X_t\beta) = \Phi(X_t\beta)\end{aligned}$$

The last equality exploits the fact that the standard normal density function is symmetric around zero. The final result, $\Phi(X_t\beta)$, is the probability that would be obtained by letting $\Phi(.)$ play the role of $F(.)$. Thus, the probit model is derived from the latent variable model. One of the advantages of the probit model is that it can be created in this way (Baltagi, 2008).

Taffler's Methodology

Estimation Method: Linear Discriminant Analysis

The analysis of variance is closely related to LDA because it attempts to express one dependent variable as a linear combination of other features or measurements. The difference between the analysis of variance and LDA is that whereas the former uses categorically independent variables with a continuous dependent variable, the latter uses continuous independent variables with a categorically dependent variable. In terms of explaining a categorical variable through continuous independent variables, LDA is closer to logistic regression and probit regression. An important feature common to logistic regression and probit regression is the lack of requirement for normally distributed independent variables, in contrast to LDA, which strictly requires these variables (Huberty & Olejnik, 2006).

The training set is the set of samples that includes the set of observations $\vec{x}$ for each sample of an event with known as class y. Finding a good predictor of the class y of any sample of the same distribution given only an observation $\vec{x}$ refers to the classification problem.

LDA assumes that the conditional probability density functions $p(\vec{x}|y=0)$ and $p(\vec{x}|y=1)$ are normally distributed with mean and covariance parameters $(\vec{\mu}, \Sigma_{y=1})$ and $(\vec{\mu}, \Sigma_{y=1})$ to solve the problem. The Bayes optimal solution is to predict second-class points if the log of the likelihood ratios falls below a threshold T under the following assumption.

$$(\vec{x}-\vec{\mu}_0)^T \Sigma_{y=0}^{-1} (\vec{x}-\vec{\mu}_0) + \ln|\Sigma_{y=0}| - (\vec{x}-\vec{\mu}_1)^T \Sigma_{y=0}^{-1} (\vec{x}-\vec{\mu}_1) - \ln|\Sigma_{y=1}| < T$$

The resulting classifier is referred to as quadratic discriminant analysis without any other assumption. By generating the co-variances that have full rank, this methodology achieves the simplification of the homoscedasticity assumption. Therefore, the above decision criterion becomes a threshold on the scalar product.

$$\vec{w} \cdot \vec{x} > c$$

for some threshold constant c, where

$$\vec{w} \propto (\Sigma_0 + \Sigma_1)^{-1} (\vec{\mu}_1 - \vec{\mu}_0)$$
$$c = \vec{w} \cdot \frac{1}{2}(\vec{\mu}_0 + \vec{\mu}_1) = \frac{1}{2}\vec{\mu}_1^T \Sigma^{-1} \vec{\mu}_1 - \frac{1}{2}\vec{\mu}_0^T \Sigma^{-1} \vec{\mu}_0$$

The result indicates that the criterion of an input $\vec{x}$ being in a class y is purely a function of this linear combination of the known observations.

4. Empirical results

The results are obtained by considering each model's variables over the original coefficients, and the coefficients re-estimated. The five models that are analyzed for Turkish industrial firms through financial distress levels, depending on two years of financial distress, and the prediction period, which covers the period from one to five years prior to the distress are considered. After the re-estimation process, the updated models are represented below and comparative coefficients in Table A.1.

Altman
$$(1.42)WC/TA + (0.31)RE/TA + (8.05)EBIT/TA + (0.00)MVE/TL - (0.02)SALES/TA$$

Ohlson
$$-(1.34) - (0.21)SIZE - (0.45)TL/TA - (2.13)WC/TA + (0.01)CL/CA - (0.30)ROA + (0.00)OCF/TA - (1.05)OENEG + (1.09)CHIN$$

Shumway
$$(2.81) - (1.44)SIZE + (0.02)RETURN - (0.25)ROA - (6.99)SIGMA + (0.26)TL/TA$$

Zmijewski
$$-(0.60) + (0.001)CA/CL - (0.13)ROA - (0.05)TL/TA$$

Taffler
$$-(0.87) - \frac{(0.09)PBT}{ACL} + \frac{(0.009)CA}{TL} + \frac{(2.59)CL}{TA} - (0.03)\frac{CA-INV-CL}{SALES-NIBT+DEPR}$$

The results indicate that the most accurate prediction results for financial distress one year in advance for Turkish manufacturing firms are derived from the original Zmijewski model (Table 2). The only model that results in an improved level of prediction accuracy when re-estimated is the Ohlson model in advance of one year before financial distress. One of the reasons for this improvement could be that the model works better with a more recent data sample, as indicated by (Begley *et al.*, 1996).

Taffler model gives the second most accurate results through its original coefficients, and its prediction ability decreases when the model is re-estimated. This result is also compatible with those of Taffler and Agarwal (2007), who aim to measure the predictive power of Taffler's (1983) model and find that the model is more effective when applied with the original coefficients for the UK sample which concludes that the longevity of the model does not mean that it is outdated. Likewise, Shumway's model prediction accuracy also falls when the model is re-estimated. Although Shumway's model differentiates itself from the other models by having market-based variables, for Turkish industrial firms, its prediction accuracy is lower than all other models, with the exception of Altman's model, which has the lowest accuracy level of all models.

Table 2 Comparison of accuracy levels of each model

Model	*Lag*	*Original*			*Re-estimated*		
		t_γ	t_θ	t_φ	t_γ	t_θ	t_φ
Altman	[1]	32.5%	35.9%	28.4%	33.5%	39.3%	26.7%
	[2]	30.4%	34.7%	26.2%	32.2%	38.2%	26.2%
	[3]	30.1%	36.1%	25.3%	31.9%	38.9%	26.2%
	[4]	28.3%	37.0%	23.1%	30.3%	40.0%	24.4%
	[5]	23.4%	31.1%	20.4%	24.7%	34.4%	20.8%
Ohlson	[1]	75.8%	70.7%	81.8%	80.6%	76.3%	85.8%
	[2]	77.3%	72.9%	81.8%	77.8%	72.9%	82.7%
	[3]	77.8%	72.8%	81.8%	77.0%	73.3%	80.8%
	[4]	78.9%	74.1%	81.8%	76.1%	69.6%	80.8%
	[5]	76.5%	71.2%	81.8%	75.2%	67.2%	80.8%
Shumway	[1]	80.6%	74.4%	88.0%	78.2%	81.1%	74.7%
	[2]	77.1%	72.0%	82.2%	68.9%	72.4%	65.3%
	[3]	76.5%	72.8%	79.6%	64.4%	70.0%	60.0%
	[4]	75.6%	69.6%	79.1%	62.5%	65.9%	60.4%
	[5]	74.1%	66.4%	77.2%	61.0%	62.1%	59.2%
Zmijewski	[1]	85.9%	85.9%	85.8%	80.0%	74.4%	86.7%
	[2]	81.2%	80.7%	81.8%	80.6%	74.4%	88.0%
	[3]	72.3%	74.4%	70.7%	77.0%	72.8%	80.4%
	[4]	69.4%	71.1%	68.4%	75.8%	69.6%	79.6%
	[5]	67.5%	69.8%	69.3%	72.9%	67.8%	78.2%
Taffler	[1]	80.6%	78.1%	83.6%	73.3%	68.1%	79.6%
	[2]	76.7%	75.6%	77.8%	74.9%	70.2%	79.6%
	[3]	75.8%	76.1%	75.6%	75.6%	70.0%	80.0%
	[4]	76.1%	75.6%	76.4%	76.4%	71.1%	79.6%
	[5]	71.5%	72.1%	74.7%	77.3%	71.6%	79.8%

Notes: t_γ, t_θ, and t_φ are the period identifiers when the auxiliary accuracy results are calculated for the full period, pre-crisis period, and post-crisis period, respectively.

When the sub-samples are considered in terms of pre- and post-financial crisis results, the models provide greater accuracy with their original coefficients, with an average increase in accuracy of 4.5% after the financial crisis of 2008, and the re-estimated model results show a corresponding increase of 2.9%. As for the results for the full sample, no improvement is shown in accuracy for the re-estimated results in relation to the original coefficients when the models are compared by considering the sub-samples of the periods before and after the financial crisis of 2008.

In order to measure the validity of the results, the matched hold out sample of 100 FD and 100 Non-FD firms are selected. The results indicate that four of the models have the predictive accuracy for Turkish publicly listed industrial firms (Table

A.2). Additionally, the type I and type II error rates (Table A.3) emphasize that Shumway,Zmijeski and Taffler models provide improved type I error classification whereas each model other than Ohlson provides deteriorated type II error results when re-estimated.

5. Conclusions

The current study analyzes the generalizability of financial distress estimation models in an emerging economy derived for developed markets. The results emphasize that all models, with the exception of Altman (1968), are generalizable and capable of classifying firms in an emerging market as distressed or not distressed, while also establishing a basis for further prediction models. Because the ratio selection process has no theoretical base, and researchers may use many different ratios, generalizable models have the potential to create a benchmark which could be used when establishing new models for prediction accuracy. On the other hand, the models' ability to classify ongoing industrial firms, rather than bankrupt firms provides practitioners with an important decision-making tool, while indicating which model provides the best accuracy for Turkish industrial market.

The results also emphasize that Altman (1968) model is not able to process distress classification for ongoing firms. However, the remaining models are appropriate for predicting the distress of listed industrial firms in Turkey through the original coefficients for ongoing firms, with an average accurate prediction rate of 81%. The re-estimation results of the models indicate that the re-estimation improves the Ohlson (1980) model results by 4.8%, but has a negative effect on all other models. The models' prediction results over original coefficients give better results after the financial crisis of 2008; in contrast, the re-estimated model predictions after the financial crisis period are mixed, and do not allow a precise interpretation to be obtained. It can therefore be concluded that the distress prediction models derived for developed markets provide robust prediction results, and are capable of classifying ongoing firms in an emerging market sample. Where the data is available, further research may be able to shed light on the prediction results of these models for other emerging market countries.

References

Agarwal, V. & Taffler, R. J. (2007) "Twenty-five years of the Taffler z-score model: does it really have predictive ability?", *Accounting and Business Research*, vol. 37 (4): 285-300

Altman, E. I. (1968) "Financial Ratios, Discriminant Analysis and the Prediction of Corporate Bankruptcy", *The Journal of Finance*, vol. 23 (4): 589-609

Altman, E. I. (1973) "Predicting Railroad Bankruptcy in America", *The Bell Journal of Economics and Management* vol. 4 (1): 184-211

Altman, E. I., Baidya, T. K. N. & Dias, L. M. R. (1979) "Assessing potential financial problems for firms in Brazil", *Journal of International Business Studies*, vol. 10 (2): 9-24

Amemiya, T. (1985) *Advanced Econometrics*, Harvard University Press

Baltagi, B. H. (2008) *Econometrics*, 4h Edition, Springer

Bauer,J., & Agarwal V. (2014) "Are hazard models superior to traditional bankruptcy prediction approaches? A comprehensive test", *Journal of Banking & Finance*, vol. 40: 432-442

Beaver, W. H. (1966) "Financial ratios as predictors of failure", *Journal of Accounting Research, Empirical Research in Accounting: Selected Studies*, vol. 4: 71-111

Begley, J., Ming, J. & Watts, S. (1996) "Bankruptcy classification errors in the 1980s: An empirical analysis of Altman's and Ohlson's models", *Review of Accounting Studies*, vol. 1 (4): 267-284

Bhatia, U. (1988) "Predicting corporate sickness in India", *Studies in Banking and Finance*, no. 7: 57-71

Bidin, A. R. (1988) "The development of a mredictive model (PNBScore) for evaluating performance of companies owned by the Government of Malaysia", *Studies in Banking & Finance*, no. 7: 91-103

Blum, M. (1974) "Failing company discriminant analysis", *Journal of Accounting Research*, vol. 12 (1): 1-25

Domencich, T. A. & McFadden, D. (1975) "Urban travel demand: A behavioral analysis", *North Holland Publishing*

Edmister, R. O. (1972) "An empirical test of financial ratio analysis for small business failure prediction", *Journal of Financial and Quantitative Analysis*, vol. 7 (2): 1477-1493

Gilbert, L. R., Krishnagopal, M. & Schwartz, K. B. (1990) "Predicting bankruptcy for firms in financial distress", *Journal of Business Finance and Accounting*, vol. 17 (1): 161-171

Grice, J. S. & Dugan, M. T. (2003) "Re-estimations of the Zmijewski and Ohlson bankruptcy prediction models", *Advances in Accounting*, vol. 20: 77-93

Grice, J. S. & Ingram, R. W. (2001) "Tests of generalizability of Altman's bankruptcy prediction model", *Journal of Business Research*, vol. 54: 53-61

Horrigan, J. O. (1968) "A short history of financial ratio analysis", *The Accounting Review*, vol. 43 (22): 84-294

Huberty C. J. & Olejnik, S. (2006) "Applied MANOVA and discriminant analysis", *John Wiley & Sons*

Judge, G. G., Griffiths, W. E., Hill, R. C., Lütkepohl, H., & Lee, T. C. (1985) "The theory and practice of econometrics, 2nd Edition", *John Wiley & Sons*

Kemsley, D. (1998) "The effect of taxes on production location", *Journal of Accounting Research*, vol. 36: 321-341

Li, H. & Sun, J. (2008) "Ranking-order case-based reasoning for financial distress prediction", *Knowledge-Based Systems*, vol. 21 (8): 868-878

McFadden, D. L. (1984) "Econometric analysis of qualitative response models", *Handbook of Econometrics*, vol. 2: 1395-1457

McLachlan, G. (2004) "Discriminant analysis and statistical pattern recognition", *John Wiley & Sons*

Ohlson, J. A. (1980) "Financial ratios and the probabilistic prediction of bankruptcy", *Journal of Accounting Research*, vol. 18 (1): 109-131

Shumway, T. (2001) "Forecasting bankruptcy more accurately: A simple hazard model", *The Journal of Business*, vol. 74 (1): 101-124

Taffler, R. J. (1983) "The assessment of company solvency and performance using a statistical model", *Accounting and Business Research*, vol. 13 (52): 295-307

Ugurlu, M. & Aksoy, H. (2006) "Prediction of corporate financial distress in an emerging market: The case of Turkey", *Cross Cultural Management: An International Journal*, vol. 13 (4): 277-295

Train, K. (1986) *Qualitative Choice Analysis*, MIT Press

Xie, C., Luo, C. & Yu, X. (2011) "Financial distress prediction based on SVM and MDA methods: the case of Chinese listed companies", *Quality and Quantity*, vol. 45: 671-686

Zmijewski, M. E. (1984) "Methodological Issues Related to the Estimation of Financial Distress Prediction Models", *Journal of Accounting Research*, vol. 22: 59-82

Appendix

Table A.1 Re-estimated coefficients of each model

X	Altman		Ohlson		Shumway	
	β	$\hat{\beta}$	β	$\hat{\beta}$	β	$\hat{\beta}$
X_1	0.012	1.419	-0.410	-0.207	-0.480	-1.439
X_2	0.014	0.312	6.030	-0.451	-1.810	0.022
X_3	0.033	8.050	-1.430	-2.129	-1.980	-0.253
X_4	0.006	-0.022	0.070	0.002	5.790	-6.994
X_5	0.999	0.003	-2.370	1.086	3.590	0.260
X_6			-1.830	-0.297		
X_7			-1.720	0.000		
X_8			- 0.520	-1.062		
	Zmijewski		**Taffler**			
X_1	β	$\hat{\beta}$	β	$\hat{\beta}$		
X_2	0.004	0.001	12.18	-0.089		
X_3	-4.500	-0.126	2.500	0.009		
X_4	5.700	-0.059	-10.68	2.587		
X_5			0.030	-0.032		

Notes: X represents the independent variables of each model, β stands for the original coefficients, and $\hat{\beta}$ indicates re-estimated coefficients.

Table A.2 Comparison of accuracy levels of each model for holdout sample

	Lag	*Model*			
		Zmijewski	Taffler	Shumway	Ohlson
Original	[1]	88.8%	77.7%	72.1%	63.1%
	[2]	83.5%	77.8%	72.2%	65.2%
	[3]	74.3%	72.9%	71.4%	67.1%
	[4]	73.0%	73.8%	71.3%	69.7%
	[5]	74.3%	72.9%	71.4%	70.8%
Re-estimated	[1]	69.3%	62.6%	77.1%	70.9%
	[2]	70.9%	64.6%	77.8%	70.9%
	[3]	71.4%	66.4%	73.6%	68.6%
	[4]	71.3%	68.9%	73.8%	69.7%
	[5]	71.4%	66.4%	73.6%	68.9%

Table A.3 Comparison of Type I and Type II results

Model	*Lag*	*Original*		*Re-estimated*	
		e_I	e_{II}	e_I	e_{II}
Ohlson	[1]	1.3%	17.9%	5.9%	13.3%
	[2]	0.6%	17.4%	5.5%	12.5%
	[3]	1.7%	15.4%	5.9%	11.1%
	[4]	2.8%	13.0%	6.3%	9.6%
	[5]	3.8%	11.1%	7.1%	7.9%
Shumway	[1]	5.2%	14.0%	2.1%	18.1%
	[2]	4.5%	13.7%	2.2%	16.2%
	[3]	8.1%	12.1%	4.4%	14.4%
	[4]	11.3%	10.6%	6.5%	12.6%
	[5]	8.1%	12.1%	4.4%	14.4%
Zmijewski	[1]	17.1%	1.7%	0.5%	19.5%
	[2]	15.4%	4.8%	2.0%	16.9%
	[3]	22.5%	4.4%	3.9%	14.9%
	[4]	25.8%	4.4%	5.5%	12.8%
	[5]	22.5%	4.4%	3.9%	14.9%
Taffler	[1]	7.6%	11.6%	0.9%	20.5%
	[2]	8.1%	11.5%	2.8%	17.4%
	[3]	11.5%	10.4%	3.9%	15.4%
	[4]	13.2%	8.7%	5.1%	13.0%
	[5]	11.5%	10.4%	3.9%	15.4%

Notes: e_I, and e_{II} represents Type I and Type II errors respectively.

8

Bank credit risk analysis with k-nearest-neighbor classifier: Case of Tunisian banks

Aida Krichene Abdelmoula[1,a]

[a]Institut des Hautes Etudes Commerciales de Carthage, University of Carthage, Tunisia

Abstract: Credit risk is defined as the risk that borrowers will fail to pay its loan obligations. In recent years, a large number of banks have developed sophisticated systems and models to help bankers in quantifying, aggregating and managing risk. The outputs of these models also play increasingly important roles in banks' risk management and performance measurement processes. In this study we try to tackle the question of default prediction of short term loans for a Tunisian commercial bank. We use a database of 924 credit records of Tunisian firms granted by a Tunisian commercial bank from 2003 to 2006. The K-Nearest Neighbor classifier algorithm was conducted and the results indicate that the best information set is relating to accrual and cash-flow and the good classification rate is in order of 88.63 % (for k=3). A curve ROC is plotted to assess the performance of the model. The result shows that the AUC (Area Under Curve) criterion is in order of 87.4% (for the first model), 95% (third model) and 95.6% for the best model with cash flow information.

Keywords: banking sector, risk assessment, default risk, k-Nearest-Neighbor classifier, ROC curve

1. Introduction

Bank credit risk assessment is widely used at banks around the world. Since, credit risk evaluation is very crucial, variety of techniques is used for risk level assessment. In addition, credit risk is one of the main functions of the banking

[1] *Corresponding author*: Department of Accounting, Carthage University 1, rue de la Paix Ain Zaghouane, Tunis, TUNISIA, 2046 mail addresses: aidakrichene@yahoo.fr; aida.krichene@iscae.rnu.tn

community (Seval, 2008). Basel Committee on Banking Supervision defined credit risk as the potential of a bank borrower or counterparty will fail to pay its obligations in accordance with agreed terms (Okan veli safakli, 2007).

Banks classify clients according to their profile. While classifying, financial background of customers and subjective factors of customers are evaluated. Financial ratios play an important role for risk level calculation (Berk *et al.*, 2011). These ratios are objective and indicate the financial statement of business. Balance sheet, income statement and cash flows are some financial statements for collecting information to calculate objective financial ratios. There are many other subjective factors too; these depend on bank decision strategy and its mission according to (Berk *et al.*, 2011). The Basel Committee on Banking Supervision, in a consultative document, tried to provide banks and supervisors with guidance on sound credit risk assessment and valuation policies and practices for loans independently of the accounting framework applied. In this document the third principle states that "A bank's policies should appropriately address validation of any internal credit risk assessment models»[1].

The implementation of this principle turns out to be a daily decision based on a binary classification problem distinguishing good payers from bad payers (Karaa & Krichène, 2012). Surely, evaluating the insolvency plays an important role since a good estimate of the quality of a borrower can help to decide whether granting the requested loans or not. The Basel Committee recommends a choice between two broad methodologies for calculating their capital requirements for credit risk, either external mapping approach or internal rating system (Karaa & Krichène, 2012).

Although the external mapping approach is difficult to apply because of the unavailability of external rating grades, the internal rating is easy and simple to implement since a lot of techniques have been proposed in the literature to develop credit-risk assessment models. Additionally, the subprime crisis, which shakes down the American and European countries and shows the fragility of banking sector and cast some doubt on the accuracy and usefulness of agency ratings (Matoussi & Abdelmoula, 2009). In fact, Credit scoring methods are used to evaluate both objective and subjective factors. These techniques spread all around the world in 50's (Abramowicz *et al.*, 2003). By these methods, information collection from customer is formalized. Besides, the scoring system forms a basis for loan approval. These models include traditional statistical techniques such as logistic regression (Steenackers & Goovaerts, 1989), multivariate discriminant analysis (MDA) (Altman, 1968), classification trees (Davis *et al.*, 1992), neural network (NNs) models (Desai *et al.*, 1996, Matoussi & Abdelmoula, 2009; Karaa and Krichène, 2012) and nonparametric statistical models like k-nearest neighbour, Henley & Hand (1997). Recent contributions have proposed the employ of Bayesian classification rules using Naïve Bayes classifiers. The results of these studies demonstrated their frequent ability to do better than the most existing techniques. In this context, Sarkar and Sriram (2001), and Sun and Shenoy (2007) had been successfully applied to bankruptcy prediction.

In this research we try to tackle the following question: how banks can develop fairly accurate quantitative prediction models that can used as very early warning signals for default risk. The most of previous research look at business failure prediction from the mid-term and long-term prospects (failure vs non failure). In our paper, we examine the short-term prospect (payment vs. non payment of the short term loan at maturity). We try also to explore the case of a bank who wants to use prediction model to assess its credit risk (see failure prediction in Tunisia by (Matoussi *et al.*, 1999), financial distress prediction using Neural Networks by (Matoussi & Krichene, 2010; Abid & Zouari, 2000), financial distress in Egypt by (El-Shazly, 2002), credit scoring model for Turkey's micro & small enterprises by (Davutyan, 2006). In this study, we use a K-Nearest Neighbour classifier model to investigate the credit–risk.

This paper is organized as follow. In section 2 we provide the theoretical framework and Empirical Modelling supporting our research question our research design respectively. In section 3, we define data and methodology. In Section 4, we present our results and discussion. Finally, Section 5 concludes the paper and presents some limits.

2. Credit risk assessment of banks: theoretical framework and empirical modelling

2.1. Theoretical framework of credit risk problem: agency theory

One of the most important applications of agency theory to the lender-borrower problem is the derivation of the optimal form of the lending contract. In credit market, there is an information asymmetry between the borrower, who usually has better information about the investment project and its potential profits and risk, and the lender (the bank) who doesn't have enough and reliable information relating to investment project. This lack of information in quantity and quality is a source of problems before and after the transaction takes place. The presence of asymmetric information normally leads to moral hazard and adverse selection problems. This situation shows a classical principal-agent problem.

The principal-agent models of the agency theory may be divided into three classes according to the nature of information asymmetry (Karel, 2006). First, we find models with ex-post asymmetric information qualified as moral hazard. In this case, agent receives some private information after signing the contract. Moral hazard refers to a situation in which the asymmetric information problem is created after the transaction occurs. Since the borrower has relevant information about the project the lender doesn't have, the lender runs the risk that the borrower will engage in activities that are undesirable from the lender's point of view because they make it less likely that the loan will be paid back (Matoussi & Abdelmoula, 2009).

Second, we find models with ex-ante asymmetric information known as adverse selection models (Karel, 2006). In these models agent has private information already before signing the contract. Adverse Selection refers to a situation in which the borrower have significant information that the lender lack (or vice versa) about the quality of the project before the transaction takes place. This happens when the potential borrowers who are the most likely to produce an adverse outcome (bad credit risks) are the ones who are most active to get a loan and are thus most likely to be selected. In the simplest case, lenders' price cannot differentiate between good and bad borrowers, because the riskiness of projects is unknown. Finally, we find the third class known as signalling models, in which the informed agent may divulge his private information through the signal which he sends to the principal (Karel, 2006).

This problem is traditionally considered in the framework of costly state verification, introduced by (Townsend, 1979). The essence of the model is that the agent, who has no endowment, borrows money from the principal to run a one-shot investment project. The agent is confronted with a moral hazard problem. Should he declare the true value or should he decrease the outcome of the project? This situation illustrates ex-post moral hazard. Moreover, we can also face a situation of ex-ante moral hazard, where the unobservable effort by agent during the project realization may impact the outcome of the project. Townsend (1979) indicated that the optimal contract which solves this problem is known as standard (or simple) debt contract. This standard debt contract is characterized by its face value, which should be repaid by the agent when the project is finished. As another theoretical justification for simple debt contract was considered by (Diamond, 1984), where the costly state verification was changed by a costly punishment.

Hellwig (2000, 2001) indicated that the two models are equivalent only under the risk neutrality assumption. However, when we consider the introduction of risk aversion, the costly state verification model still working, but the costly punishment model does not survive.

In the real world, credit institutions can use either guarantee (collateral) or bankruptcy prediction modelling or both to face out the asymmetric information problem and its consequences on credit risk evaluation (Karaa & Krichène, 2012). We deal with this aspect in the next subsection.

2.2. Credit Risk Assessment and Bankruptcy Prediction: Related studies (works)

After the high number of profile bank failures in Asia, the regulators recognize the need and urge banks to employ advanced technology to assess the credit risk in their portfolios. Assessing the credit risk correctly also permits banks to engineer future lending transactions, so as to achieve targeted return/risk characteristics. The evaluation of credit risk needs the development of fairly accurate quantitative prediction models that can serve as very early warning signals for counterparty defaults.

Many researchers proposed two main approaches to deal with credit scoring in the literature. The first approach proposed by (Merton, 1974) and known as the structural or market based models where the default probability derivation is based on modelling the underlying dynamics of interest rates and firm characteristics. Initially, this approach is based on the asset value model, where the default process is endogenous, and relates to the capital structure of the firm. Default happens when the value of the firm's assets drops below some critical level (Crouhy *et al.*, 2000). The second approach is centered on the empirical or accounting based models where the relationship between default probability and characteristics of a firm is learned from the data instead of modelling this relationship. Raymond (2007), Thomas *et al.* (2002), Galindo and Tamayo (2000) synthesized some methods used in this context. In this regard we can cite the studies of Beaver (1966) and Altman (1968), bankruptcy prediction has been investigated intensively by academics and practitioners. Several models have been developed and tested empirically. Altman's popular Z-Score (Altman, 1968) is an illustration based on linear discriminant analysis, and was used to predict the probability of default of firms. Ohlsons O-Score (Ohlson, 1980) is based on generalized linear models or multiple logistic regression which have been used either to detect the best determinants of bankruptcy and the predictive accuracy rate of their occurrence. Neural network models were adapted and used in bankruptcy prediction (Atya, 2001; Matoussi & Abdelmoula, 2009). Their high power of prediction makes them a widely held alternative with the ability to integrate a very large number of features in an adaptive nonlinear model (Kay & Titterington, 2000).

A lot of researches have focused on the non-parametric methods class (e.g. k-nearest neighbor) (Henley & Hand, 1996), decision trees (Quinlan, 1992) and neural networks (Mcculloch & Pitts, 1943) have also been largely applied in the field of credit scoring. There are also some other approaches that combine several techniques to create a classification model such as Support Vector Machine (e.g. Lee and Chen, 2005; Lee *et al.*, 2002). West (2000) tried to compare the accuracy of credit scoring of five Artificial Neural Network models namely multilayer perceptron, radial basis function, fuzzy adaptive resonance, mixture-of-experts and learning vector quantization. In his study, West (2000) used two real world data sets Australian and German. He employed 10 fold cross validation for improving his predictive power. He indicated both good and bad credit rates. Finally, he compared the results against five other traditional techniques including linear discriminant analysis, logistic regression, k nearest neighbor, kernel density estimation and decision trees. The results indicate that the multilayer perception may not be the most accurate Artificial Neural Network model and that both the combination-of-experts and radial basis function Neural Network models should be considered for credit scoring applications. Also, between traditional methods, logistic regression is more accurate method and more precise than Neural Network models in average case.

According to Vera *et al.* (2012) "Despite the intense study of credit scoring, there is no consensus on the most appropriate classification technique to use." Baesens *et al.* (2003b) revealed that some conflicts can occur when comparing the findings of different studies. However Thomas *et al.* (2002) also suggested that most methods applied in credit scoring have similar levels of performance. In fact, for banks and financial institutions the reasons that may motivate the preference for a certain methods are the interpretability and the transparency (Martens *et al.*, 2009). According to Vera *et al.* (2002) "two aspects of methods for credit scoring are very important: that is the predictive performance, as well as the insights or interpretations that are revealed by the model."

2.3. Empirical research design

2.3.1. K-NN classifier algorithm

Banks are in a very competitive environment; thereby the service quality during credit risk assessment is very important. When customer demands for credit from bank, bank should evaluate credit demand as short as possible (Berk *et al.*, 2011) to gain competitive advantage. Additionally for each credit demand, the same process is repeated and constitutes a cost for the bank. Since the importance of credit risk analysis, most of techniques and models are developed by financial institution to decide whether to grant or not to grant credit (Çinko, 2006).

The classification methods can be classified into parametric and non-parametric problems. In fact, parametric methods are based upon the assumptions of normally distributed population and estimate the parameters of the distributions to solve the problem (Zhang *et al.*, 2007). However, according to Berry and Linoff (1997) non-parametric methods make no assumptions about the specific distributions involved, and are therefore distribution-free. The k-nearest neighbor classifier serves as an illustration of a non-parametric statistical approach. When given an unknown case, a K-NN classifier seeks the pattern space for the k training (Pranab & Radha, 2013) (cases that are similar to unknown cases. These k training cases are the K-nearest neighbors" of the unknown cases (Ravinder & Aggarwal, 2011).

K-NN classifier can be useful when the dependent variable takes more than two values such as high risk, medium risk and low risk. Moreover K-NN classifier requires an equal number of good and bad sample cases for better performance (Hand & Henley, 1997). According to Berry and Linoff (1997) "the choice of ***k*** also affects the performance of the k-NN algorithm. This can be determined experimentally. Starting with k=1, we use a test case to estimate the error rate of the classifier. This process is repeated each time by incrementing k to allow for one more neighbors. The K-value that gives the minimum error rate may be selected. In general, larger the number of training samples is, the larger the value of k will be."

2.3.2. ROC curve as a classifier performance

A Receiver Operating Characteristics (ROC) is a generally useful performance graphing method. In other word, ROC graph is a method for visualizing, organizing and selecting classifiers based on their performance Fawcett (2006). Spackman (1989) was the earliest adopters of ROC graphs in machine learning. He demonstrated the value of ROC curves in evaluating and comparing algorithms (Fawcett, 2006). In fact, the use of ROC graphs in the machine learning community has increased in recent years. Since that simple classification accuracy is often a poor metric for measuring performance (Provost & Fawcett, 1997; Provost *et al.*, 1998). Besides, they have properties that make them especially useful for domains with skewed class distribution and unequal classification error costs (Fawcett, 2006).

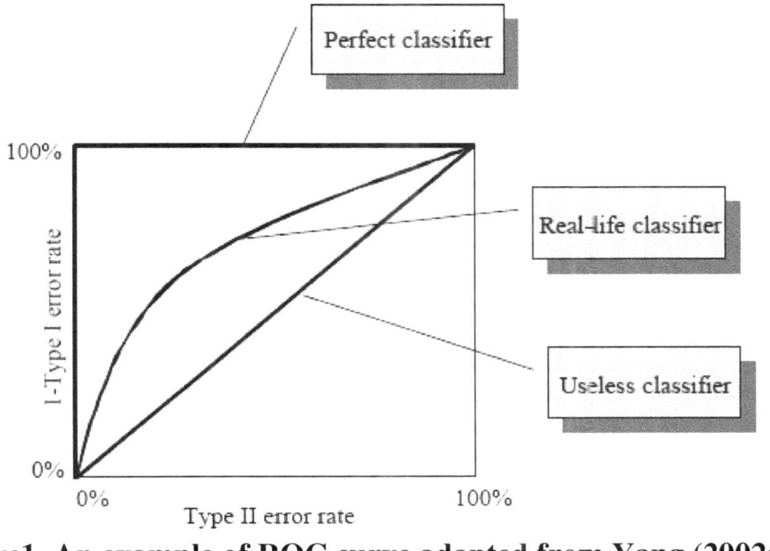

Figure1. An example of ROC curve adapted from Yang (2002: 18)

2.3.3. The criterion of the area under a curve ROC (AUC)

A ROC curve is a two-dimensional representation of classifier performance. According to Fawcett (2006), "to compare classifiers we may want to reduce ROC performance to a single scalar value representing expected performance". To do so, many researchers such as Bradley (1997) and Hanley and McNeil (1982) recommend the use of a common method which is to calculate the area under the ROC curve, abbreviated AUC. The AUC is defined as a portion of the area of the unit square; its value will always be between 0 and 1.0. However, because random guessing produces the diagonal line between (0, 0) and (1, 1), which has an area of 0.5, no realistic classifier should have an AUC less than 0.5 (Fawcett, 2006).

3. Methodology

The need for models that predict defaults correctly is very important, because in commercial bank the credit risk measurement is crucial for each client to discriminate reliable clients from not reliable. Among the quantitative methods for solving credit risk evaluation problems, the simple Bayesian classifier was applied for estimating the posterior probabilities of default. In fact, Antonakis and Sfakianakis (2009) showed that the posterior probability of an event is the probability of an event after collecting some empirical data. Rosner (2006) demonstrated that the posterior probability is obtained by integrating information from the prior probability with additional data related to the event in question. According to Mileris (2010) "often analysis begins with initial or prior probability estimates for specific events of interest. Then from sources such as a sample we obtain additional information about the events. Given this new information the prior probability values can be updated by calculating revised probabilities, referred to as posterior probabilities". Anderson *et al.* (2007) demonstrated that Bayesian theorem provides a means for making these probability calculations.

In our research we use a sample of the bank credit files composed of 924 files of short term loan granted to Tunisian companies from 2003 to 2006.

3.1. Sample and data

Let's recall that our objective is to use k-NN[2]classifier methodology for default prediction of bank's commercial loans. But, in order to solve a problem using k-NN algorithm, we have to collect data for training purposes. The training data set includes a number of cases, each containing values for a range of input and output variables. The first decision we need to make is which variables to use. The second one concerns the subjects we want to predict their behaviour. For our case the variables are indicators of default risk and the subjects are borrowers. The data collected for our investigation came from a large private commercial bank (BIAT)[3]. We choose a private bank in order to avoid the potential inefficiency of public banking sector, whose decision is sometimes dictated by government choices. Our choice to work with short-term commercial credits is motivated by the fact that this type of credits represents the major part of loans granted by commercial bank and is subject to renewal every year. In fact, loans with maturities of one year or less comprise more than half of all commercial bank loans (Revsine *et al.,* 1999). For the case of the BIAT this ratio was around 40% during 2006 and 2007.

In our investigation, we use a database of 924 files granted to industrial Tunisian companies by a commercial bank from 2003 to 2006. This period was chosen because it corresponds to a central bank instruction, in which it asks bank to provide credit risk classes for their borrowers. For the case the BIAT, by the end of every quarter, it classifies these files into five clusters, each one corresponding to a risk class. Files without delay of payment correspond to the healthy firms. The four remaining classes correspond to four riskier classes of three, six, nine and one year (or more) delay of payment respectively. We group these four classes in one class (risky companies).

3.2. Variables measurement

3.2.1. Dependent variable

In this research, we try to study the probability of default. The dependent variable is a dummy variable, which equals 0 if the classified is healthy and 1 if the classified is risky. Hence:

Y = 0 if no delay of payment (healthy)

Y = 1 if more there is more than 3 month delay (risky)

3.2.2. Independent variables

Default risk prediction depends on a good evaluation of the couple risk-return of a company. Financial ratios, commonly used, are calculated from financial statements (balance sheet, income and cash flow statement). Financial ratio analysis classifies the ratios into groups which states about different facets of a company's finances and operations (liquidity, activity or operational, leverage and profitability).

In our experiment we keep the same variables used in the study of (Karaa & Krichène, 2012). So the database is composed of 24 financial and non-financial indicators. The financial indicators are inspired from Altman's popular Z-Score and recommended textbooks in financial statement analysis and valuation (Berstein

& Wild, 1998; Revsine *et al.*, 1999; and Palepu *et al.*, 2000). The financial indicators measure liquidity (working capital, operating activity and cash flow), Leverage, long term solvency and Profitability. The non-financial variables used in this research are firm size and collateral (Karaa & Krichène, 2012).

Table 1. Variables definition and measure[4]

RISK FACET	CODE	VARIABLE DEFINITION	VARIABLE MEASURE
Liquidity indicators	R1	Long term financing of Working capital	(Shareholders'equity+non current liabilities)- non current assets
	R2	Working capital requirement	Working capital / (Shareholders'equity+non current liabilities)-non current assets
	R3t	Account receivable liquidity	Provision for doubtful accounts / Gross account receivables
	R4	Current ratio	Current assets / Current liabilities
	R5	Quick ratio	Current assets-inventories / Current liabilities
	R6	Cash flow ratio	Operating cash flow / Current liabilities
	R7	Inventory turnover	Sales / inventories
Leverage and solvency indicators	R8	Debt Cash Flow Coverage Ratio	Cash flow / Total debts = Net income +depreciation / Total debts
	R9	Liabilities to equity ratio	Total liabilities / Shareholders' equity
	R10	Net debt to equity ratio	Short term debt+long term debt – cash and marketable securities / Shareholders' equity
	R11	Debt to capital ratio	Short term debt+long term debt / Short term debt+long term debt + Shareholders'equity
	R12	Long term debt to assets	Long term debt / Total assets

	R13	Long term debt to tangible assets	$\frac{\text{Long term debt}}{\text{Total tangible assets}}$
	R14	Interest coverage ratio	$\frac{\text{Operating income before taxes and interest}}{\text{Interest expense}}$
Profitability indicators	R15	Net profit margin	$\frac{\text{Net income}}{\text{Total operating revenue}}$
	R16	Gross profit margin	$\frac{\text{Earnings before interest and taxes}}{\text{Total operating revenue}}$
	R17	Return on invested capital	$\frac{\text{Net income}}{\text{Total assets}}$
	R18	Return On Equity (ROE)	$\frac{\text{Net income}}{\text{Stockholders equity}}$
Ratios used by the bank	R19	Fixed asset to debt ratio	$\frac{\text{Net fixed assets}}{\text{Total debt}}$
	R20	Short term debt to sales ratio	$\frac{\text{Short term debt}}{\text{Total sales}}$
	R21	Financial expenses to revenue ratio	$\frac{\text{Financial expenses}}{\text{Total revenue}}$
	R22	Fixed asset turnover	$\frac{\text{Sales}}{\text{Fixed assets}}$
Other variables	V01	collateral	LOG(GUARANTEE)
	V02	Firm size	LOG(TOTAL ASSETS)

4. Empirical results

4.1. Descriptive analysis

To get an insight about our data before performing the k-NN classifier models, we will achieve a test of mean differences between the two risks classes defined above (table 2). The summary statistics and the mean differences can be seen as an analysis similar to Beaver (1963). In Table 2 we expose the descriptive statistics of our data. When we run mean differences analysis between the two risks classes (healthy and risky groups). Such analysis allows us to verify if there is a difference between the two classes in terms of financial ratios. Table 2 presents some summary statistics for the two risks classes.

Table 2. Group means

Ratios	Code	Mean	Std. Deviation
R2:	,00	***16,8191***	58,85241
	1,00	***8,5990***	15,69326
R3:	,00	,0471	,13891
	1,00	,0568	,14135
R4:	,00	***2,9623***	7,05638
	1,00	***3,2328***	8,05572
R6:	,00	***2,0391***	22,41881
	1,00	***-,6450***	38,61664
R7:	,00	,0439	,10179
	1,00	,0757	,14164
R8:	,00	***1,4900***	2,00318
	1,00	***1,0742***	,91636
R10:	,00	,0452	,33929
	1,00	,0347	,16519
R11:	,00	***,0569***	,15137
	1,00	***,0166***	,10049
R12 :	,00	***,4993***	2,33091
	1,00	***,2348***	1,14838
R13:	,00	,7708	,97464
	1,00	,7151	,58013
R14:	,00	***,2274***	1,06959
	1,00	***,0588***	,74966
R15:	,00	***5,0372***	55,16137
	1,00	***13,4255***	16,99936
R18:	,00	***,6227***	2,93441
	1,00	***7,4529***	54,44136
R19:	,00	1,8072	2,80796
	1,00	1,7822	3,89486
R20:	,00	1,1982	2,38237
	1,00	1,1215	3,14473
R21:	,00	***,0634***	,30944
	1,00	***,2492***	2,91846
R22:	,00	***,0115***	,43979
	1,00	***-,0284***	,25000

00: corresponds to healthy group
01: corresponds to risky group

Table 2 presents significant mean differences between the two groups for some ratios (R_2; R_4; R_6; R_8 R_{11}; R_{12}; $R_{14;}$ R_{15}; R_{18}; $R_{21}$and R_{22}) and no significant differences for others (R_1; R_3; R_5; R_7; R_9; R_{10}; R_{11}; R_{13}; R_{16}; R_{17}; R_{19} and R_{20}). Globally, they tell us that the liquidity risk does not differentiate the two groups (Karaa & Krichène, 2012). The leverage and solvency ratios do better in discriminating the two groups. For others indicators (coverage and profitability), the results are mitigated. For example, while return on equity (R_{18}) shows a significant difference gross profit margin (R_{16}) and return on invested capital (R_{17}) are not.

When we look at the significance of mean differences, we notice that globally the good indicators are superior in the healthy group, while the bad indicators are higher in the risky group. For example the mean of cash flow ratios (R_6), Working capital requirement (R_2), leverage and solvency ratios (R_{11}, R_{12}, R_{14} and R_8) is bigger in health group. Current ratio (R_4), profitability ratios (R_{18} and R15), have a higher mean in the risky group.

4.2. Results and discussion

In our experiment, we build up three types of K-NN classifier. The first classifier uses data on financial ratios (cash-flows excluded). It will be referred as 'Non cash-flow model'. The second model uses data on all ratios indicators (cash-flows included, collateral excluded). It will be referred as 'Cash-flow model'. The third model uses all indicators of the study. It will be referred as 'full information model'.

According to Rafiul *et al.* (2008) "the *k*-nearest neighbor (*k*-NN) technique, due to its interpretable nature, is a simple and very intuitively appealing method to address classification problems. However, choosing an appropriate distance function for *k*-NN can be challenging and an inferior choice can make the classifier highly vulnerable to noise in the data". In our investigation, we tested using different values of *k* (2, 3, 4 and 5). Based on this testing, for *k*-NN we identified the best value of *k* which produced the best classification performance and this is what is reported in the result tables 3, 4 and 5.

Table 3. Results for Non Cash-Flow models (Appendix 1)

Panel 1: k-NN classifier with variation of the parameter k=2 (appendix 1 panel 1)

	K=2	
	Healthy	**Risky**
Healthy companies	**358**	**100**
Risky companies	**100**	**366**
% Total Good and Bad Classification		
Good classification	78.35%	
Bad classification	21.64%	

Panel 2: K-NN with k=3 (appendix 1 panel 2)

	K=3	
	Healthy	**Risky**
Healthy companies	364	94
Risky companies	78	388
% Total Good and Bad Classification		
Good classification	**81.38%**	
Bad classification	18.62%	

Panel 3: K-NN with k=4 (Appendix 1 panel 3)

	K=4	
	Healthy	**Risky**
Healthy companies	**332**	**126**
Risky companies	**122**	**344**
% Total Good and Bad Classification		
Good classification	73.16%	
Bad classification	26.84%	

Panel 4: K-NN with k=5 (Appendix 1 panel 4)

	K=5	
	Healthy	**Risky**
Healthy companies	**331**	**127**
Risky companies	**124**	**342**
% Total Good and Bad Classification		
Good classification	**72.83%**	
Bad classification	**27.16%**	

We can see from these results (panel 1, 2, 3 and 4) that the global good classification rate is getting better when we fixed the number of the parameter k to 3. In fact, the good classification rate is in order of 81.38% for the best model with k=3 for the other models with k=2, 4 and 5 the good classification rate is respectively of 78.35%, 73.16% and 72.83%. A lot of researches have examined the criterion of type I and II errors. According to Yang (2002) «Type I error rate is also called a rate or credit risk, it is the rate of 'bad' customers being categorized as 'good'. When this happens, the miss-classified 'bad' customers will become default. Therefore, if a credit institution has a high a rate, which means the credit granting policy, is too generous, the institution is exposed to credit risk».

Type II error rate is called also a commercial risk; it is the rate of 'good' client being classified as 'bad'. When this happens, the miss-classified 'good' client are rejected, the bank supports (endure) therefore an opportunity cost caused by the loss of 'good' customers. Bogess (1967) showed that if a credit institution has a high type II error for a long period, which means it takes a long time restrictive credit granting policy Yang (2002), it may lose its share in the market. The credit institution is therefore exposed to commercial risk.

Table 4. Results for Cash-Flow models (Appendix 2 panels 1,2,3 and 4)

	K=2		K=3		K=4		K=5	
	Healthy	**Risky**	**Healthy**	**Risky**	**Healthy**	**Risky**	**Healthy**	**Risky**
Healthy companies	**395**	**63**	**409**	**49**	**387**	**71**	**375**	**83**
Risky companies	**59**	**407**	**56**	**410**	**72**	**394**	**92**	**374**
% Total Good and Bad Classification								
Good classification	**86.79%**		**88.63%**		**84.52%**		**81.06%**	
Bad classification	**13.20%**		**11.37%**		**15.48%**		**19.94%**	

Table 5. Results for full information models (Appendix3 panels 1, 2, 3 and 4)

	K=2		K=3		K=4		K=5	
	Healthy	**Risky**	**Healthy**	**Risky**	**Healthy**	**Risky**	**Healthy**	**Risky**
Healthy companies	**393**	**65**	**406**	**52**	**381**	**77**	**383**	**75**
Risky companies	**69**	**397**	**69**	**397**	**99**	**367**	**113**	**353**
% Total Good and Bad Classification								
Good classification	**85.5%**		**86.90%**		**80.95%**		**79.65%**	
Bad classification	**14.50%**		**13.10%**		**19.05%**		**20.35%**	

The classification results for the two models (cash flow and full information models) are presented in Table 4 and 5. The best performances among that of the reported classifiers are marked in bold and red.

From tables 4 and 5 we can see that the best model which shows the best classification rate is the one associating accrual and cash flow information (table 4) with a good classification rate of 88.63% versus 86.90% for the third model with full information. Let's recall that our objective is to find the class label for the new point. The algorithm has different behavior based on k and in this research we choose the value of K. We can also conclude that the best parameter k –NN is set to 3 for all models in this research.

The variation of the parameter k to 3 has improved the results. The good classification rate is getting better. Moreover, the model has reduced the error type

I from 16.73% to 12% (Table 6) and the error type II is reduced from 20.52% to 10.69% when we introduce cash flow information.

Table 6. Criterion of the type I and II error

	ERROR	K=2	K=3	K=4	K=5
NON CASH FLOW MODEL	Type I	**21.83%**	**16.73%**	**27.51%**	**27.25%**
	Type II	**21.45%**	**20.52%**	**26.18%**	**27.72%**
CASH FLOW MODEL	Type I	**12.66%**	**12.01%**	**15.45%**	**19.74%**
	Type II	**13.75%**	**10.69%**	**15.50%**	**18.12%**
FULL INFORMATION MODEL	Type I	**14.8%**	**14.80%**	**21.24%**	**24.24%**
	Type II	**14.19%**	**11.35%**	**16.81%**	**16.37%**

In this research, we would like to assess credit risk using a selection of financial ratio recommended in debt contracts. The predictions on the selection of financial ratio illustrate relation between financial ratios and credit risk. This evidence is well known in the practitioner and academic literature (Demerjian, 2007). In fact, textbooks emphasize the role of ratios in evaluating credit quality (Lundholm & Sloan, 2004), while academic studies conclude that financial ratios serve to provide signals about borrower credit risk when used as covenants (Smith & Warner, 1979; Dichev & Skinner, 2002).

4.3. The ROC curve

A ROC curve for the perfect classifier, which orders all 'bad' cases before 'good' cases, is the curve follows the two axes. It would classify 100% 'bad' cases into class 'bad' and 0% 'good' cases into class 'bad' for some value of the sill. According to Yang (2002) "a classifier with a ROC curve which follows the 45° line would be useless. It would classify the same proportion of the 'bad' cases and 'good' cases into the class 'bad' at each value of the threshold; it would not separate the classes at all. Real-life classifiers produce ROC curves which lie between these two extremes".

To evaluate the performance of the curve we have to use a measure given by the Area under the ROC Curve (denoted as AUC) (Hand, 1997). The curve that has a larger AUC is better than the one that has a smaller AUC.

We can note that the criterion of AUC is of the order of 95.6% for the best model (cash flow model). This score is larger than 50% and it is a good score. This result confirms the good classification rate found in the previous section. We can conclude that cash flow information is a good indicator for bankers who want to evaluate credit applicant.

Figure 2. ROC curve of three models

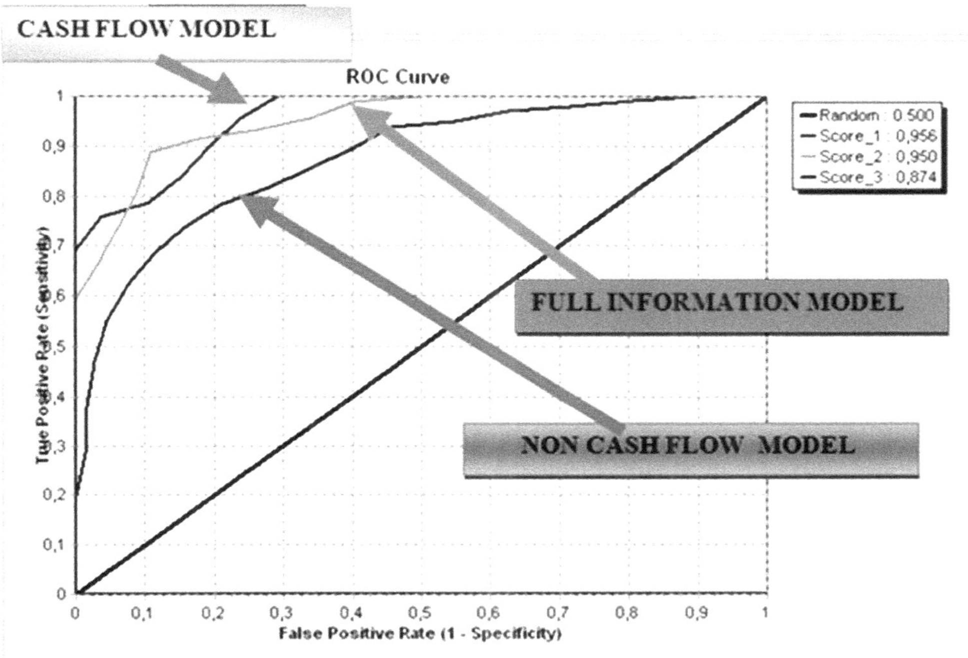

5. Conclusion

Commercial banks that grant client borrower loans need consistent models that can correctly detect and predict defaults. Moonasar (2007) emphasized that the one of the fundamental tasks which any bank has to deal with, in the current competitive and turbulent business environment, is to reduce its credit risk. Traditionally, we employ scoring methods to estimate the credit worthiness of a credit applicant. In fact, the quantitative method known as credit scoring has been developed for the credit assessment problem (Yang, 2002). Credit scoring is basically an application of classification methods, which classify borrower into different risk groups. The objective of Scoring methods is to predict the probability that a borrower or counterparty will default (Komor´ad, 2002). In credit risk evaluation, Credit scoring is a key methods, that help financial institution to make decision whether or not to grant credit to customer Thomas (2002). According to Moonasar (2007) "a common approach of credit scoring is to apply a classification technique on data of previous customers (both good credit customers and delinquent customers) in order to find a relationship between the customers characteristics and potential failure to service their debt. Institutions use credit scoring techniques (utilizing information from the consumers past credit history and current economic conditions) to determine which applicants will pay back their liabilities". An accurate classifier is necessary to differentiate between new potential good and bad credit applicant.

In this article we evaluate the credit risk for a Tunisian bank through modelling the default risk of its short term loans. We used a data base of 924 credit files from 2003 to 2006. In our evaluation, a K- Nearest Neighbor classifier algorithm was conducted and we tested using different values of k (2, 3,4 and 5). The criterion used for assessing performance is the minimization of the bad risk rate. We build up three types of K-NN classifier:

❶ The first classifier is non cash-flows model

❷ The second classifier is cash-flows model

❸ The third classifier is full information model

The main results show that the best K-NN with k=3 for the three models, and the best global classification rate is in order of 88.63% (second classifier). Moreover, to evaluate the performance of the model curve ROC is plotted. The result shows that the AUC (**A**rea **U**nder **C**urve) criterion is in order of 95.6%. Our study is, however, incomplete in the sense that it didn't show how one can use these results in the implementation of the Basel II or III accord in Tunisia.

References

Abid, F. & A. Zouari (2000) "Financial distress prediction using neural networks", http://ssrn.com/abstract=355980 or DOI: 10.2139/ssrn.355980.

Abramowicz, W. M. Nowak, J. Sztykiel (2003) "Bayesian networks as a decision support tool in credit scoring domain", Idea Group Publishing

Altman, E. I. (1968) "Financial ratios, discriminant analysis and the prediction of corporate bankruptcy", *Journal of Finance* , vol. 23: 589–609

Anderson, D.R., Sweeney, D.J., Freeman, J., Williams T.A. & Shoesmith, E. (2007) "Statistics for business and economics", London: *Thomson Learning EMEA*

Antonakis, A. C. & Sfakianakis, M. E. (2009) "Assessing naive bayes as a method for screening credit applicants", *Journal of Applied Statistics*, vol. 36: 537-545

Atiya, A.F. (2001) "Bankruptcy prediction for credit risk using neural nets: a survey and new results", *IEEE Transactions on Neural Nets*, vol. 12 (4): 929-935

Baesens, B., Van Gestel, T., Viaene, S., Stepanova, M., Suykens, J. & Vanthienen, J. (2003) "Benchmarking state-of-the-art classification algorithms for credit scoring", *Journal of the Operational Research Society*, vol. 54 (6): 627–635

Beaver, W. (1966) "Financial ratios as predictors of failure. Empirical research in accounting: Selected studies", *Journal of Accounting Research,* vol. 5: 71–111

Berk Bekiroglu Hidayet Takci1 & Utku Can Ekinci (2011) " Bank credit risk analysis with bayesian network decision tool" *International Journal Of Advanced Engineering Sciences And Technologies,* vol. 9, no. 2: 273-279

Berry. M.J.A. & Linoff, G.S (1997) *Data mining techniques for marketing, sales, and customer support*, John Wiley & Sons, Inc.

Berstein, L. A. & Wild J.J. (1998) *Financial statement analysis: theory, application, and interpretation*, sixth Edition, McGraw-Hill

Bogess, W. P. (1967) "Screen -test your credit risks", *Harvard Business Review*, vol. 45, no. 6: 113-122

Bradley, A.P. (1997) "The use of the area under the ROC curve in the evaluation of machine learning algorithms", *Pattern Recogn*, vol. 30(7): 1145-1159

Çinko, M. (2006) "Comparison of credit scoring tecniques: Istanbul ticaret üniversitesi sosyal bilimler", *Dergisi,* vol. 9: 143-153

Crouhy, M.; Galai, D.; Mark, R. (2000) "A comparative analysis of current credit risk models", *Journal of Banking and Finance,* vol. 24, no. 1: 59-117

Davis R. H., Edelman, D.B. & Gammerman, A.J. (1992) "Machine learning algorithms for credit-card applications", *IMA Journal of Management Mathematics*, vol. 4: 43-51

Davutyan, N. & Özar, S. (2006) "A credit scoring model for Turkey's micro & small enterprises (MSE's)," *13th Annual ERF Conference, Kuwait*, 16 – 18 December 2006

Demerjian, P. R. W (2007) "Financial ratios and credit risk: the selection of financial ratio covenants in debt contracts", working paper, workshop Stephen M. Ross School of Business University of Michigan, January 11

Desai, V. S., Crook, J. N. & Overstreet, G. A. (1996) "A comparison of neural networks and linear scoring models in the credit union environment", *European Journal of Operational Research*, vol. 95(1): 24–37

Diamond, D.W (1984) "Financial intermediation and delegated monitoring", *Review of Economic Studies*, vol. 51: 393–414

Dichev, I. & Skinner, D. (2002) "Large-sample evidence on the debt covenant hypothesis", *Journal of Accounting Research*, vol. 40 (4): 1091-1123

El-Shazly, A. (2002) "Financial distress and early warning signals: a non-parametric approach with application to Egypt", *9th Annual ERF Conference*, Emirates, October 2002

Fawcett, T. (2006) "Roc analysis in pattern recognition", *Pattern Recognition Letters*, vol. 27; no. 8: 861-874

Galindo, J. & Tamayo, P. (2000) "Credit risk assessment using statistical and MachineLearning: basic methodology and risk modeling applications", *Computational Econ*omics, vol. 15(1-2): 107- 143

Hand, D. J. (1997) *Construction and assessment of classification rules*, Wiley series in probability and statistics, John Wiley & Sons

Hand, J. & Henley, W. (1997) "Statistical classification methods in consumer credit scoring", *Computer Journal of the Royal Statistical Society Series a Statistics in Society*", vol. 160, no. 3: 523-541

Hanley, J.A. & McNeil, B.J. (1982) "The meaning and use of the area under a receiver operating characteristic (ROC) curve", *Radiology*, vol. 143: 29–36

Hellwig, M. (2000) "Financial intermediation with risk aversion", *Review of Economic Studies*, vol. 67(4): 719–742

Hellwig M. (2001) "Risk aversion and incentive compatibility with ex post information Asymmetry", *Economic Theory*, vol. 18 (2):415–438.

Henley, W.E. & Hand, D.J. (1997) "Statistical classification methods in consumer credit scoring: a review", *Journal of the Royal Statistical Society. Series A* (Statistics in society), vol. 160, no. 3: 523- 541

Henley, W. E. & Hand, D. J. (1996) "A k-Nearest-Neighbour classifier for assessing consumer credit risk", *The Statistician*, vol. 45(1): 77

Karaa,A. & Krichène, A. (2012) "Credit–risk assessment using support vectors machine and multilayer neural network models: a comparative study case of a Tunisian bank", *Accounting and Management Information Systems,* vol. 11, no. 4: 587–620

Karel.J. (2006) "Agency theory approach to the contracting between lender and borrower" *Acta Oeconomica Pragensia,* 14/3

Kay, J. & Titterington, M. (eds) (2000) "*Statistics and Neural Nets, Advances at the Interface"*, Oxford University Press

Komorad, K. (2002) "On credit scoring estimation", Institute for statistics and econometrics, Humboldt University, Berlin

Lee, T. & Chen, I. (2005) "A two-stage hybrid credit scoring model using artificial neural networks and multivariate adaptive regression splines", *Expert Systems with Applications*, vol. 28(4): 743–752

Lee, T., Chiu, C., Lu, C. & Chen, I. (2002) "Credit scoring using the hybrid neural discriminant technique", *Expert Systems with Applications*, vol. 23(3): 245-254

Lundholm, R. & Sloan, R. (2004) *Equity valuation & analysis*, New York; McGraw-Hill/Irwin

Martens, D., Van Gestel, T., De Backer, M., Haesen, R., Vanthienen, J. & Baesens, B. (2009) "Credit rating prediction using ant colony optimization", *Journal of the Operational Research Society*, vol. 61(4): 561–573

Matoussi, H. & Abdelmoula,A. (2009) "Using a neural network-based methodology for credit–risk evaluation of a Tunisian bank", *Middle Eastern Finance and Economics* Issue 4

Matoussi, H. & Krichène Abdelmoula, A. (2010) "Credit risk evaluation of a Tunisian commercial: Bank: logistic regression versus Neural Network Modelling", *Accounting and Management Information Systems*, vol. 9, no. 1

Matoussi, H., Mouelhi, R. & Salah, S. (1999) "La prédiction de faillite des entreprises tunisiennes par la régression logistique", *Revue Tunisienne des Sciences de Gestion*, vol. 1: 90-106

Mcculloch, W. & Pitts, W. (1943) "A logical calculus of the ideas immanent in nervous activity", *Bulletin of Mathematical Biophysic*, vol. 5: 115-133

Merton, R. (1974) "On the pricing of corporate debt: The risk structure of interest rates," *Journal of Finance*, vol. 29: 449-470

Mileris, R. (2010) "Estimation of loan applicants default probability applying discriminant analysis and simple bayesian classifier", *Economics and Management*, vol. 15: 1078-1084

Moonasar, V. (2007) "Credit risk analysis using artificial intelligence: evidence from a leading South African banking institution", *Research Report: Mbl3*

Ohlson, J. A. (1980) "Financial ratios and the probabilistic prediction of bankruptcy", *Journal of Accounting Research*, vol. 18: 109-131

Okan veli şafakli (2007) "Credit risk assessment for the banking sector of Northern Cyprus", Banks and Bank Systems, vol. 2

Palepu K.G., Healy, P.M. & Bernard, V.L. (2000) *Business analysis & valuation using financial Statements*, second Edition, South – Western College Publishing

Pranab Kumar D. G., Radha Krishna, P., (2013) «Database management system oracle SQL AND PL/SQL" *PHI Learning Pvt. Ltd.*, 576 pages

Provost, F. & Fawcett, T. (1997) "Analysis and visualization of classifier performance: Comparison under imprecise class and cost distributions", In: *Proc. Third Internat. Conf. on Knowledge Discovery and Data Mining (KDD-97). AAAI Press, Menlo Park*

Provost, F., Fawcett, T. & Kohavi, R. (1998) "The case against accuracy estimation for comparing induction algorithms", In: Shavlik, J. (Ed.) *Proc. ICML-98. Morgan* Kaufmann, San Francisco, Available from: <http://www.purl.org/NET/tfawcett/papers/ICML98-final.ps.gz>.

Quinlan, J. R. (1992) *C4.5 "programs for machine learning"*, Morgan Kaufmann Publishers Inc., California

Rafiul, H., Marufhossain, M., Bailey, J. & Kotagiri Ramamohanarao (2008) "Improving k-Nearest Neighbour classification with distance functions based on receiver operating characteristics", *Proceeding ECML PKDD '08 Proceedings of the 2008 European Conference on Machine Learning and Knowledge Discovery in Databases* - Part I, pp. 489-504, Springer-Verlag Berlin Heidelberg

Ravinder, S. & Aggarwal, R.R. (2011) "Comparative Evaluation of Predictive Modeling Techniques on Credit Card Data", *International Journal of Computer Theory and Engineering*, vol. 3, no. 5

Raymond, A. (2007) *The Credit Scoring Toolkit: Theory and Practice for Retail Credit Risk Management and Decision Automation*, Oxford University Press, United States of America, 1st edition.

Revsine, L., Collins, D.W. & Johnson, W.B. (1999) *Financial Statement and Analysis*, Prentice Hall, New Jersey.

Rosner, B.A. (2006) *Fundamental of Biostatistics*, Taunton: Quebecor World

Rumelhart, D.E., Hinton, G.E. & McClelland, J.L. (1986) "A general framework for parallel distributed processing", In "Parallel Distributed Processing: explorations in the microstructure of cognition", vol. 1, pp. 45-75

Sarkar, S. & Sriram, R.S. (2001) "Bayesian models for early warning of bank failures", *Management Science*, vol. 47(11): 1457-1475

Seval, S. (2008) "Credit risk and Basel II", Credit Risk Solutions Inforsense

Smith, C. & Warner, J. (1979) "On financial contracting", *Journal of Financial Economics,* vol. 7: 117-161

Spackman, K.A. (1989) "Signal detection theory: Valuable tools for evaluating inductive learning", In: Proc. Sixth Internat. Workshop on Machine Learning, Morgan Kaufman, San Mateo, CA, pp. 160-163.

Steenackers, A. & Goovaerts, M.J. (1989) "A credit scoring model for personal loans", *Insurance Mathematics and Economics*, vol. 8: 31-34

Sun, L. & Shenoy, P. (2007) "Using bayesian networks for bankruptcy prediction", *European Journal of Operational Research*, vol. 180, no. 2: 738-753

Thomas, L. C., Edelman, D. B. & Crook, J. N. (2002) *Credit scoring & its applications*, *Society for Industrial Mathematics*, Philadelphia, 1st edition.

Thomas, L.C. (2002) "A survey of credit and behavioral scoring: forecasting financial risk of lending to consumers", *International Journal of Forecasting*, vol. 15: 149-172

Townsend, R. M. (1979) "Optimal contracts and competitive markets with costly state verification", *Journal of Economic Theory*, vol.21 (2): 265-293

Vera L. M., Dries F.B. & Van den Poel, D. (2012) "Enhanced decision support in credit scoring using bayesian binary quantile regression", Working Paper August

West, D. (2000) "Neural network credit scoring", *Computer & Operations Research*, vol. 27 (11): 1131-1152

West, D. (2000) "Neural network credit scoring model", *Computational Operation Research* vol. 27: 1131-1152

Yang, L. (2002) "The evaluation of classification models for credit scoring", Working Paper no. 02/2002 Edit. Matthias Schumann University of Göttingen Institute of computer science

Zhang, D., Huang, H., Chen, Q. & Jiang, Y. (2007) "Comparison of credit scoring models", *Third international conference of Natural Computation*, vol. 1

APPENDIX

APPENDIX 1: NON CASH FLOW MODEL

Panel 1: K-NN with k=2

Supervised Learning 1 (K-NN)

Parameters

k-NN parameters

Neighbors	2
Distance	Euclidian

Results

Classifier performances

Error rate	0,2165

Values prediction

Value	Recall	1-Precision
RISKY	0,7854	0,2146
HEALTHY	0,7817	0,2183

Confusion matrix

	RISKY	HEALTHY	Sum
RISKY	366	100	466
HEALTHY	100	358	458
Sum	466	458	924

Panel 2: K-NN with k=3

Supervised Learning 1 (K-NN)

Parameters

k-NN parameters

Neighbors	3
Distance	Euclidian

Results

Classifier performances

Error rate	0,1861

Values prediction

Value	Recall	1-Precision
RISKY	0,8326	0,1950
HEALTHY	0,7948	0,1765

Confusion matrix

	RISKY	HEALTHY	Sum
RISKY	388	78	466
HEALTHY	94	364	458
Sum	482	442	924

Panel 3: K-NN with k=4

Supervised Learning 1 (K-NN)

Parameters

k-NN parameters

Neighbors	4
Distance	Euclidian

Results

Classifier performances

Error rate	0,2684

Values prediction

Value	Recall	1-Precision
RISKY	0,7382	0,2681
HEALTHY	0,7249	0,2687

Confusion matrix

	RISKY	HEALTHY	Sum
RISKY	344	122	466
HEALTHY	126	332	458
Sum	470	454	924

Panel 4: K-NN with k=5

Supervised Learning 1 (K-NN)

Parameters

k-NN parameters

Neighbors	5
Distance	Euclidian

Results

Classifier performances

Error rate	0,2716

Values prediction

Value	Recall	1-Precision
RISKY	0,7339	0,2708
HEALTHY	0,7227	0,2725

Confusion matrix

	RISKY	HEALTHY	Sum
RISKY	342	124	466
HEALTHY	127	331	458
Sum	469	455	924

APPENDIX 2: CASH FLOW MODEL

Panel 1: K-NN with k=2

Supervised Learning 1 (K-NN)

Parameters

k-NN parameters

Neighbors 2

Distance HEOM

Results

Classifier performances

Error rate	0,1320

Values prediction

Value	Recall	1-Precision
RISKY	0,8734	0,1340
HEALTHY	0,8624	0,1300

Confusion matrix

	RISKY	HEALTHY	Sum
RISKY	407	59	466
HEALTHY	63	395	458
Sum	470	454	924

Panel 2: K-NN with k=3

Supervised Learning 8 (K-NN)

Parameters

k-NN parameters

Neighbors 3

Distance HEOM

Results

Classifier performances

Error rate	0,1136

Values prediction

Value	Recall	1-Precision
RISKY	0,8798	0,1068
HEALTHY	0,8930	0,1204

Confusion matrix

	RISKY	HEALTHY	Sum
RISKY	410	56	466
HEALTHY	49	409	458
Sum	459	465	924

Panel 3: K-NN with k=4

Supervised Learning 6 (K-NN)

Parameters

k-NN parameters

Neighbors	4
Distance	HEOM

Results

Classifier performances

Error rate	0,1548

Values prediction

Value	Recall	1-Precision
RISKY	0,8455	0,1527
HEALTHY	0,8450	0,1569

Confusion matrix

	RISKY	HEALTHY	Sum
RISKY	394	72	466
HEALTHY	71	387	458
Sum	465	459	924

Panel 4: K-NN with k=5

Supervised Learning 7 (K-NN)

Parameters

k-NN parameters

Neighbors	5
Distance	HEOM

Results

Classifier performances

Error rate	0,1894

Values prediction

Value	Recall	1-Precision
RISKY	0,8026	0,1816
HEALTHY	0,8188	0,1970

Confusion matrix

	RISKY	HEALTHY	Sum
RISKY	374	92	466
HEALTHY	83	375	458
Sum	457	467	924

APPENDIX 3: FULL INFORMATION MODEL

Panel 1: K-NN with k=2

Supervised Learning 1 (K-NN)

Parameters

k-NN parameters

Neighbors 2

Distance HEOM

Results

Classifier performances

Error rate	0,1450

Values prediction

Value	Recall	1-Precision
RISKY	0,8519	0,1407
HEALTHY	0,8581	0,1494

Confusion matrix

	RISKY	HEALTHY	Sum
RISKY	397	69	466
HEALTHY	65	393	458
Sum	462	462	924

Panel 2: K-NN with k=3

Supervised Learning 2 (K-NN)

Parameters

k-NN parameters

Neighbors 3

Distance HEOM

Results

Classifier performances

Error rate	0,1310

Values prediction

Value	Recall	1-Precision
RISKY	0,8519	0,1158
HEALTHY	0,8865	0,1453

Confusion matrix

	RISKY	HEALTHY	Sum
RISKY	397	69	466
HEALTHY	52	406	458
Sum	449	475	924

Panel 3: K-NN with k=4

Supervised Learning 3 (K-NN)

Parameters

k-NN parameters

Neighbors	4
Distance	HEOM

Results

Classifier performances

Error rate			0,1905			
Values prediction			**Confusion matrix**			
Value	**Recall**	**1-Precision**		**RISKY**	**HEALTHY**	**Sum**
RISKY	0,7876	0,1734	**RISKY**	367	99	466
HEALTHY	0,8319	0,2063	**HEALTHY**	77	381	458
			Sum	444	480	924

Panel 4: K-NN with k=5

Supervised Learning 4 (K-NN)

Parameters

k-NN parameters

Neighbors	5
Distance	HEOM

Results

Classifier performances

Error rate			0,2035			
Values prediction			**Confusion matrix**			
Value	**Recall**	**1-Precision**		**RISKY**	**HEALTHY**	**Sum**
RISKY	0,7575	0,1752	**RISKY**	353	113	466
HEALTHY	0,8362	0,2278	**HEALTHY**	75	383	458
			Sum	428	496	924

[1] "Sound Credit Risk Assessment and Valuation for Loans », Consultative Document, Bank for International Settlements Press & Communications, Basel (November 2005).

[2] *k*-Nearest Neighbors

[3] BIAT :Banque Internationale Arabe de Tunisie

[4] See (Karaa & Krichène, 2012 ; Matoussi & Abdelmoula, 2009)

9

The usefulness of accounting information on financial instruments to investors assessing non-financial companies: An empirical analysis on the Bucharest Stock Exchange

Maria Carmen Huian [a,1]

[a] *Alexandru Ioan Cuza University of Iaşi, Romania*

Abstract: The aim of this paper is to study the value relevance of IFRS-based accounting information regarding financial instruments provided by non-financial Romanian groups quoted on Bucharest Stock Exchange for the period 2011-2013. Data from both consolidated and parent-only accounts are tested using a modified Ohlson model to show the empirical correlation between stock market prices and accounting numbers. We find that at parent company level, the information about financial assets is more value relevant than the one about financial liabilities. At group level, investors rely mostly on information about financial assets, ignoring the one about financial liabilities. Moreover, results show the superiority of parent company's individual accounts over the consolidated ones in terms of value relevance of financial instruments information.

Keywords: financial instruments, value relevance, IFRS, regression analysis

1. Introduction

In the Conceptual Framework for Financial Reporting, the International Accounting Standards Board (IASB), states that the primary objective of general purpose financial reporting is to provide useful information about the reporting entity to investors and creditors to enable them to make proper economic decisions.

[1] *Corresponding author*: Maria Carmen Huian, Department of Accounting, Information Systems and Statistics, e-mail: maria.huian@uaic.ro

To meet this objective, accounting information must be relevant and representational faithful. Whether this goal is achieved or not has become a recurrent theme of research in the accounting field. There is a significant stream of literature that investigates the role played by the accounting information provided through financial statements in market-based economies, known as value relevance research (Holthausen & Watts, 2001 and Beisland, 2009 provide comprehensive literature reviews on the subject of value relevance).

Value relevance is defined as the ability of accounting information to capture and summarize information that determines the firm's value (Francis & Schipper, 1999). For an investor, accounting information is value relevant if it is reflected in stock prices and/or stock returns. For a value relevance researcher, accounting information is value relevant if it is empirically connected to financial market equity prices/returns (or changes in these prices/returns). The stronger the correlation to market prices, the more value relevant accounting information is (Filip & Raffournier, 2010).

Our study investigates value relevance of accounting information about financial instruments reported by non-financial Romanian groups. This is of particular importance as, according to Beaver (2002) single country studies are preferrable to cross-country ones because they are based on a more in-depth knowledge of national standard-setting bodies and allow for a better control of institutional, socio-economic and political factors that affect the companies' reporting and the investing behaviour. Moreover, Romania is an Eastern-European country, with a less developed capital market and an original process of IFRS adoption that provides an interesting setting for value relevance research.

Firstly, we examine the connection between stock market price and financial instruments information at both individual and consolidated level. Accounting for financial instruments has been a strongly debated subject for more than 20 years already. Although it raises more interest among financial institution, it is also a matter of concern for non-financial firms companies. The voice of non-financial firms was heard pretty loudly at the discussions about the new IFRS 9 "Financial instruments". They sent 13% of all comment letters to the IASB exposure draft ED/2009/7 "Financial instruments: classification and measurement" (Huian, 2013a) and 14% to the ED/2009/12 "Amortized cost and impairment of financial assets" (Huian, 2013b). These responses represent a recognition of the significant impact of financial instruments (and their corresponding accounting and reporting rules) on their financial position and performance. We believe that this is also applicable to Romanian companies that, to our knowledge, have not been involved in the aforementioned debates so far.

Secondly, we examine whether information about financial instruments provided through consolidated financial statements is deemed by investors more useful than the one from the individual accounts of the parent company. There has been a longstanding debate in financial reporting theory about which set of financial statements provide more meaningful information (for this paper, meaningful is synonymous to value relevant): consolidated accounts or unconsolidated accounts of the parent company? According to the entity approach, the group is the dominant economic unit and thus, consolidated accounts are deemed to be the most suitable format for providing information about the financial position and performance of the parent (Abad *et al.*, 2000). We believe that this is not applicable to Romania, where consolidated statements are quite a recent requirement to which investors are less accustomed.

The findings of the 1st test show that, at parent company level, the information about financial assets is more value relevant than the one about financial liabilities. As far as consolidated accounts are concerned, investors rely only on information about financial assets, ignoring the one about financial liabilities. The 2nd test reports a superiority of parent company's individual accounts over the consolidated ones in terms of value relevance of financial instruments information.

Our contribution to the literature mainly consists of: i) addressing the subject of value relevance of accounting information provided by both consolidated and parent's individual accounts in emerging markets such as Romania. We contribute to the debate regarding consolidated versus unconsolidated financial statements in Europe, in general, and in emerging markets, in particular; ii) investigating the impact of financial instruments information on the price of non-financial companies' equity instead of the usual emphasis on the financial industry (as dominant user of financial instruments); iii) assessing value relevance of all financial instruments information. To our knowledge, prior studies addressed only financial instruments at fair value; iv) extending previous studies on one of the most controversial and debated accounting issue in the last decades: accounting and financial reporting of financial instruments.

The rest of the paper is organized as follows: section 2 deals with the literature review and the development of the 2 research hypotheses, section 3 describes the data used and the corresponding statistics, while section 4 discusses the results. Section 5 concludes the paper.

2. Literature review and hypotheses development

Value relevance literature has known a tremendous development over the last 20 years. Analyzing the explanatory power of several accounting variables (computed according to local GAAP) on stock prices, a significant number of studies report that earnings and cash flows are value relevant. Examples include Barth *et al.* (1996), Lev and Sougiannis (1996) and Ayers (1998). Others tackle the subject of the effects of the IFRS adoption on the accounting information quality, by comparing it to accounting numbers resulting from national standards. Some examples are Hung and Subramanyam (2007) for the IFRS adoption in Germany; Callao *et al.* (2007) for Spain, Morais and Curto (2008) for Portugal; Leonrmand and Touchais (2009) for France; Iatridis (2010) for Great Britan, and Klimczak, (2011) for Poland. They show mixed findings, consisting of weak evidence or no. evidence at all on the improvement of value relevance due to the adoption of a new accounting system – the IFRS.

Our paper investigates an emergent economy from Eastern Europe. These economies provide an institutional and accounting setting that favors the unambiguous prediction of value relevance testing results. According to Hellstrom (2006), the possibility of confirming the predicted results (which is higher in emergent countries) is a supportive evidence of the validity of value relevance methodology, enabling the development of the theoretical aspect of the research. Our paper is to be included in the current stream of literature on Eastern European countries, alongside other studies such as: Polish market (Grabinski *et al.*, 2014), Czech market (Hellstrom, 2006), and Baltic States market (Jarmalaite Pritchard, 2002).

In Romania, value relevance is investigated by Filip and Raffournier (2010) and Takacs (2012) who study the association between stock market prices and earnings reported by companies listed on the Bucharest Stock Exchange. They find a rather limited level of value relevance. More recently, Mironiuc *et al.* (2015) examine the value relevance of the comprehensive income in relation to that of net income, after the IFRS adoption in Romania in 2012. They find an increase in value relevance that could also be explained by the influence of the auditing performed by the Big 4 companies.

Value relevance literature dealing with financial instruments indicate a better correlation between fair value amounts and stock prices than that of historical cost figures (Barth, 1994; Ahmed *et al.*, 2006; Koonce *et al.*, 2011). Other studies argue that quality disclosures of financial instrument are value relevant (Venkatachalam, 1996, Kolev, 2009; Song *et al.*, 2010).

Based on the previously presented state of knowledge, we consider that our research extends a rather scant value relevance literature regarding both the Romanian capital market and the financial instruments information reported by non-financial companies. To our knowledge, value relevance of financial instruments information has never been addressed in Romania before. Instead of investigating value relevance in general, we choose to test value relevance of financial instruments information for both consolidated and parent's individual accounts. This leads to our first hypothesis:

> **H_1**: *Information about financial instruments reported in the financial statements of non-financial companies is value relevant.*

Although not explicitly stated as part of H_1, we also test the value relevance of financial instruments information by grouping the entities according to their results (i.e. profit or loss). In order to prepare the field for the second hypothesis, we further develop H_1 in 2 sub-hypotheses, tested separately:

> **H_{1a}**: *Information about financial instruments reported in the individual financial statements of a parent company is value relevant.*
> **H_{1b}**: *Information about financial instruments reported in the consolidated financial statements is value relevant.*

With the development of groups of companies in the USA, towards the end of the 19th century, financial reporting shifted its focus from individual financial statements to consolidated accounts (Epstein & Jermakowicz, 2010). This paradigm change has made that the USA and UK no. longer require publication of the parent's separate financial statements. Nevertheless, many countries require a dual reporting: parent companies must provide separate financial statements but, at the same time, they have the obligation to prepare consolidated accounts. Each set of accounts meets different reporting demands. According to Goncharov *et al.* (2009), group accounts exist to provide a faithful representation of the entity's financial position, while the single accounts exist not only to inform about the financial position but are the starting point both for taxation and computation of distributable income.

The existence of dual reporting provides an interesting research field for value relevance scholars all over the world. Previous studies that have investigated which statements are more important show mixed results. On the one hand, some have agreed that consolidated statements are more value relevant than parent's unconsolidated statements. Niskanen *et al.* (1998), using a sample of 35 Finnish companies, conclude that consolidated data is more informative than the parent-only earnings. Abad *et al.* (2000) investigate the topic on Spanish listed companies suggesting that consolidated financial statements provide incremental value relevant information over parent-only accounts. A study conducted by Okuda and Shiiba (2006) in Japan finds that subsidiary return on equity affects stock returns more than the parent-only returns. Goncharov *et al.* (2009) examine the German companies, pointing to higher predictive ability, value relevance and timeliness of consolidated accounts as well as higher earnings management in individual accounts. Muller (2011) studies value relevance of consolidated and parent company accounting information of listed entities on the largest 3 stock markets in Europe and reports an increase in superiority of the relevance of consolidated statements (in the detriment of individual ones). On the other hand, other studies find weak or no. evidence of value relevance superiority of the consolidated accounts. Darrough and Harris (1991) argue that consolidated statements provide very little incremental information content in Japan. Harris (1997) obtain the same result while using data from German companies. Srinivasan and Narasimhan (2012) find that annual consolidated statements of 59 Indian groups are not value relevant, whereas annual parent-only financial statements are.

In Romania, as well as in other European countries, until recently, the reporting of consolidated financial statements has been the exception rather than the rule (Abad *et al.*, 2000). To be more precise, in Romania consolidated reporting practice has existed for no. more than 2 decades (Malciu & Feleagă, 2004). Even though several orders issued by the Ministry of Finance (such as Order 772/2000 or Order 1752/2005) approved rules regarding consolidation and consolidated accounts, it was not until 2007 that the Accounting Law no. 82/1991 imposed sanctions for failing to prepare and publish annual consolidated financial statements. 2007 is also the year of Romania's adhesion to the European Union and, consequently, the starting date of the mandatory application of the IFRS in the consolidated financial statements of the listed groups. Therefore, investors are not very accustomed to this type of reporting and, we expect, pay less attention to consolidated information. This leads to our second hypothesis:

> **H_2**: *Information about financial instruments reported in the individual financial statements of the parent company is deemed more value relevant by investors than the one provided by the consolidated financial statements.*

To confirm the 2nd hypothesis, the explanatory power of model used for Sample A, unconsolidated accounts, quantified by adjusted R^2, must be greater than the explanatory power of sample B's model.

3. Data and descriptive statistics

This section deals with the financial data used in the research and the most significant descriptive statistics.

3.1 Financial data

The population consists of all non-financial groups listed on the main board of Bucharest Stock Exchange (BSE) in 2012 (the year of the IFRS mandatory application in the individual accounts). The financial groups are excluded as they have a different structure and follow different accounting practices from the non-financial firms (Hellstrom, 2006). A breakdown of data by industries is presented in table 1.

Table 1. Composition of data by industry

Groups by industry	Number of groups	Firm-year observations (financial statements)	
		Consolidated	Individual
Mining and quarrying	2	6	6
Manufacturing	12	36	36
Electricity, gas, steam supply	1	3	3
Construction	3	9	9
Wholesale and retail trade	3	9	9
Accommodation and food service	2	6	6
Total	***23***	***69***	***69***

Financial data is hand-collected from the annual consolidated financial statements and the parent's separate financial statements available on the companies' websites and/or the BSE's website. The chosen period is 2011-2013 to ensure the comparability of the accounting data. Even though 2012 is the first year of the IFRS mandatory application in the individual accounts, the 2012 financial statements include restated data for 2011 according to the new rules. 2013 is the only year included in our analysis in which IFRS were used as basis of accounting. Therefore, all data is prepared based on the IFRS. Only companies that have been listed on the BSE for the whole period analyzed are included. Stock market prices are also hand-collected from the BSE's website. In addition, price is taken as of 30th of June next year in order to ensure that both consolidated and separate annual reports are publicly available.

As the main purpose is to demonstrate that investors use information about financial instruments when assessing a non-financial company's value, all consolidated and individual statements of financial positions are reclassified to properly show the application of IAS 39 "Financial instruments: recognition and measurement". The IAS 39's version endorsed by the European Commission is used, and not IFRS 9 "Financial instruments", that is yet to be adopted. The reclassification consists of dividing assets and liabilities into 2 major classes: financial assets within the scope of IAS 39 (FAIAS39) and all the other assets that are considered non-financial assets (NFA); the same goes for liabilities: financial liabilities within the scope of IAS 39 (FLIAS39) and non-financial liabilities (NFL). These data are structured following both IAS 39 and IFRS 7 "Financial instruments: disclosures", as the information from the balance sheets is doubled by the one provided in the footnotes.

3.2 Descriptive statistics

Table 2 provides descriptive statistics on the relative size of financial assets and financial liabilities from 69 individual and 69 consolidated observations. Compared to total assets and liabilities, the mean financial assets and liabilities within the scope of IAS 39 (FAIAS39 and FLIAS39) are about 21% (22% at consolidated level) and 73% (76% at consolidated level), respectively. While non-financial assets (NFA) represent the most consistent portion of total assets, financial liabilities (FLIAS39) are the majority of total liabilities. The results regarding financial assets are comparable to those reported by Gebhardt (2012).

Table 2. Relative size of financial assets and financial liabilities

Variables N	Mean	Median	Std. Deviation	Minimum	Maximum
NFA/Total Assets	0.7832	0.8335	0.19418	0.0360	0.9946
FAIAS39/Total Assets	0.2056	0.1664	0.17139	0.0054	0.6990
NFL/Total Liabilities	0.2675	0.2092	0.19131	0.0214	0.7380
FLIAS39/Total Liabilities	0.7324	0.7907	0.19131	0.2620	0.9786
Variables C_N	**Mean**	**Median**	**Std. Deviation**	**Minimum**	**Maximum**
C_NFA/Total Assets	0.7773	0.8312	0.17669	0.3138	0.9917
C_FAIAS39/Total Assets	0.2226	0.1688	0.17669	0.0083	0.6862
C_NFL/Total Liabilities	0.2661	0.1984	0.25479	0.0244	1.5905
C_FLIAS39/Total Liabilities	0.7569	0.8016	0.17335	0.2885	0.9756

N = Number of observations - 69 Individual Financial Statements
C_N = Number of observations - 69 Consolidated Financial Statements
NFA and NFL indicate non-financial assets and liabilities. FAIAS39 and FLIAS39 are financial assets and financial liabilities within the scope of IAS 39. C_NFA/C_NFL, C_FAIAS39/C_FLIAS39 are the same abbreviations for the consolidated accounts.

In this paper, financial assets within the scope of IAS 39 (FAIAS39) fall in one of the 4 categories: receivables, derivative assets, other investments, cash and cash equivalents. In most cases, receivables and cash & cash equivalents are the only types of financial assets. Accordingly, financial liabilities within the scope of IAS 39 (FLIAS39) are divided into: accounts payable, derivative liabilities and debt. Overall, derivative liabilities are almost non-existent. Table 3 provides descriptive statistics on the relative size of receivables, cash & cash equivalents, accounts payable and debt from 69 individual and 69 consolidated observations.

Table 3. Relative size of major categories of financial assets and liabilities

Variables N	Mean	Median	Std. Deviation	Minimum	Maximum
Receivables/FAIAS39	0.7111	0.8080	0.26481	0.0723	0.9901
Cash/FAIAS39	0.2328	0.1710	0.21894	0.0099	0.9201
Accounts Payable/FLIAS39	0.4677	0.4005	0.30089	0.0346	1.0000
Debt/FLIAS39	0.4940	0.5654	0.31649	0.0000	0.9422
Variables C_N	**Mean**	**Median**	**Std. Deviation**	**Minimum**	**Maximum**
C_Receivables/FAIAS39	0.7137	0.8036	0.25210	0.0526	0.9809
C_Cash/FAIAS39	0.2487	0.1877	0.21552	0.0186	0.9203
C_Accounts Payable/FLIAS39	0.4475	0.3676	0.28574	0.0357	1.0000
C_Debt/FLIAS39	0.5070	0.5844	0.29088	0.0000	0.9643

N = Number of observations - 69 individual financial statements
C_N = Number of observations - 69 consolidated financial statements
FAIAS39 and FLIAS39 are financial assets and financial liabilities within the scope of IAS 39. C_FAIAS39/C_FLIAS39 are the same abbreviations for consolidated accounts.

According to the data in table 3, the most significant financial asset reported by non-financial companies are receivables with a mean of 71% (for both individual and consolidated level), while mean financial liabilities are almost equally split between accounts payable (47% - individual data and 45% - consolidated data) and debt (49%, 51% respectively).

Table 4 provides descriptive statistics on the variables used to test value relevance of accounting information regarding financial instruments under IFRS. All variables are per-share numbers.

Table 4. Per share value of financial and non-financial assets, financial and non-financial liabilities

Sample A Individual Statements		Variables	Sample B Consolidated Statements	
Mean	Std Deviation		Mean	Std Deviation
0,6867	2,8016	NFA	0,6950	2,7648
0,1207	4,4712	FAIAS39	0,1377	4,1315
0,0651	3,3965	NFL	0,0620	3,5037
0,2205	5,0312	FLIAS39	0,2454	4,7829
0,1810	4,0171	Price	0,1858	4,0269

NFA and NFL - non-financial assets and liabilities. FAIAS39 and FLIAS39 - financial assets and financial liabilities within the scope of IAS 39. All amounts are per share numbers.

The mean of non-financial assets (NFA), which is 0.69 for individual statements of the parent company (sample A), is more than 5 times higher than the mean of financial assets within the scope of IAS 39 (FAIAS39), which is 0.12 (the same goes for consolidated accounts – sample B). In terms of liabilities, the situation is reversed. Financial liabilities within the scope of IAS 39 (FLIAS39) have a mean of 0.22 (sample A) which is 3 times higher than the mean of non-financial liabilities (NFL), that is 0.07. For sample B, the mean of financial liabilities is 4 times higher than the mean of non-financial liabilities. Table 4 shows results for 66 observations for each sample: sample A - the individual financial statements of the parent company and sample B - the consolidated financial statements. The 2 samples were adjusted for outliers because both databases included some extreme cases of observations. Outliers were identified according to the labeling method developed by Hoaglin *et al.* (1986). Thus, 3 observations were eliminated from both samples, reducing the number of observations from 69 to 66 each.

4. Research design and results

This section comprises the description of the model used and the results obtained by testing the proposed hypotheses.

4.1 Research Design

The model used to test the value relevance of accounting information regarding financial instruments is the one applied by Song, Thomas and Yi, 2010 when testing value relevance of fair value hierarchy. It is based on the Ohlson, 1995 model that is modified by partitioning the book value into financial assets and liabilities and non-financial assets and liabilities. We further modified the Song, Thomas and Yi model by transforming the other variable from the original Ohlson model, net income, into a dummy variable - PL (1 for profit and 0 for loss), because the net income data were not normally distributed. Around 40% of net income data are negative (the parent company or the group report losses) and range over several orders of magnitude. All techniques used (such as adding a constant value to the data prior to applying the natural logarithm transformation or the reflection of data prior to the natural log transformation) failed to make the data normally distributed.

A multiple linear regression model is applied to estimate the association between stock market price (that is the dependent variable) and accounting numbers (the independent share-deflated variables), for both sample A and B. The equation of the model is:

$$P_{it} = \alpha_0 + \alpha_1 NFA_{it} + \alpha_2 FAIAS39_{it} + \alpha_3 NFL_{it} + \alpha_4 FLIAS39_{it} + \alpha_5 PL_{it} + \varepsilon_{it} \quad (1)$$

The dependent variable, P, is stock market price of the firm i, measured 6 months after the individual and consolidated annual financial statements are released for the year (the period taken into account is 2011-2013). All others are independent variables defined, as previously stated, on a per share basis. Moreover, to ensure a normal distribution of the data, all variables (except for the dummy one – PL – profit or loss) are natural log transformed. According to Osborne, 2002, the natural-log transformation reduces the skewness and kurtosis in the raw data and does not change the relationship between variables.

4.2 Results

We first analyze the degree of linear dependence between variables. Pearson's correlation coefficients (table 5) reveal the existence of direct correlations of strong intensity between price and assets and a moderate dependence between price and liabilities for parent's accounts.

Table 5. Correlation matrix of variables – Sample A - individual accounts

Pearson Correlation	Pnatlog	NFA natlog	FAIAS39 natlog	NFL natlog	FLIAS39 natlog	Profit or loss
Pnatlog	1.000					
NFAnatlog	0.734**	1.000				
FAIAS39 natlog	0.739**	0.571**	1.000			
NFL natlog	0.315*	0.662**	0.488**	1.000		
FLIAS39 natlog	0.380**	0.617**	0.665**	0.704**	1.000	
Profit or loss	0.459**	0.143	0.239	-0.168	-0.143	1.000

** Correlation is significant at the 0.01 level (2-tailed).

* Correlation is significant at the 0.05 level (2-tailed).

This conclusion holds for consolidated accounts too (table 6), but overall, the coefficients are lower than those from table 5. This means that the relationship between price and accounting information, in the case of consolidated statements – Sample B, is of weaker intensity (Jaba & Grama, 2004).

Table 6. Correlation matrix of variables – Sample B - consolidated accounts

Pearson Correlation	Pnatlog	NFA natlog	FAIAS39 natlog	NFL natlog	FLIAS39 natlog	Profit or loss
Pnatlog	1.000					
NFAnatlog	0.691**	1.000				
FAIAS39 natlog	0.685**	0.517**	1.000			
NFLnatlog	0.278*	0.658**	0.465**	1.000		
FLIAS39 natlog	0.379**	0.620**	0.640**	0.742**	1.000	
Profit or loss	0.418**	0.148	0.201	-0.177	-0.212	1.000

** Correlation is significant at the 0.01 level (2-tailed).
* Correlation is significant at the 0.05 level (2-tailed).

Table 7 presents the results of the equation (1) applied to sample A: parent companies' separate financial statements.

Table 7. Value relevance of financial instruments information – Sample A - individual accounts

Sample A Parent company individual statements N = 66	Unstandardized Coefficients		Standar-dized Coefficients	t	Sig.	Collinearity Statistics	
	B	Std. Error	Beta			Tol	VIF
(Constant)	-1.440	0.245		-5.877	0.000		
NFAnatlog	0.913	0.106	0.676	8.581	0.000	0.438	2.281
FAIAS39 natlog	0.554	0.074	0.596	7.516	0.000	0.432	2.313
FLIAS39 natlog	-0.224	0.079	-0.260	-2.848	0.006	0.326	3.071
NFLnatlog	-0.245	0.094	-0.216	-2.599	0.012	0.395	2.533
Profit or loss	0.408	0.173	0.146	2.352	0.022	0.707	1.415
	R	R Square	Adjusted R Square	Std. Error of Estimate/ Durbin-Watson		ANOVA F	Sig.
	0.915	0.837	0.823	0.5849	1.531	61.475	0.000

Table 7 shows that the model has a high explanatory power. The adjusted R^2 is 82.30%, which means that more than 82% of variation in the dependent variable, stock market price, is explained by the independent variables chosen. The p-value of the F statistic of the ANOVA test is less than 0.05, which means that the model is fit. Moreover, all independent variables have coefficients that are statistically significantly different from zero (the p-value for the regression coefficient is less than 0.05), meaning that they are significant predictors of stock market price. In table 7, beta expresses the relative importance of each individual variable in standardized terms. According to this, the information about non-financial assets (NFA) has a higher power for investors than the one about financial assets within the scope of IAS 39 (FAIAS39). The information regarding financial liabilities within the scope of IAS 39 (FLIAS39) has only a slightly higher power than the one about non-financial liabilities (NFL).

Because all variables are natural-log transformed, the regression coefficients are analyzed as partial elasticity coefficients of the dependent variable in relation to the independent ones (e.g. a 1% increase in FAIAS39 is associated with an average 0.554% increase in price when all other independent variables are constant). The dummy variable's coefficient shows that if it switches from 1 to 0 (from profit to loss), the % impact of the dummy on price is a negative one of 33.5%. This percentage is the back-transformed coefficient after using the formula $100*(e^{-0.408}-1)$. This transformation is necessary as the dependent variable is natural-log transformed. Therefore, stock price decreases by 33.5% if a company no. longer reports profits and all other variables remain constant.

Hence, H_{1a} is supported. Information about financial assets and, to a lesser degree, information about financial liabilities are used by investors to assess the value of a non-financial parent company.

The results of the equation (1) applied to consolidated financial statements (sample B) are presented in table 8.

Table 8. Value relevance of financial instruments information – Sample B – consolidated accounts

Sample B Consoli-dated statements N = 66	Unstandardized Coefficients		Standardized Coefficients	t	Sig.	Collinearity Statistics	
	B	Std. Error	Beta			Tol	VIF
(Constant)	-1.752	0.273		-6.416	0.000		
NFAnatlog	0.876	0.129	0.640	6.783	0.000	0.469	2.131
FAIAS39 natlog	0.466	0.078	0.475	5.990	0.000	0.665	1.504
NFLnatlog	-0.370	0.106	-0.333	-3.478	0.001	0.455	2.199
Profit or loss	0.477	0.203	0.170	2.345	0.022	0.797	1.254
	R	R Square	Adjusted R Square	Std. Error of Estimate/	Durbin-Watson	ANOVA F	ANOVA Sig.
	0.863	0.745	0.729	0.7256	1.560	44.631	0.000

The explanatory power of the model is lower than the one of sample A, but it is still very high (adjusted R^2 is 72.9%). In addition, financial liabilities within the scope of IAS 39 (FLIAS39) are excluded from the model as they are not deemed to be significant predictors of stock market price.

Hence, H_{1b} is partially confirmed. There is an association only between price and financial assets, therefore investors only use accounting information about financial assets when assessing the value of a non-financial group. As far as H_2 is concerned, it is supported. Because the explanatory power of Sample A is slightly greater than the one of sample B, we conclude that Romanian investors deem the parent's individual financial statements to be more value relevant than the consolidated accounts. These results are consistent to those reported by Srinivasan and Narasimhan (2012) for emerging markets or Herrman *et al.* (2001) for developed markets.

Both models were checked for any violations of the multiple regression assumptions. They both passed the normality test (i.e. Kolmogorov-Smirnov test), but also multicollinearity, non-constant variance (heteroscedasticity) and auto-correlation of residuals tests. Multicollinearity can be detected using the variance inflation factor (VIF) that measures the degree to which a variable is contributing to the standard error in the fitted regression model. When the independent variables included have a statistically significant linear correlation, the variance inflation factor is very large. In our paper, we used a level of 5 and above for VIF to indicate a multicollinearity problem, according to Jermacowicz *et al.* (2007). Tolerance (TOL) is the reversed version of VIF: a TOL below 0.2 indicates a multicollinearity problem. According to tables 7 and 8, variables are correlated (when they are not correlated, the variance inflation factor is 1), but there is no. evidence of multicollinearity.

To examine heteroscedasticity (see table 9), we used a Breusch-Pagan test and a Koenker test which show if the standard deviations of the error terms (residuals) are constant and do not depend on the values of the independent variables. For sample A, Breusch-Pagan test calculates a value of 5.171 with a significance value of 0.3935, which is >0.05, therefore the null hypothesis of homoscedasticity is accepted (there is no correlation between independent variables and residuals). The same interpretation is given to the Koenker test result (Koenker has more rigorous results for small sample sizes). Therefore, the null hypothesis is also accepted for sample B. To check for the auto-correlation of residuals, we performed the Durbin Watson test (tables 7 and 8) and Runs Test (table 9) on both samples. As the Durbin Watson test is between 1.5 and 2.5, we conclude that there is no. serial correlations among residuals (Jaba & Grama, 2004). Moreover, the Runs test has a significance level >0.05, which shows that the null hypothesis is accepted (i.e. residuals do not auto-correlate).

Table 9. Heteroscedasticity and auto-correlation of residuals

Breusch-Pagan test	Sig.	Koenker test	Sig.	Runs test (sig.)
Sample A - Parent company's individual financial statements				
5.171	0.3953	4.906	0.4275	0.457
Sample B - Consolidated financial statements				
6.328	0.2756	7.990	0.1568	0.215

To better examine the influence of reported earnings, we repeat the analysis with subsamples partitioned by the "profit or loss" characteristic (entities reporting profits versus entities reporting losses). The model used is described in equation 2:

$$P_{it} = \alpha_0 + \alpha_1 NFA_{it} + \alpha_2 FAIAS39_{it} + \alpha_3 NFL_{it} + \alpha_4 FLIAS39_{it} + \varepsilon_{it} \quad (2)$$

Results obtained for individual financial statements of the parent companies are provided in table 10. The adjusted R^2 of both subsamples are equal (79.1%) and they both deem non-financial and financial assets to be significant predictors of stock market price. With liabilities, the situation is different: for companies reporting profits – subsample A_1 - only financial liabilities are kept within the model, while for the A_2 subsample, only non-financial liabilities are taken into consideration.

Table 10. Value relevance of financial instruments information reported in individual accounts according to the profit/loss criterion

Sample A Parent company individual statements	Unstandardized Coefficients		Standardized Coefficients	t	Sig.	Collinearity Statistics	
	B	Std. Error	Beta			Tol	VIF
Subsample A_1 - entities reporting **profits** (N = 38)							
(Constant)	-0.479	0.119		-4.022	0.000		
FAIAS39 natlog	0.516	0.084	0.829	6.117	0.000	0.307	3.256
NFAnatlog	0.680	0.114	0.547	5.963	0.000	0.670	1.492
FLIAS39 natlog	-0.244	0.086	-0.402	-2.835	0.008	0.281	3.561
	R	R Square	Adjusted R Square	Std. Error of Estimate		ANOVA F	Sig.
	0.899	0.808	0.791	0.47881		47.739	0.000
Subsample A_2 - entities reporting **losses** (N = 28)							
(Constant)	-1.759	0.518		-3.392	0.002		
NFAnatlog	0.987	0.202	0.828	4.883	0.000	0.269	3.721

Sample A Parent company individual statements	Unstandardized Coefficients		Standardized Coefficients	t	Sig.	Collinearity Statistics	
	B	Std. Error	Beta			Tol	VIF
FAIAS39 natlog	0.635	0.174	0.473	3.654	0.001	0.461	2.171
NFLnatlog	-0.584	0.155	-0.523	-3.775	0.001	0.403	2.480
	R	R Square	Adjusted R Square	Std. Error of Estimate		ANOVA F	ANOVA Sig.
	0.903	0.815	0.791	0.67293		35.150	0.000

Results obtained for sample B, consolidated financial statements, are provided in table 11.

Table 11. Value relevance of financial instruments information reported in consolidated accounts according to the profit/loss criterion

Sample B Consolidated statements	Unstandardized Coefficients		Standardized Coefficients	t	Sig.	Collinearity Statistics	
	B	Std. Error	Beta			Tol	VIF
Subsample B_1 - entities reporting **profits** (N= 39)							
(Constant)	-0.428	0.142		-3.020	0.005		
NFAnatlog	0.446	0.130	0.362	3.419	0.002	0.740	1.351
FAIAS39 natlog	0.382	0.068	0.593	5.598	0.000	0.740	1.351
	R	R Square	Adjusted R Square	Std. Error of Estimate		ANOVA F	ANOVA Sig.
	0.837	0.701	0.685	0.58240		42.243	0.000
Subsample B_2 - entities reporting **losses** (N = 27)							
(Constant)	-2.213	0.504		-4.389	0.000		
NFAnatlog	1.268	0.197	0.994	6.423	0.000	0.353	2.834
NFLnatlog	-0.773	0.162	-0.671	-4.761	0.000	0.424	2.356
FAIAS39 natlog	0.612	0.176	0.400	3.476	0.002	0.637	1.569
	R	R Square	Adjusted R Square	Std. Error of Estimate		ANOVA F	ANOVA Sig.
	0.898	0.806	0.780	0.73028		31.817	0.000

The adjusted R^2 is lower for the profit subsample B_1 (68.5%) when compared to the loss subsample B_2 (78%). For B_1 only assets (both non-financial and financial) are deemed to be significant predictors of stock market price. For the B_2 - loss subsample, non-financial liabilities are added to the model, while financial liabilities are excluded.

5. Conclusions

This study had two major motivations: (1) to test whether the accounting information regarding financial instruments provided by individual and consolidated accounts was value relevant to investors in the case of non-financial companies; and (2i) to test which of the 2 sets of financial statements is more value relevant to investors (especially in terms of financial instruments information). These research questions are even more challenging when posed for non-financial companies that use financial instruments to a lesser degree than financial entities. Moreover, as shown by empirical results, they use less sophisticated financial instruments such as accounts receivables and accounts payable, cash and deposits, short and long-term debt.

This leads to the following question: do investors place weight on the accounting information about financial instruments when estimating the value of a non-financial company? To answer it, we use data from the annual separate financial statements of the parent companies and the consolidated financial statements of the non-financial groups listed on the Bucharest Stock Exchange between 2011 and 2013. Firstly, we investigate whether financial instruments recognized in the individual accounts are deemed value relevant or not. Secondly, we do the same for consolidated accounts. Thirdly, we address whether parent company's statements provide value relevant information about financial instruments in excess of consolidated statements.

We find the following. At parent company level, investors place more weight on information about assets than liabilities and, among assets, on non-financial ones (which have the highest regression coefficient, almost equal to 1). This is not surprising given the industry to which the analyzed companies belong to. Also interesting to notice is that, in terms of liabilities, the importance placed on financial liabilities is very similar to non-financial liabilities (and quite small when compared to assets). We conclude that, of all financial instruments, financial assets are better market predictors than financial liabilities. At group level, coefficients are smaller for both types of assets (when compared to individual accounts) and greater for non-financial liabilities. Furthermore, investors seem to ignore any information regarding financial liabilities. This is rather puzzling as in terms of relative size of liabilities, the financial liabilities are more significant than the non-financial ones. One explanation could be that investors perceive financial liabilities as "less risky" as they are contracted after a thorough analysis made by banks, which reassures investors that companies are creditworthy.

When the analysis is detailed based on the results obtained by the parent company, it is noticeable that investors heavily rely on non-financial assets and non-financial liabilities in determining the stock price of unprofitable firms. Correlation with the market price is lower if firms are profitable, the existence of profits decreasing the importance of other accounting variables. In addition, financial instruments weigh more heavily in determining stock prices. The same can be seen at group level. Accounting variables correlation with stock price is two or three times higher for groups reporting losses, the detached winners being the non-financial assets and liabilities, followed by financial assets. For profitable groups, only assets (financial and non-financial) are taken into account and, as in the case of parent companies, the importance of the two types of assets is similar (there is no. big difference between the regression coefficients of financial assets and non-financial assets).

Based on the results of the test performed at group level, it is worth noting that our initial suspicion regarding the superiority of parent-only accounts in terms of value relevance has been confirmed. This makes us believe that on the Romanian stock exchange, investors see the consolidated annual accounts as an extension of the individual annual accounts of the parent company rather than the main source of information about the reporting entity. Therefore, they treat the consolidated information as a complement to the information disclosed in the parent company's accounts. These results are consistent with those obtained by Srinivasan and Narasimhan (2012) or Herrman *et al.* (2001).

There are some limitations to our research, such as: size of the sample, which is small compared to other studies, but common to emerging economies; inefficiency of the Romanian stock exchange that might influence the interpretation of results. However, Hellstrom (2006) and Filip and Raffournier (2010) downgrade the importance of market efficiency in emerging markets where stock prices and accounting numbers are correlated, arguing that it matters mainly for developed markets, where stock prices are derived from the accounting figures. These limitations will be addressed in the future as we intend to expand our research to bigger samples and more efficient markets.

Acknowledgements

This paper was presented at the 10th edition of the International Conference on Accounting and Management Information Systems (AMIS) which was held at the Bucharest University of Economic Studies, on June 10-11, 2015. The authors would like to thank to the AMIS participants for their precious recommendations and to the anonymous reviewers.

References

Abad, C., Garcia-Borbolla, A., Garrod, N., Laffarga, J., Larran, M. & Pinero, J. M. (2000) "An evaluation of the value relevance of consolidated versus unconsolidated accounting information: Evidence from quoted Spanish firms", *Journal of International Financial Management and Accounting*, vol. 11, no. 3: 156-177

Ahmed, A. S., Kilic, E. & Lobo, G.J. (2006) "Does recognition versus disclosure matter? Evidence from value –relevance of banks' recognised and disclosed derivative financial instruments", *The Accounting Review*, vol. 81, no. 3: 567-588

Ayers, B.C. (1998) "Deferred tax accounting under SFAS No. 109: An empirical investigation of its incremental value-relevance relative to APB No. 11", *Accounting Review*, vol. 73, no. 2: 195-212

Barth, M. E., Beaver W.H. & Landsman, W. R. (1996) "Value-relevance of banks' fair value disclosures under SFAS No. 107", *The Accounting Review*, vol. 71: 513-537

Barth, M. E. (1994) "Fair value accounting: Evidence from investment securities and the market valuation of banks", *The Accounting Review*, vol. 69: 1-25

Beaver, W. H. (2002) "Perspectives on recent capital market research", *The Accounting Review*, vol. 77, no. 2: 453-474.

Beisland, L. A. (2009) "A review of the value relevance literature", *The Open Business Journal*, vol. 2: 7-27

Callao, S., Jarne, J. I. & Laínez, J. A. (2007) "Adoption of IFRS in Spain: Effect on the comparability and relevance of financial reporting", *Journal of International Accounting, Auditing and Taxation*, vol. 16, no. 2: 148-178

Darrough, M.N. & Harris, T.S. (1991) "Do management forecasts of earnings affect stock prices in Japan?" in Ziemba, W.T., Bailey, W. & Hamao, Y. (Eds.) *Japanese Financial Markets Research*, Amsterdam: North Holland, Elsevier Science, pp. 197-229

Epstein, B. J. & Jermakowicz, E. K. (2010) *Wiley 2010 Interpretation and Application of International Financial Reporting Standards*, New Jersey: John Wiley & Sons.

Filip, A. & Raffournier, B. (2010) "The value relevance of earnings in a transition economy: the case of Romania", *The International Journal of Accounting*, vol. 45, no. 1: 77-103

Francis, J. & Schipper, K. (1999) "Have financial statements lost their relevance?", *Journal of Accounting Research*, vol. 37, no. 2: 319-352

Gebhardt, G. (2012) "Financial instruments in non-financial firms: what do we know?", *Accounting and Business Research*, vol. 42, no. 3: 267-289

Goncharov, I., Werner, J.R. & Zimmermann, J. (2009) "Legislative demands and economic realities: Company and group accounts compared", *The International Journal of Accounting*, vol. 44, no. 4: 334-362

Harris, T.S., Lang, M.H. & Moller, H.P. (1997) "Unconsolidated versus consolidated accounting measures: empirical evidence from listed German companies", Paper presented at the 20th Annual Congress of the European Accounting Association, Graz

Hellstrom, K. (2006) "The value relevance of financial accounting information in a transition economy: The case of the Czech Republic", *European Accounting Review*, vol. 15, no. 3: 325-349

Herrmann, D., Inoue, T. & Thomas, W.B. (2001) "The relation between incremental subsidiary earnings and future stock returns in Japan", *Journal of Business, Finance, and Accounting*, vol. 28, no. 9-10: 1115-1139

Hoaglin, D.C., Iglewicz, B. & Tuckey, J. W. (1986) "Performance of some resistant rules for outliers labeling", *Journal of American Statistical Association*, vol. 81: 991-999

Holthausen, R. & Watts, R. (2001) "The relevance of the value-relevance literature for financial accounting standard setting", *Journal of Accounting and Economics*, vol. 31: 3–75

Huian, M. C. (2013a) "Analysis of the constituents' participation in the development of the 1st Phase of IFRS 9 Financial Instruments", *Annals of the „Constantin Brâncuşi" University of Târgu Jiu, Economy Series*, vol. 1: 209-216

Huian, M. C. (2013b) "Stakeholders' participation in the development of the new accounting rules regarding the impairment of financial assets", *Business and Management Dynamics*, vol. 2, no. 9: 23-35

Hung, M. & Subramanyan, K. R. (2007) "Financial statement effects of adopting internationalaccounting standards: the case of Germany", *Review of Accounting Studies*, vol. 12, no. 4: 623-671

Grabinski, K., Kedzior, M. & Krasodomska, J. (2014) "The Polish accounting system and IFRS implementation process in the view of empirical research", *Accounting and Management Information Systems*, vol. 13, no. 2: 281-310

Iatridis, G. (2010) "International Financial Reporting Standards and the quality of financial statement information", *International Review of Financial Analysis*, vol. 19, no. 3, pp. 193-204

Jaba, E. & Grama, A. (2004) *Analiza statistică cu SPSS sub Windows* [Statistical Analysis with SPSS in Windows], Iaşi: Polirom

Jarmalaite Pritchard, N. (2002) "The relationship between accounting numbers and returns in the Baltic stock markets", *Working paper, CERT, Heriot-Watt University, Edinburgh*

Jermakowicz, E. K., Prather-Kinsey, J. & Wulf, I. (2007) "The value relevance of accounting income reported by DAX-30 German companies", *Journal of International Financial Management and Accounting,* vol. 18, no. 3, pp. 151-191

Klimczak, K. M. (2011) "Market reaction to mandatory IFRS adoption: evidence from Poland", *Accounting and Management Information Systems*, vol. 10, no. 2: 228-248

Kolev, K. (2009) "Do investors perceive marking-to-model as marking-to-myth? Early evidence from FAS 157 Disclosure", *Working paper, New York University*, vol. 1: 1-51

Koonce, L., Nelson K. K. & Shakespeare, C. M. (2011) "Judging the Relevance of Fair Value for Financial Instruments", *The Accounting Review,* vol. 86, no. 6: 2075-2098

Leonrmand, G. & Touchais, L. (2009) "Les IFRS améliorent-elles la qualité de l'information financière? Approche par la value relevance", *Comptabilite. Audit*, vol. 15, no. 2: 145-163

Lev, B. & Sougiannis, T. (1996) "The capitalization, amortization, and value-relevance of R&D", *Journal of Accounting and Economics*, vol. 21, no. 1: 107-138

Malciu, L. & Feleagă, N. (2004) *Reglementare şi practici de consolidare a conturilor. Din orele astrale ale Europei contabile* [Regulations and Practices of Consolidation. The Astral Hours of European Accounting], Bucureşti: CECCAR

Mironiuc, M., Carp M. & Chersan I.C. (2015) "The relevance of financial reporting on the performance of quoted Romanian companies in the context of adopting the IFRS", *Procedia Economics and Finance*, vol. 20: 404-413

Morais, A. I. & Curto, J. D. (2008) "Accounting quality and the adoption of IASB standards – Portuguese evidence", *Revista Contabilidade & Finanças*, vol. 19, no. 48: 103-111

Müller, V. O. (2011) "Value relevance on consolidated versus parent company financial statements: evidence from the largest three European capital markets", *Accounting and Management Information Systems*, vol. 10, no. 3: 326-350

Niskanen, J., Kinnunen, J. & Kasanen, E. (1998) "A note on the information content of parent company versus consolidated earnings in Finland", *The European Accounting Review*, vol. 7, no. 1: 31-40

Ohlson, J. A. (1995) "Earnings, book values, and dividends in equity valuation", *Contemporary Accounting Research*, vol. 11, no. 2: 661-687

Okuda, S. & Shiiba, A. (2006) "An evaluation of the relative importance of parent-only and subsidiary earnings in Japan: a variance decomposition approach", available on-line at: http://www.papers.ssrn.com/sol3/papers.cfm.abstract_id¼944740 [March 12, 2015]

Osborne, J. (2002) "Notes on the use of data transformations", *Practical Assessment, Research & Evaluation*, vol. 8, no. 6

Song, C. J., Thomas, W.B. & Yi, H. (2010) "Value relevance of FAS No. 157 Fair value hierarchy information and the impact of corporate governance mechanisms", *The Accounting Review*, vol. 85, no. 4: 1375-1410

Srinivasan, P. & Narasimhan M.S. (2012) "The value relevance of consolidated financial statements in an emerging market. The case of India", *Asian Review of Accounting*, vol. 20 no. 1: 58-73

Takacs, L.M. (2012) "The value relevance of earnings in a transition economy: evidence from Romanian stock market", *Annales Universitatis Apulensis Series Oeconomica*, vol. 14, no. 1: 88-103

Venkatachalam, M. (1996) "Value-relevance of banks' derivatives disclosures", *Journal of Accounting and Economics*, vol. 22: 327-355

10

An analysis framework for defining the required IT&C competencies for the accounting profession

Cătălin Georgel Tudor, Mirela Gheorghe, Mirela Oancea & Robert Şova

The Bucharest University of Economic Studies, Romania

Abstract: In the current economic context, the issue of IT&C competencies indissoluble to the accounting profession gets special meanings: accounting skills and those associated with the quality of professional accountant must be completed with the specific use of advanced technologies to address this profession. This paper proposes an analysis of key competencies concerning the use of information and communication technology by the professional accountant, by defining a multidimensional analysis framework following, from different perspectives considered to be essentials, the opportunity to include IT&C competencies into training and professional development programs for accountants and auditors. This framework captures IT&C competencies located at the intersection of three axes (Roles, Levels of experience and Information technologies) that will guide the definition of thematic areas and specific competences. Finally, we identified correlations between the IT&C competencies and some important information technologies addressing the training programs for the accounting profession at different levels of expertise.

Keywords: IT&C competencies, skills, knowledge of IT, IT technologies, accounting profession

[1] *Correspondence address:* The Bucharest University of Economic Studies, PiaţaRomană nr. 6, sector 1, Bucharest, Romania, Email: catalin.tudor@cig.ase.ro

1. Introduction

In the actual economical context, every entity is trying to rediscover itself, in order to define new coordinates in the process of restructuring and adapting to the new requirements imposed by the new realities with which the economic environment is confronted in the present. Technological proliferation and, especially, information technology proliferation has led to requirements of the work market that are more and more diverse in relation to the competencies of the accountant as a profession.

The problematic of the competencies and their evaluation has become a subject of major interest in the professional educational preparation in any field. The term competency has a major impact also in the accountant education, with a powerful influence upon the way the future accountants will be evaluated. A fundamental characteristic of the competencies-based education is that the definition of offer and of the educational program starts from the purpose of obtaining certain results identified beforehand.

Discussing in terms of efficiency of the accounting profession as a central and centralizing element of a business, the economics and business environment accepts the professional qualification of the members of the accountant body as being acquired in accordance to a performance standard expected by employers in all the specific fields. The approach based on competencies represents a systematic and efficient manner of accomplishing this goal.

By competency we understand the ability to complete the tasks and the acts attributed to professional accountants (the newly qualified accountants as well the experienced ones) according to the standards demanded by the employers and general public. The reputation, the value and significance of the accounting profession depend on the ability of their members to answer to the expectations of the organizations that they are working for, through providing adequate services which bring added value in a certain time window. Lately, the academics environment as well as the business environment has reached a common conclusion in which concerns the teaching of the accountants, in general, but more precisely, the experts in this field: a separation cannot be made between the knowledge and the gathered experience in the field of accounting and in the fields associated to the information technology domain. The accounting competencies and those associated to the quality of professional accountant must be completed with those specific to the advanced use of technologies that are related to this field. Following the same idea, bodies and communities of accountants have constantly and continuously supported the need for change of the education in accounting through the growth and improvement of the knowledge regarding information accounting systems or the techniques and the most frequent practices that concern the application of the advantages of instruments specific to the information technology in the activities the accountant performs.

The present paper wishes to answer to the following questions: Which should be the competencies from the Information and Technology Communication (IT&C) field indissoluble to the accounting profession? and how can these competencies be analyzed with respect to the existing information technologies in the present time and keeping track of the parts played by the accountant with respect to the internal environment of an organization but as well to the interaction with the external environment?

2. Research Methodology

The present paper proposes an analysis of the main competencies that target the professional accountant regarding the usage of information and communication technology in his activity, by defining a multidimensional analysis framework which supervises, from a series of perspectives considered essential, the opportunity of including the IT&C competencies in the education programs and the professional development of the accountants and the auditors.

The present paper follows the authors concerns from the research point of view regarding the discovery of new methods to align the competencies associated to information technology to the requirements imposed by exercising their profession as accountants inside the organizations. In the step towards the definition of a coherent analysis framework for the educational necessity described through efficient formation programs based on identifying competencies requested in order to practice the accounting profession, there have been analyzed several relevant opinions from the specialist literature, as bedrock on which the proceeding of the research is based, following at the same time the way in which these converge to the purpose of the present paper. In the end, correlations have been identified between the identified competencies and the existing information technologies that can answer to these competencies through their inclusion in the framework of the formation programs in the accounting field on several levels of experience.

3. Literature Review

Literature review had the purpose of identifying the ways in which the issue of the topic discussed was previously addressed, but to identify also the amount of interest raised by the competencies in IT&C in the field of education at different levels but also in the business environment, as a recipient of the product of accounting training.

A large number of professional organizations have stressed the importance of introducing information and communication technology in the subject areas specific to accounting education. Even since 1993, The Association to Advance

Collegiate Schools of Business (AACSB) stresses the need for complete knowledge of accounting professionals with specific tools and techniques of information technology (AACSB, 1993). Similarly, The Institute of Management Accountants (IMA) places competencies in the field of use and exploitation of information technology (in terms of knowledge, skills and techniques learned) among the top 10 accounting profession skills required (IMA, 1996). Also, The American Accounting Association, in a report aiming at a target group of accounting faculties, suggests completing learning techniques with informatics tools of professional training assistance (AAA, 1986).

As shown in the official views expressed by the Commission of changes in accounting education - The Accounting Education Change Commission (AECC), "because organizations are affected by rapidly growing dependence on technology, professional accountants should understand current and future roles of the information and communication technology in organizations " (AECC, 1990). The American Institute of Certified Public Accountants (AICPA) suggests as primary the need to complete the knowledge of individual professional accountant with the skills and competencies necessary in order to use effectively and easily the computer tools that are suitable for this area (AICPA, 1998).

IFAC has stressed very concise the need to complete the accountant education with information technology, through the educational standard IEG-11 International Education Guideline on "IT and Accounting Curriculum": "Information technology is universal in the business world. Competence with this technology is imperative for the Accounting Profession "(IFAC, 2003). The understanding of educational needs in this area should be seen in terms of the need to adapt to the new challenges, techniques and opportunities of development of the accounting profession. Involvement of the IT component in this education requires a shift in the accounting thinking and the specific actions towards improving the activity efficiency through automation and computer assistance.

The collection and growing of IT&C skills by the professional accountant may be justified at least through the level of expertise required to use financial and accounting informatics systems, but also with the tools that enhance the ability to make decisions in an environment that is increasingly computerized. This relationship is demonstrated by research based on various empirical studies (Eliot, 1992; Cooper, 1996; McKinnon & Bruns, 1992; Borthick, 1996) emphasized the idea that managers generally rely on skilled accountants to obtain information from disparate sources and on analyzing them in a useful and understandable manner.

Chen *et al.* (2009) were concerned in identifying the key knowledge necessary for the accounting profession after completing a training and refinement program in the field. A number of other reference papers treat in depth the topic of IT&C skills required for the accounting profession, through empirical studies conducted on different populations, or only through studies at a conceptual level, emphasizing the usefulness and necessity of acquiring skills in the IT&C domain for exercising the accounting function (Harrison *et al.*, 2004; Wessels, 2005; Cardoş, 2011; Ku Bahador *et al.*, 2012; Havelka & Merhout, 2009).

In the research topic of implementing training programs that would take into account the need for symbiosis between information technologies and accounting when speaking of professional accountants training, there can be identified several specialized studies designed to emphasize the main themes that could be a common body of knowledge necessary to the professional regarding the obtaining of competencies in the use of IT&C (AAA, 1986; Daigle, 2007; Borthick, 1996). Besides these, other possible proposals can be found regarding learning objectives and possible training activities related to the IT&C component of the training necessary for the professional accountants (Heagy & Rakow, 1991; Jackson & Cherrington, 2002). All these studies highlight the main issues related to the accounting training in the field of informatics systems that should be included in any training program: business cycles, control and auditing, analyzing and designing of the financial-accounting system (Jackson & Cherrington, 2002). Based upon the recommendation of IFAC, Wessels (2008) proposes a series of strategies for the implementation of IT skills in the education of professional accountants.

Looking at it more pragmatically, Novak and Beckman (2008), define a multi-layered model for improving the knowledge of an organization, through a skill based approach. The authors underline the idea according to which IT&C represents an activator factor in the retention of organizational knowledge (and implicitly associated to the accounting profession), the usage of information technologies leading to the organizational memory growth of an enterprise.

Following a review of the literature on IT&C technologies applicable to the accounting profession, Wessels (2005) analyzed the results of research conducted by Greenstein and McKee (2004) and Theuri and Gunn (1998), along with the proposals set out by IEG 11 issued by IFAC (2003a). Thus, in a first step the author noted 22 major IT technologies important for the accounting profession, only to later recommend 36 critical technologies in conducting of daily work tasks of the professional accountant, and also in the process of innovating and creating new products through the IT&C component.

Even though there are several specialist studies trying to prove the necessity of completing the training programs in the field of accounting with disciplines orientated towards gaining IT&C competencies, we could not identify a coherent analysis framework of these competencies against the demanded expertise level and accordingly to the parts played by the professional accountant inside and outside of the organization in which he performs. Also, there are no studies to present the need for the implementation of a training program at a national level following the IT&C skills associated to the accounting profession in Romania, taking into account the IFAC recommendations through its broadcasted standards and proposals regarding the homogenizing of knowledge and competencies in the field.

4. The Analysis of the Actual Status of Professional Accountants Training Through the IT&C Component

The accounting profession, viewed traditionally, is subject, in the present, to some threats coming from the emergence on the labor market of new categories, not specialized in accounting, but with university and post-graduate studies and mastering very well the IT field. Non-specialists in accounting may be able to develop internal analysis of data from the available information sources of the organization. It was found that these competitors are sometimes preferred by the accounting firms. If non-accountants learn to respond better than professional or authorized accountants to the management information requirements issued by an organization, it can be deduced very simply, that the value of the accounting profession falls within that organization. Interpretation of accounting information significance, and ensuring the completeness and the integrity of it, is a task that falls, however, to the accounting profession. This creates an opportunity to prepare accounting professionals today given the specifics of the work done by them: accounting, control, auditing, and so on, in a computer-intensive environment – environment about which Siegel (1996) stated that "creative analysis is more valuable than encyclopedic knowledge specific to accounting procedures."

4.1. The need of IT&C component for the professional accountants

The role of the accountant follows the same trend as for the other professionals from business, recording a major change oriented towards technology. After completing a training and refinement program in the field, the accounting professionals expect to know the use of spreadsheets in financial analysis, business graphs construction and interpretation, word processing, how to make a business presentation or one on the financial-accounting statements, the use of tools to assist in auditing, financial reporting, and so on, business systems, databases management systems or using communication solutions in a virtual environment, at an advanced level (Chen *et al.*, 2009). They are anticipating, also, skills in evaluating IT security needs at the organizational level, in the organization and management of computing resources within the enterprise where they evolve, along with protection against unauthorized access to or against vulnerabilities concerning the IT&C environment of the organization. Once aware of the need to adjust the accounting profession in order to accept and adopt evolutionary computing environment from the business field, the training of the experts in this field must be concerned, equally, and about gaining the IT skills (expressed in terms of knowledge, technical skills and abilities).

4.2. Complementarity between IT&C competencies and those associated to the accounting profession

Lately, we are witnessing an expansion of the accounting part inside an organization, the latter evolving from supplying financial information to seconding the business decision, becoming a component part of the organization's management structure. The accountants have changed their priorities from the analysis of past events to acting as strategic partners, advisors and providers of financial-accounting information. The Institute of Management Accountants (IMA, 1996) has identified four activities that define the present accounting profession: long term strategic planning, internal advisor, information systems and computer operations, and the improvement of business processes. We can admit that the accounting profession is a supplier of not only financial information, but technological and strategic also, at any organization's level.

Information technology has completed the professional accountant mission, who does not only uses the information system through exercising his given part, but starts to play a growing part in determining the design and realization requests of such a system, in all the stages it goes through, and of the evaluation of its functionalities, or in knowing and using some information technologies that help him exercise his functions as economist, manager, auditor or evaluator, in certain stages of his career.

The role of the accountant changes continuously while the world becomes more and more information and technology oriented. As technology continues to have a major impact onto the way to lead a business, the inclusion of IT&C in the education and in the teaching of the accounting profession, at any level of preparation, proves to have a critical importance for any institution of formation in this field.

The professional accountant will be asked to provide a wide variety of services based on software applications, together with the involvement in activities that regard the information system of an organization: the information system analysis, the information management, the information security and so on. Analyzing this aspect, we can observe the need of a high enough level of knowledge of the IT aspects: the professional accountants have to not only be acquainted with techniques of using software applications, but must show a good understanding of the fundamental concepts associated to the term of financial-accounting information system, in all its life cycle stages, and furthermore they have to demonstrate a high level of experience when it comes to using IT instruments associated to the status of economist in general. In an article presented in the journal of the body of professional accountants from the US, Albrecht and Robert (2001) foretold that the demands for advanced IT competencies, explained through the need of involvement of the accountants in issuing judgments based on the analysis of information, will become a critical point in the future. Analyzing the expansion trends of the information technology towards more and more professions from the economical field, we can say for sure that the forecast could have been extended to activities that target an entire business, from the operational level to the management level, but, with a majority, it has been confirmed mainly for the accounting profession.

The globalization has represented the phenomenon that led to a harmonization of practices, of standards and professional qualifications in the accounting field. With the globalization of markets, there was an acute need for professional accountants with specific skills and abilities who can perform specialized tasks in different jurisdictions. This exchange of professional accountants across countries requires not only mastering of the international accounting norms and standards in this area, but also of a number of business tools currently used extensively. Information technology has proven to be an indispensable and activating factor for the implementation of these tools in an efficient manner.

4.3. The analysis of IT&C competencies usage against the functions at organization level that concern the accounting profession

Today the information systems have become an integrated part of any activity performed within the organization. Given this feature, the usefulness of IT&C knowledge has become a *sine qua non* condition for professional accountants.
Over time, accounting education has continued to be quite limited, focusing on practical accounting skills (Boyce, 2004). Delmond and Lebas (IFAC, 1998), cited by Wessels (2005) reinforce this claim, arguing that the role of the professional accountant was constrained to that of reviewing the financial data of an organization, detaching him as important in decision making.

Traditionally, the professional accountants have been called in functions such as: *chief accountant, financial manager, financial or operational internal auditor, external auditor or external consultant*. Current developments in the business environment have led to a natural change of the role of the professional accountant so that today his abilities are not just those of user of information and communication technologies (IT&C), but rather he can play an important role in an evaluation team, design or management of information systems.

In the vision of the IES 2 standard (IFAC, 2003a:44) "all professional accountants are expected to participate in at least one of the ***roles of manager, designer or evaluator of information systems***, or, a cluster of these roles". These generic roles do not demand the professional accountant to be an expert in the IT field, but rather we can state that it proposes the development of a set of abilities and basic competencies in the IT field that can help in securing decisions, in the identification and evaluation of new opportunities and risks generated by the IT component at the organizational level, the usage of the informatics instrument in completing daily tasks for the business activities. Clearly, one must not ignore the fact that there exists a **golden rule**, stated Druckman (2008), when we analyze the performance of the professional accountant, especially at the mid organizational level, there were in practice they play various parts at the same time – *„their competencies must answer to the organization needs*".

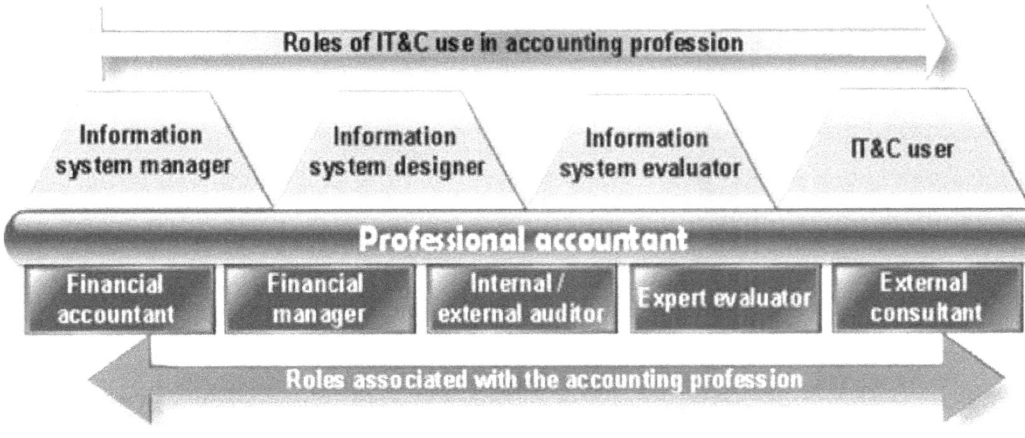

Figure 1. The functions of the professional accountant in the organizational environment

5. Defining A Conceptual Analysis Framework for Competencies in the IT&C Field for the Accounting Profession

The conceptualization of the term IT competence in the accounting profession requires, first, to highlight the meaning of the term competence in general. As it is presented, the basic psychological theory designates the correlation between skills, attitudes, knowledge and habits that enable a person to work effectively in a great variety of situations and which helps the person carry out his role. In the training based on competence the defining three factors (knowledge, attitudes and skills) have to be managed effectively and in an integrated manner so that they can lead to performance and success.

Associated with the term professionalism, competence may designate the group of knowledge, attitudes and skills that affects a major part of a person's activity, is correlated with performance in the activity, it can be measured by generally accepted standards and it can be improved through training and development (Lucia & Lepsinger, 1999:2). All three elements combined give the individual the opportunity to excel in a particular field. The latter sense may be found usually in management and focuses on cultivating the three elements (knowledge, attitudes and skills) to the level of excellence through various programs and courses using learning methods and techniques adapted to the subject in discussion.

Under the general international education standards for the accounting profession, IFAC defines competency as the ability of the individuals to meet the expected standards of the accounting profession, fact which requires an adequate level of knowledge, skills, values, ethics and attitudes to build and develop those skills. Appropriate level of competence will depend on certain factors, such as the complexity of the working environment, the complexity and type of tasks to be solved, the required expertise knowledge, the dependencies related to teamwork, the level of autonomy, or the level of analysis required. (IFAC, 2009).

While the attitudes are related to the individual's personal characteristics, the skills and the knowledge are the two aspects that accounting education should be based on when defining the appropriate training programs. Often accounting training at an advanced level requires a distinction between the concept of competence and that of knowledge when developing the professional accounting skills to deal effectively with the tasks assigned to him in the exercise of his roles. Awareness of differences in educational goals related to the development of knowledge and to those related to competencies (Carter, 1985) has become essential in designing effective training programs by the preparation institutions of professional accountants (Stone *et al.*, 1996). In the context of vocational education, knowledge is assimilated to the state of holding relevant information in a particular context, while the ability (the one that is closest to the meaning of the term competency viewed from a practical standpoint) is seen as the ability to use the knowledge in the process of performing a task. The competencies can be identified on multiple levels (novice, beginner, practitioner, expert, professional), while the knowledge in a certain field can be considered as having a dichotomous character (present or absent). In the vocational development of a person, the relation between knowledge and competencies goes both ways: the competencies cannot exist without the due knowledge, while the knowledge is considered necessary (but not sufficient) for competencies. The accounting teaching based on knowledge is preoccupied, in general, with the development of skills for the target group, which concern gathering as much information as possible which is associated to some specific concepts and scenarios. The training that relies on obtaining and growing competencies (viewed from the point of view of abilities and habits) aims at the ability of using the various concepts gained through enhancement of knowledge during specific tasks carried out and at the increase of the capabilities to apply abstract principles in solving some specific problems (Angelo & Cross, 1993).

For many analysts, today's training of the accounting profession focuses on the acquisition of knowledge and it is only tangentially addressed to acquiring and cultivating the necessary competencies in relation to the real needs imposed by permanent changes in the business environment. The need for accounting practitioners at an advanced level of expertise transcends, therefore, the limit of the knowledge based education, requiring the orientation of the training process in this field in the direction imposed by today's reality. This designates a recalibration of curriculum and curricular areas after an analysis of the necessary competencies. Competency levels should also be carefully analyzed in designing any training programs on the acquisition of skills and knowledge, and techniques and learning methods can be built upon this hierarchy.

In the process of identifying the competencies that a professional accountant must possess in the field of information and communication technology (IT&C), we propose a general analysis framework based on a structure that defines the dimensions according to which the term of IT&C competency can be addressed. This framework captures the IT competencies located at the intersection of three main axes that will guide the process of definition of thematic areas and areas of competence. The three axes, together with a three-dimensional representation of their components, can be observed graphically in Figure 2. Thus, the IT&C competency necessary for the accounting profession will be analyzed in relation with the part played by the accountant user within the organizational informatics system, with his level of expertise in manifesting the competency and in relation with the training modules destined for education with the purpose of acquiring the identified IT&C competency. The competency identification must be followed, usually, by its description through a list of thematic and content courses, the success in defining these being a direct consequence of identifying the best combination of values among the three vectors in relation with the competency's need.

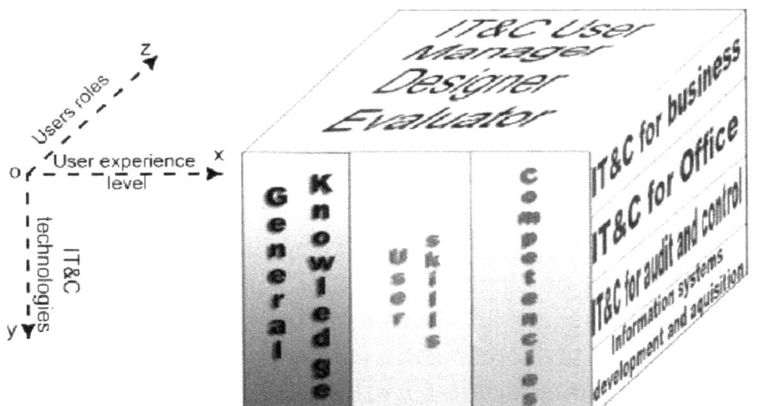

Figure 2. General analysis framework of the ICT competencies in the accounting profession

Even though the level of experience vector can present multiple levels of detail in relation with the perceived IT&C competency importance in the performance of the professional accountants, the proposed framework limited itself to evaluating the necessary experience level over three levels of hierarchy:

- general knowledge – the individual knows the general aspects and specific basic concepts and he is capable of realizing certain correlations between the identified problems and these concepts, implying a somewhat cognitive activity which will allow him to act effective in certain situations;

- ability in usage – the individual manages to carry out a certain task through the use of necessary knowledge previously acquired, acting aware through applying some defined plans on a certain time window by following precise goals;
- competencies – the person manages to build the solution of any problem, exhaustively analyzing the situational components and acting with conviction, guided by experience and by the intuitive comprehension of the details of the problem and of the scenario in which the problem appears.

In defining the transverse axis of analysis of IT&C competencies there have been used the roles defined in the educational standard IES 2 (IFAC, 2003b) on the use of information systems and, by extrapolation, of the information and communication technology: the user role, that of manager, of designer and that of evaluator. Grouping competencies over these types of functions is guided by the need to correlate competencies with the designated responsibilities in relation to ensuring the accuracy of financial-accounting information obtained by using the IT&C component.

The vertical axis proposes identified competencies evaluation in relation to the educational training modules. These were defined on the basis of the main responsibilities of the accounting profession, expressed through associated activities.

Placing a competency in agreement with a training module is a prerequisite for defining an educational offer that is consistent with the real-world usage needs of concepts, methods, techniques and IT tools in the accountant activities, on all three fundamental levels of the organizational pyramid: operational, strategic and management. Defining an educational offer must detail the content areas of the training programs in the field, which need to match those relevant from the competition.

The three perspectives of the analysis converge each time to a certain key point in which the IT competencies destined to the accounting profession are explained through function descriptor, through the appropriate level of training for that function and through the educational offer (defined through curricular fields with certain study disciplines) necessary for assimilating and developing the concerned competency.

5.1. The dimension of IT&C specific competencies that target the accounting profession

Table 1. Dimension of general competencies needed for information and communication technology usage

IT&C General knowledge	• IT Strategy • IT architecture • The IT impact on the business process • Information systems development process or IT&C acquisition process • IT&C management • Business communication by the means of IT&C use	• IT control standards • IT control objectives • IT control environment • Roles and responsibilities • IT risks assessment • IT&C risk treatment • It control activities • Monitoring IT&C control compliances	**Knowledge associated with IT&C control**
IT&C control competencies	• The methods selection for assessing IT&C control • Assessing the IT&C control environment • Assessing the IT&C control in the Information Systems developing / acquisition process • The IT&C risks analysis and assessment • IT&C control evaluation • The evaluation of IT&C control monitoring.	• IT&C business and accounting systems • IT&C integrated systems for business management (ERP, SAP, CRM) • Ensuring security organization assets.	**IT&C use competencies**

(Adapted from IFAC, 2003b)

Regarding IT&C competencies relative to the accounting profession, the IES 2 (IFAC, 2003b:44) standard groups them into several key areas:

- General knowledge about IT.
- Knowledge about the control in the IT field.
- Competencies (practical skills) in IT control.
- IT user competencies.
- A competency or a group of competencies associated to the functions of manager, evaluator or designer of SI.

These fields can be detailed, further, into main areas of content specific to the abilities and knowledge needed by the professional accountants. The areas of content can be looked at, firstly, from a general point of view, following specific competencies especially in the function of user of information and communication technology, but, addressing in equal measure to the other functions also. Table 1 presents the main knowledge and competencies directed at the accountants from the point of view of information and communication technology usage in the field where they perform.

In the process of identification of knowledge and general abilities, the main fields of competencies have been grouped into two axes: general and specific knowledge in the IT field and competencies in IT use and control.

5.2. The dimension of the functions related to the accounting profession in the IT&C field

IEG 11 (IFAC, 2003a) recommends packages of competencies diversified in relation to the IT&C functions specific to the accounting profession (Table 2).

Table 2. The dimension of competencies in IT&C functions specific to the accounting profession

IT manager Role	• The business entity IT&C strategy administration • The management of IT&C organizational structures; • Efficient and effective management of IT&C operational environment; • Achieving financial control over IT&C resources; • Conducting the IT&C controls; • Managing the Information Systems acquisition, development, and implementation process; • Efficient change management; • Managing efficiently IT&C critical issues	• Analysis and evaluation of information from organizational environment • Use project management methods • Use techniques for initiating an IT&C project and to evaluate the existing information system • Use methods for determining user requirements and system design • Understand the process of system maintenance and change management	**IT designer Role**
IT user Role	• Using business specific programs packages • Understanding Business Process Management Systems • Applying control measures to protect organization assets	• Define an information system evaluation plan; • System assessment by applying CAATs techniques; • Communicate the results of assessment and monitoring the implementation of recommendations.	**IT evaluator Role**

(Adapted from IFAC, 2003b)

These competencies packages will be completed with inter-personal communication abilities needed for an efficient communication with all the involved actors from the organizational environment: organization's board, employees, suppliers and customers.

5.3. The dimension of IT technologies needed for IT&C competencies deployment

In the present paper we refer to the research of Wessels (2005) regarding the definition of a reference list comprising the IT technologies considered essential for the accounting profession, some of them being found trough the standards elaborated by IFAC for the IT&C field. In the present study, the technologies used for obtaining and practicing the IT&C competencies for each role have been grouped according to the tasks performed by the professional accountant.

Table 3. The main identified technologies that can answer to the IT&C competencies required for the accounting profession

Business activities	• Small Business Accounting Software • Tax Return Preparation Software • Time Management & Billing Systems • Firewall Software/Hardware • External Network Configurations • User Authentication Systems • Internal Network Configurations • Intrusion Detection & Monitoring • Wireless Communications • Digital Communications • Encryption Software • EDI-Traditional • EDI-Web Based	• Cooperative Client/Server Environment • Test Data • Database Search & Retrieval • Flowcharting/Data Modeling • Enterprise Resource Planning • Simulation Software • Workflow Technology • Database Design & Installation • Application Service Providers • Computer-Aided Systems Engineering (CASE) Tools	**IT evaluation, design and management activities**
Office activities	• Word Processing • Electronic Spreadsheets • E-Mail • Internet Search & Retrieval • Image Processing • Electronic Presentations • Groupware	• Electronic Working Papers • Generalized Audit Software • Embedded Audit Modules/Real-time Audit Modules • Expert Systems	**Control and audit activities**

(Adapted from Wessels, 2005)

Thus the technologies answer to the business activities, office activities, control or audit (both financial and IT) activities, and to those specific to involvement in the evaluation, design and IT management teams. Synthetizing the most important stressed technologies as being critical in relation to the competencies specific to IT functions of the accounting profession can be tracked in Table 3.

Each of the three cases in the above tables surprise IT&C skills from different perspectives obtained by combining the dimensions stated in the aforementioned framework analysis. Educational needs in this area for the accounting profession must be identified through an integrated approach of all three dimensions, considering, equally, the level of experience required to acquire these competencies. Therefore, the formulation of relevant educational offerings must start from the formulation of the specific competencies, the technologies needed to put them in practice and the required level of experience.

6. A Questionnaire-Based Analysis on the Perception of Professional Accountants on IT&C Use in the Financial-Accounting Field

In order to identify an opinion on the use of ICT component at professional level in financial accounting field, an analysis based on a questionnaire was conducted with the purpose to lead to the provision of an image on the professional accountants' perception on the correlations imposed by the abovementioned analysis framework.

The objective of the questionnaire is to identify correlations that can be made between information technologies useful in the financial-accounting domain and the associated competencies. Thus, the questionnaire was structured based on the conceptual framework of analysis that tries to capture specific IT&C competencies necessary to the accounting profession at the crossroads of the accounting roles in relation to IT&C component, with the technologies used in the field and with the level of experience needed to use them.

A number of 1510 people accepted the invitation to respond to the questionnaire, having an average age of 38 years and an average professional experience in accounting field of about 12 years, most presenting undergraduate and post-graduate education. The questionnaire was divided into several parts that can identify correlations regarding the proposed analysis model: Implementation of ICT in financial accounting activities; Types of technologies; Knowledge, skills and competencies and Accounting roles. Several important aspects were followed. First, the perception of the level the IT&C component use in accounting activity was analyzed as a whole and in detail. The majority of respondents stated the level of IT&C use in the activity specific to accounting and auditing profession as being adequate or high. It was noted, overall, that the percentage of responses suggesting a degree of low or very low usage is very modest (only 5% of all responses combined), which demonstrates the importance of the perceived usefulness of IT&C in accounting and audit activities. Thus, we can conclude that the respondents are aware that a separation between information and communication technology and the specific accounting profession cannot be achieved.

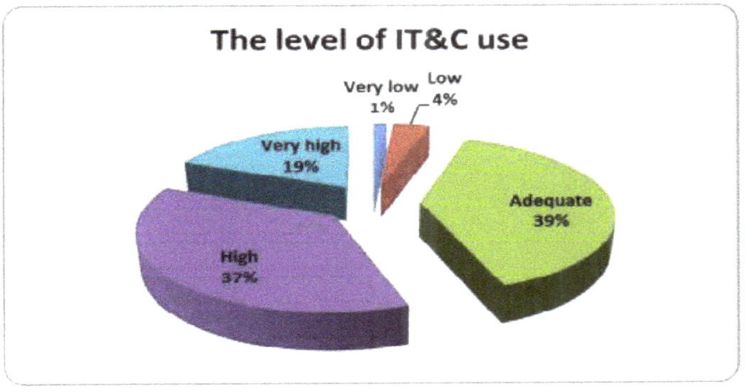

Figure 3. The overall representation of responses for the level of IT&C use

The level of importance perceived by the respondents on type of software could be followed by a comparative analysis of those technologies considered appropriate in the financial, accounting and auditing activity.

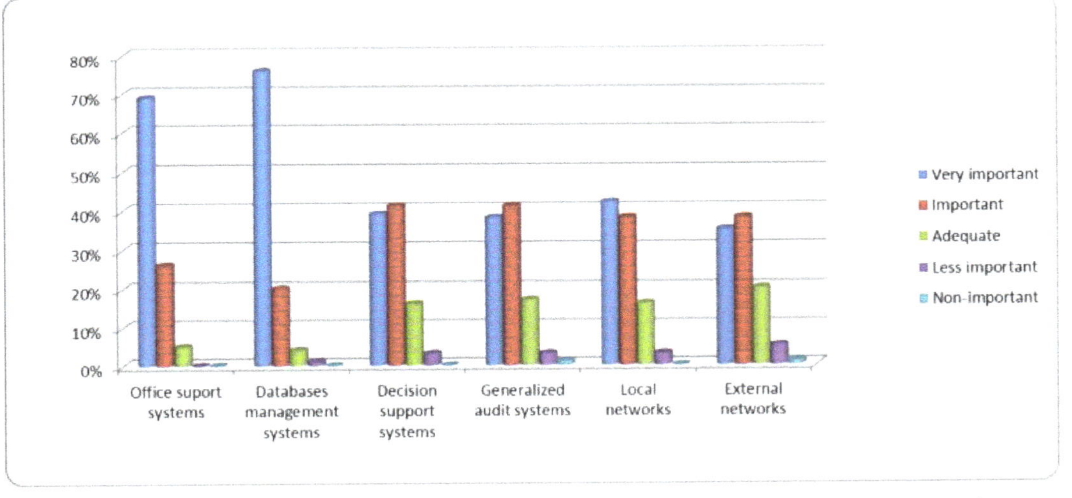

Figure 4. The importance of software applications from the perspective of their usefulness in the work of accountants / auditors

From this comparative analysis of the covered categories, best represented remain office support systems, followed by the databases management systems, then by decision support systems. External networks and local networks are less representative in order of importance, but nevertheless, from the total number of respondents, most stated that it is important to know these technologies for the effective exercise of the accounting profession.

Regarding the level of knowledge and skills in the use of the main categories of technologies, the largest share (about 60%) of respondents stated a good degree of knowledge for the Office applications. Furthermore, this type of ICT applications recorded the highest percentage for Excellent response, which suggests that this type of applications are most common in the work of accountants and auditors. Regarding the category of databases, the most frequent level of knowledge is Good, only 13% of respondents saying that excels in this area.

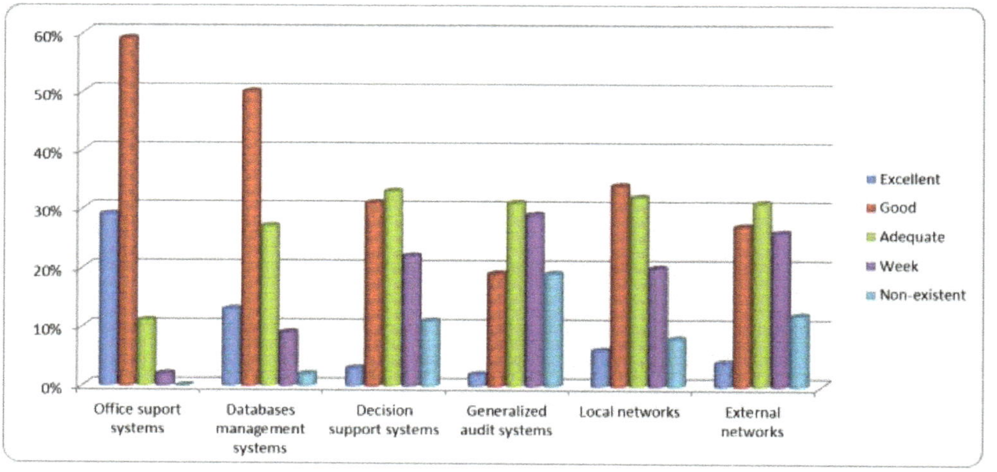

Figure 5. The level of knowledge and competencies in using software applications

It should be noted, also, the very small percentages of respondents who consider they do not have any knowledge in Office and databases fields. Decision support systems and audit systems own a relatively close structure in terms of responses, the most frequent occurrence having the response with an appropriate level of knowledge and skills. The use of local and external networks has a relatively uniform distribution of responses across the five levels of knowledge, most respondents saying that their level of knowledge and skills in use can be classified as good or appropriate and very few considering that they have an excellent level of knowledge.

Another line of analysis targeted the degree of IT&C use, taking into account five categories of common software applications. Summarizing the responses situation, we note high percentage (over 50% cumulative) of respondents who use office support systems and databases frequently or very frequently (most declaring a high and very high utilization level for these two types) and an adequate usage level for users who use other types of software applications taken into account.

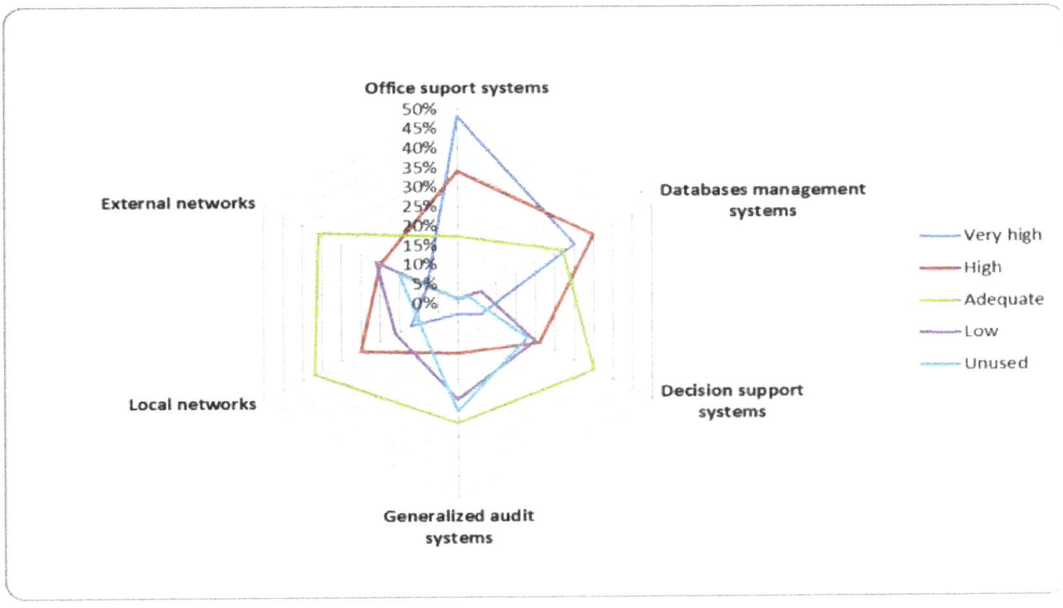

Figure 6. The level of IT&C use by software categories

A more complex view of reality can be obtained by highlighting the correlations established between responses that analyze distinct phenomena for the same variables. It can be seen, thus, how differ the responses regarding the importance in relation to the need for knowledge, usefulness and to the current level of use in practice for each of the software applications analyzed in this survey.

Table 4. The overall situation of responses analyzing different phenomena for distinct software categories

	Excellent	Good	Adequate	Week	Absent
The level of importance from the perspective of utility	69%	26%	5%	0%	0%
The actual level of knowledge and competencies	29%	59%	11%	2%	0%
The actual level of use	48%	34%	17%	1%	1%

It can be seen how responses corresponds in most situations for the three analyzed events. A significant difference can be observed, however, in the light of responses to the question which analyzes the level of importance assigned to this type of application and the current level of knowledge. In this sense, we can make the observation that, although respondents felt that the level of importance and implicitly, the level of use is very high in terms of usefulness of these software categories in their work, however, only a third of respondents consider the current level of their knowledge as being excellent, most qualifying the level of skills and knowledge in this field as being good.

Moreover, the differences in responses can be observed by analyzing the correlations between the pairs of events analyzed. Thus we have seen a strong correlation between the answers to the question of importance and the one that questions the current level of use in practical applications such as office support (Office), while the correlation between the knowledge and the other two phenomena analyzed (importance and level of use) is much lower, as can be seen bellow:

Table 5. The linear correlation between importance, knowledge and level of use for the chosen software categories

Analyzed phenomena	Linear correlation coefficient
Correlation between importance and knowledge	0,54
Correlation between importance and level of use	0,93
Correlation between knowledge and level of use	0,76

Positive values of the correlation coefficient indicates a direct link between the phenomena under analysis, more pronounced among importance perceived by the respondents and the level of use and less pronounced in the other two cases. Nevertheless, analysis of the correlation between the responses reflects only the degree of connection between the responses of the same kind for the three events analyzed. A weighting of responses to the three questions for this type of software reveals a much more suggestive image of the actual situation on the respondents' assessments. Thus, for each choice has been assigned a score (5 excellent, 1 for non-existent), the answers to these questions being weighted with the percentages represent the share in total responses, thus obtaining a weighted average showing which is the average level of respondents assessments in terms of three analyzed phenomena. It could be seen, following this analysis, that the average response is placed between good and excellent option for all the analyzed factors. However, one can observe a lower average value for the current level of knowledge and skills from the other two values, suggesting a possible improvement of this situation by increasing the competencies and knowledge in the field of office applications.

Table 6. Weighted averages analysis for software categories by the means of the three indicators

	5	4	3	2	1	Weighted average
The level of importance from the perspective of usefulness	69%	26%	5%	0%	0%	**4,64**
The current level of knowledge and skills	29%	59%	11%	2%	0%	**4,18**
The current level of use	48%	34%	17%	1%	1%	**4,30**

Regarding the technologies used in practice, the level of importance perceived in terms of usefulness in the work of accountants and auditors was considered high for technologies used in office activities and business activities and less to those used in the control and audit activities, respectively in the evaluation, design and management of IT&C systems. The answers, however, must be correlated with those concerning the skills and knowledge for each category of technology analyzed and with the evaluation of the degree of using IT&C in practice. Thus, regarding the technologies for the office activities we found a strong correlation (0.85) between the responses on the importance and the use of technologies in office work, while the correlation between the level of importance and the level of knowledge is much lower (0.66). The fact that the three correlation coefficients have positive values demonstrates a direct relationship between the three phenomena analyzed here.

About the technology that can be used in business activities, we can conclude that the respondents are aware of the importance of these technologies in their work, although the level of knowledge and use are much lower.

Analyzing correlations established between the three events, although the three factors have positive values, denoting a linear dependence, a strong correlation can be observed between the level of knowledge and the level of use.

Table 6. The linear correlation between the importance, level of use and knowledge for the technology dimension

Analyzed phenomena	Linear correlation coefficient
Correlation between importance and knowledge	0,318
Correlation between importance and level of use	0,105
Correlation between knowledge and level of use	0,773

As regards the technology for audit and control activities, as well as those on the design, evaluation and management of ICT, the answers reveal a linear correlation between the positive and the use of knowledge, but a negative dependence among the other phenomena. This can be interpreted as follows: although the practical experience of the respondents for this category of technology is low, the degree of importance perceived by respondents is high.

From the perspective of the role of ICT in accounting or auditing work, the analysis was done in terms of the importance of skills related to each of the user, designer, evaluator or IT manager roles, and in terms of current knowledge and level of use. Best represented in this respect remains IT user role, the correlation between perceived importance and level of use being high for the categories of technologies for office and business activities. It was found that the level of knowledge perceived as necessary in exercising the roles of evaluator, designer or manager of IT&C systems should be a high one, involving skills in all areas of technologies. Nevertheless, from the analysis of the responses, has been observed that, although the level of perceived importance of these roles is considered by the most of respondents as being adequate or high, the utilization degree of these specific technologies is low, demonstrating a possible direction of action in the education concerning these roles.

7. Conclusions

The demand of education regarding the development of the IT&C component that targets accounting professionals is highlighted and widely accepted by IFAC members worldwide. Normally, IT knowledge and competencies development must be integrated with education from the areas of accounting, auditing and taxation. In the short term, it is likely that this goal cannot be realized due to the time needed to restructure courses, training of qualified instructors, and so on. In the long term, implementation of a training program that takes into account the need of symbiosis between information technologies and accounting in the case of professional accountants training requires an integrated approach for improving the quality of training stages through the IT&C component.

The reality of the modern economic environment indicates that, in Romania, the training program of professional accountants destined for IT competencies development that is offered by the CECCAR organism does not meet the worldwide acknowledged standards (IES2 and IEG11 – IFAC, 2003).

The accounting profession training emphasizes knowledge gathering (especially from the financial, accounting and tax domains) and only slightly does it address acquiring and growing the necessary competencies for the IT&C field. Starting from this goal, through the present paper, an analysis of the actual status regarding professional accountants training through the IT&C component has been conducted, and a conceptual analysis framework for IT&C competencies in this field has been proposed.

The contribution of the research is focused on two dimensions: one theoretical and one practical. At a theoretical level we have conducted an analysis of the state of knowledge in the field of the development of IT&C training and competencies for professional accountants. Based on the literature review there are specified and we have justified the importance of introducing information and communication technology in subject areas specific to accounting education. Many authors (Harrison *et al.*, 2004; Wessels, 2005; Cardoş, 2011; Ku Bahador *et al.*, 2012, Havelka & Merhout, 2009) deal with this issue, through either empirical studies conducted on different populations, or only through studies at a conceptual level. Other authors (Wessels, 2005; Greenstein & McKee, 2004; Theuri & Gunn, 1998) address the issue regarding IT&C technologies applicable for the accounting profession. Our findings on the state of knowledge have determined in us the development of pragmatic side.

Thus, in practice, research has focused on designing a framework for analyzing IT&C competencies required for the professional accountants from Romania to implement training/development programs in line with international standards requirements. This framework captures IT competencies located at the intersection of three priority axes (Functions, Levels of experience and IT&C Technologies) that will guide the process of definition of thematic areas and specific competence domains. In our opinion, alongside the specific issues of the financial accounting system, an adequate attention should be paid to the use of general IT tools in achieving and interpretation of financial situations or situations specific to the other accounting roles within enterprises. A relevant analysis of the IT tools that professional accountants need to know must present, along with the usefulness of each technology required, the level of experience needed for each of the functions.

The three perspectives of analysis always converge to a certain central point in which the IT competencies regarding the accounting profession are explained by role descriptors, through level of training that is adequate for that role and through the education offer (defined by curricula areas with specific subjects) that is necessary to the understanding and the development of the competence in question.

The analysis based on questionnaire has emphasized the perception of the accounting professionals in Romania on the need for IT&C training and competencies development through the proposed IT technologies in the analysis framework. It revealed a strong relationship between the dimension of ICT competencies related to the accounting profession and the perceived importance on the utility of various technologies which were the subject of analysis. As for the roles played by the professional accountant, we could outline a possible direction of action on accounting education in IT&C field associated with the roles of evaluator, designer or manager of accounting information systems, based on their importance in relation to the degree of knowledge.

Overall, the interpretation of the questionnaire responses led to the enunciation of a clear conclusion: the educational needs analysis should take into account the existing and the necessary level of knowledge of certain technologies related to the duties expressed through the roles they perform in a professional way.

Acknowledgements

The present paper had as a starting point the research conducted by the authors for the POSDRU project no. 81/3.2/S/59664, "Using IT&C for quality services in the accounting-financial field".

References

AAA (1986) *Future Accounting Education: Preparing for the Expanding Profession.* American Accounting Association, Committee on the Future Structure, Content, and Scope of Accounting Education (The Bedford Committee), Spring

AACSB (1993) *Achieving Quality and Continuous Improvement through Self-Evaluation and Peer Review: Standards for Business and Accounting Accreditation: Guidance for Self-evaluation*, American Assembly of Collegiate Schools of Business

AECC (1990) *Objectives of Education for Accountants: Position Statement No. One*, Accounting Education Change Commission

AICPA (1998) *AICPA Core Competency Framework for Entry Into the Accounting Profession*, American Institute of Certified Public Accountants

Albrecht, W. S., & Robert, J. (2001) "The Perilous Future of Accounting Education", *The CPA Journal*, vol. 7, no. 3: 17-23

Angelo, T. A. & Cross, K. P. (1993) *Classroom Assessment Techniques: A Handbook for College Teachers*, (2nd ed.) San Francisco: Jossey-Bass

Borthick, A. (1996) "Helping accountants to get the information managers want: the role of accounting information systems course", *Journal of Information Systems,* vol. 10, no. 2: 75-85.

Cardoş, V.D., (2011) "How Romanian financial and internal auditors acquire accounting information systems knowledge and competences?", *Annals of Faculty of Economics, University of Oradea, Faculty of Economics*, vol. 1, no.1: 545-551

Carter, R. (1985) "A taxonomy of objectives for professional education", *Studies in Higher Education*, vol. 10, no. 2: 135-149

Chen, J., Damtew, D., Banatte, J.-M., Mapp, J. (2009) "Information technology competencies expected in undergraduate accounting graduates", *Research In Higher Education Journal,* vol. 3, available online at: http://www.aabri.com/manuscripts/09146.pdf

Cooper, R. (1996) "Look out, management accountants", *Management accounting*, vol. 77: 35-41.

Daigle, R., Hayes, D. & Hughes, K. E. (2007) "Assessing student learning outcomes in the introductory accounting information systems course using the AICPA's core competency framework", *Journal of Information Systems*, vol. 21, no. 1:149-169

Davis, J. R. & Leitch, R. (1988) "Accounting information systems courses and curricula: New perspectives", *Journal of Information Systems* (Fall), 153-166.

Druckman, P. (2008) "Four types of finance professionals", *IFAC Information Paper: The Crucial Roles of Professional Accountants in Business Mid-Sized Enterprises,* available online at:http://www.apesb.org.au/uploads/feb-2012-bm/attachment-17d-the-crucial-roles-of-professional-accountants-in-business-in-mid-sized-enterprises-2008.pdf[accessed 12.03.2013]

Eliot, R. (1992) "The third wave breaks on the shore of accounting", *Accounting Horizons*, vol. 6, no. 2: 61-85

Greenstein, M. & McKee, T.E. (2004) "Assurance practitioners' and educators' selfperceived IT knowledge level: an empirical assessment", *International Journal of Accounting Information Systems*, vol. 5: 213-243

Harrison, D., McPeak, D. & Greenberg, S. (2004) "Validating competencies underlying a professional accounting credential, paper presented at the ABER 3rd Global Conference on Business and Economics", Amsterdam, Netherlands, July 9-11, available online at: http://www.cga-canada.org/en-ca/ResearchReports/ca_rep_2004-07-09_competencies_Harrison_McPeak.pdf [last accessed:11.03.2013]

Havelka, D. & Merhout, J.W. (2009) "Towards a theory of information technology professional competence", *The Journal of Computer Systems*, vol. 50, no. 2: 106-116

Heagy, C. D. & Rakow, E. (1991) "Course content of accounting information systems: Do professors agree?", *Accounting Education Journal* (winter): 140-158.

IFAC (1998) *Into the 21st century with Information Management*, New York, IFAC

IFAC (2003 a) International Education Guideline - IEG 11: *Information technology for professional accountants Information Technology for Professional Accountants*, International Federation of Accountants Education Committee, available online at https://www.imanet.org/pdf/ITPA.pdf, [accessed 30 December 2012]

IFAC (2003 b) *International Education Standard IES 2 - Content of professional accounting education programs*, IFAC Education Commitee

IFAC (2009) *Framework for International Education Standards for Professional Accountants*, New York: International Accounting Education Standard Board

IMA (1996) *The Practice Analysis of Management Accounting*, Institute of Management Accountants

Jackson, R.B. & Cherrington, J.O, (2002) "IT Instruction Methodology and Minimum Competency for Accounting Students", *Journal of Information Systems Education*, vol. 12, no. 4: 213-222

Ku Bahador, K. M, Haider, A & Wan Mohd Saman, W.S. (2012) "Information technology and accountants – what skills and competencies are required?", paper presented at European, Mediterranean & Middle Eastern Conference on Information Systems, June 7-8, Munich, Germany, pp 770-780, available online at: http://www.iseing.org/emcis/emcis2012/EMCISWebsite/proceedings/120.pdf [last accessed 12.03.2013]

Lucia, A. D. & Lepsinger, R. (1999) *The Art and Science of Competency Models*, San Francisco: Jossey-Bass / Pfeiffer

McKinnon, S. & Bruns, W. (1992) *The Information Mosaic*, Boston, MA: Harvard Business School Press

Novak, M. & Beckman, T. (2008) "A Multi-tiered competency-based approach to knowledge retention in organizations", paper presented at Knowledge Management Conference, April, 28, 2008, available online at: http://events.fcw.com/events/2008/KM/Downloads/KM08_2-2_Novak_20080411_Multi-tiered_Competency-based_K_Retention.pdf [last accessed: 11.03.2013].

Siegel, G. (1996) *The practice analysis of management* accounting, Montvale, NJ: Institute of Management Accountants

Stone, D.N., Arunachalam, V. & Chandler, J.S. (1996) "An empirical investigation of knowledge, skill, self- efficacy, and computer anxiety in accounting education", *Accounting Education*, vol. 11, no. 2: 345-376

Theuri, P.M. & Gunn, R. (1998) "Accounting information systems course structure and employer system skills expectations", *Journal of Accounting Education*, vol. 16, no.1: 101-121

Wessels, P.L. (2005) "Critical information and communication technology (IT&C) skills for professional accountants", *Meditari Accountancy Research*, vol. 13, no. 1: 87-103

Permissions

All chapters in this book were first published in JAMIS, by Bucharest University of Economic Studies; hereby published with permission under the Creative Commons Attribution License or equivalent. Every chapter published in this book has been scrutinized by our experts. Their significance has been extensively debated. The topics covered herein carry significant findings which will fuel the growth of the discipline. They may even be implemented as practical applications or may be referred to as a beginning point for another development.

The contributors of this book come from diverse backgrounds, making this book a truly international effort. This book will bring forth new frontiers with its revolutionizing research information and detailed analysis of the nascent developments around the world.

We would like to thank all the contributing authors for lending their expertise to make the book truly unique. They have played a crucial role in the development of this book. Without their invaluable contributions this book wouldn't have been possible. They have made vital efforts to compile up to date information on the varied aspects of this subject to make this book a valuable addition to the collection of many professionals and students.

This book was conceptualized with the vision of imparting up-to-date information and advanced data in this field. To ensure the same, a matchless editorial board was set up. Every individual on the board went through rigorous rounds of assessment to prove their worth. After which they invested a large part of their time researching and compiling the most relevant data for our readers.

The editorial board has been involved in producing this book since its inception. They have spent rigorous hours researching and exploring the diverse topics which have resulted in the successful publishing of this book. They have passed on their knowledge of decades through this book. To expedite this challenging task, the publisher supported the team at every step. A small team of assistant editors was also appointed to further simplify the editing procedure and attain best results for the readers.

Apart from the editorial board, the designing team has also invested a significant amount of their time in understanding the subject and creating the most relevant covers. They scrutinized every image to scout for the most suitable representation of the subject and create an appropriate cover for the book.

The publishing team has been an ardent support to the editorial, designing and production team. Their endless efforts to recruit the best for this project, has resulted in the accomplishment of this book. They are a veteran in the field of academics and their pool of knowledge is as vast as their experience in printing. Their expertise and guidance has proved useful at every step. Their uncompromising quality standards have made this book an exceptional effort. Their encouragement from time to time has been an inspiration for everyone.

The publisher and the editorial board hope that this book will prove to be a valuable piece of knowledge for researchers, students, practitioners and scholars across the globe.

List of Contributors

Ruslana Kuzina
Odessa National University of Economics, Ukraine

Can Öztürk
Çankaya University, Ankara, Turkey

Ioan-Bogdan Robu, Mihaela-Alina Robu and Marilena Mironiuc
Alexandru Ioan Cuza University of Iasi, Romania

Florentina Olivia Bălu
University of Geneva, Switzerland

Sihem Khemakhem and Younés Boujelbène
University of Sfax, Tunisia

Florin Dobre, Laura Brad and Radu Ciobanu
Bucharest University of Economic Studies, Romania

Corina Grosu, Alina Almăşan and Cristina Circa
West University of Timişoara, Romania

Ibrahim Onur Oz
Central Connecticut State University, United States

Tezer Yelkenci
Izmir University of Economics, Turkey

Aida Krichene Abdelmoula
Institut des Hautes Etudes Commerciales de Carthage, University of Carthage, Tunisia

Maria Carmen Huian
Alexandru Ioan Cuza University of Iaşi, Romania

Cătălin Georgel Tudor, Mirela Gheorghe, Mirela Oancea and Robert Şova
The Bucharest University of Economic Studies, Romania

Index

CPSIA information can be obtained
at www.ICGtesting.com
Printed in the USA
LVHW062023100122
708212LV00002B/405

9 781639 872251